THE EVOLUTION
OF
GREEK PROSE STYLE

The Evolution
of
Greek Prose Style

Kenneth Dover

CLARENDON PRESS · OXFORD
1997

Oxford University Press, Great Clarendon Street, Oxford OX2 6DP
Oxford New York
Athens Auckland Bangkok Bogotá Bombay
Buenos Aires Calcutta Cape Town Dar es Salaam Delhi
Florence Hong Kong Istanbul Karachi
Kuala Lumpur Madras Madrid Melbourne
Mexico City Nairobi Paris Singapore
Taipei Tokyo Toronto Warsaw
and associated companies in
Berlin Ibadan

Oxford is a trade mark of Oxford University Press

Published in the United States
by Oxford University Press Inc., New York

British Library Cataloguing in Publication Data
Data available

Library of Congress Cataloging in Publication Data
The evolution of Greek prose style / Kenneth Dover.
Includes bibliographical references.
1. Greek prose literature—History and criticism.
2. Greek language—Style.   I. Title
PA3557.D68 1997   888'.010809—dc21   97-2022
ISBN 0-19-814028-2

1 3 5 7 9 10 8 6 4 2

Typeset by John Waś, Oxford
Printed in Great Britain on acid-free paper by
Bookcraft (Bath) Ltd., Midsomer Norton

PREFACE

ALTHOUGH the study of style is commonly regarded as the province of the literary critic, I do not profess to be a literary critic at all, but a historian of literature and language. 'Literary history' has a bad press nowadays, because it tends to be associated with a diversion of interest from literary works to minutiae of their authors' lives. In dealing with Greek literature there is no possibility of such diversion, because what we know for sure about the life even of a famous author would go on a postcard; indeed, in many cases it would go on the back of a stamp, and some works of great importance for the history of Greek literature are of unknown authorship. Literary critics are a blend of historian, autobiographer, and (why not, indeed?) preacher. They are historians in so far as a text is a thing which came into existence at a specifiable point in time and space, and they try to determine and explain what caused it to be what it is (causes, naturally, include ideologies). Autobiographers, in so far as they reveal their own reactions to a text. Preachers, in so far as they try to persuade us that of all the questions that can be asked about a text some have more relevance than others to good and evil.

My primary concern is the history of linguistic differences between texts. My aesthetic reactions are numerous and strong, and now and again I have judged it harmless to reveal them, but I recognize that the reactions of any individual at a given time are determined by the sum of that individual's formative experiences up to that time. A value-judgement is never likely to be unanimous, and cannot be commanded. For similar reasons, I do not expect the questions about language and literature which interest me most to interest everyone else to the same degree. My preaching is confined to the field of method, and I think it is defensible. I offer no apology for using analogies from different cultures at different times; it reflects my interest in continuities.

Readers of a book entitled 'The Evolution of Homo Sapiens' would not expect to find much in it about Dante or Napoleon, and

I hope that readers of this book will not be shocked at my silence on some of the greatest Greek prose authors (notably Plutarch). The principal question to which I have addressed myself is: how did Greek prose, with a long history of poetry behind it, evolve during the fifth and fourth centuries until—to borrow the expression used by Aristotle of mid-fifth-century tragedy—it 'attained its proper nature' in Plato and Demosthenes?

An account of *all* the stylistic differences observable within the extant corpus of Greek prose would be the work of a lifetime if the validity of all statements about them were founded on the requisite quantification. Denniston's splendid book *Greek Prose Style* deals with a selection of phenomena, and the questions I have posed are in some material respects different from his. Some of his (e.g. asyndeton) I have chosen not to cover afresh. As for word-order, a topic on which the influence of current interest in pragmatics has been consistently beneficial, I judged that although a lot more work would contribute something to our understanding of the Greek *language* as a whole it would not necessarily be equally helpful to the study of *style*, where *difference* between texts is crucial.

I formed a vague intention of writing this book in 1977, but ten years passed before I set to work on it systematically, and even then completion of my edition of *Frogs* had precedence. I spent the equivalent of many months on lines of enquiry which in the end yielded only negative results. At a comparatively late stage I devoted much time to wide reading in the general literature of stylistics. I do not think that in the course of that reading I came upon anything that had not already occurred to me in studying Greek, but I found plenty of welcome support and nothing that required me to change my mind on any matter of importance.

In the Winter Quarter of 1987/8 I held a graduate seminar on Greek prose style at Stanford, and I gladly express a debt of gratitude to the students whose criticisms and positive contributions helped me to construct my line of argument: Denise Greaves, Kirk Ormand, Tasha Spencer, Livia Tenzer, Kathy Veit, and Gregory Wilsdon. I am indebted also to the observations and criticisms offered by staff and students in the universities of Ioannina, Alexandroupolis, Rome, Genoa, Madrid, Salamanca, and Coimbra; more recently, to comments by Professor Martha Nussbaum; and above all, to acute observations by the copy-editor, Dr Leofranc Holford-

Strevens, the typesetter, Dr John Waś, and Professor Stephen Halliwell and Dr Helma Dik for their help with correction of the proofs.

I once noticed in a class of first-year graduate students that deficiency in knowledge of the Greek language did not necessarily inhibit perception of stylistic subtleties. That experience encourages me to think that readers who have very little Greek may nevertheless find something to interest them in this book.

I must end with a confession which is very painful for me. After the death of Sophie Trenkner in 1958 her files and card-indexes on phenomena of Greek prose style were entrusted to me, and it was my intention to use her material, with adequate acknowledgement, in writing this book. Professor Fehling very kindly worked through the material, put it in order, and gave notice in *Gnomon* of its availability to anyone who might be interested in it (no one responded). I had a very cursory look at it in the mid 1970s, and intended to address myself to it properly in the late 1980s. Unfortunately, it proved then impossible to locate.

University of St Andrews   KENNETH DOVER
May 1997

CONTENTS

x   *Contents*

LIST OF FIGURES

LIST OF TABLES

BIBLIOGRAPHY AND
ABBREVIATIONS

All works to which any reference is made in this book (except for Shakespeare and the like) are included in the bibliography.

ADAMS, CHRISTOPHER, *The Worst English Poets* (London, 1958).

ALLEN, JAMES T., and ITALIE, GABRIEL, *A Concordance to Euripides* (Cambridge, 1964); Supplement by C. Collard (Groningen, 1971).

ALY, WOLF, *Volksmärchen, Sage und Novelle bei Herodot und seinen Zeitgenossen* (Göttingen, 1921).

—— 'Herodots Sprache: Ein Beitrag zur Geistesgeschichte der Jahre 450–430', *Glotta*, 15 (1927), 84–117.

—— *Formprobleme der früheren griechischen Prosa* (*Philologus*, Suppl. 21/3; Leipzig, 1923).

AMMANN, A. N., *-ικός bei Platon* (Fribourg, 1953).

ARDIZZONI, ANTHOS, *Ποίημα: Ricerche sulla teoria del linguaggio poetico nell'antichità* (Bari, 1953).

ARMBRUSTER, C. H., *Initia Amharica*, i (Cambridge, 1908).

AS = Ludwig Radermacher (ed.), *Artium Scriptores* (Vienna, 1951).

AUERBACH, ERICH, *Mimesis*, trans. Willard Trask (New York, 1953).

AYRES, LEWIS (ed.), *The Passionate Intellect: Essays on the Transformation of Classical Tradition Presented to Professor I. G. Kidd* (New Brunswick and London, 1995).

BALLY, CHARLES, *Traité de stylistique française*, 2 vols., 3rd edn. (Geneva and Paris, 1951).

BANNIER, W., 'Zur Stilistik der älteren griechischen Urkunden', *RhM*, NF 67 (1912), 515–55.

—— 'Wiederholungen bei älteren griechischen und lateinischen Autoren', *RhM*, NF 69 (1914), 481–514.

BARRETT, W. S. (ed., comm.), *Euripides' Hippolytos* (Oxford, 1964).

BECHTEL, FRIEDRICH, *Die griechischen Dialekte*, 3 vols. (Berlin, 1921–4).

BERS, VIKTOR, *Greek Poetic Syntax in the Classical Age* (New Haven and London, 1984).

BJÖRCK, GUDMUND, *Das Alpha impurum und die tragische Kunstsprache* (Uppsala, 1950).

BLASS, FRIEDRICH, *Die attische Beredsamkeit*, 4 vols., 2nd edn. (Leipzig, 1887–98).

—— *Die Rhythmen der attischen Kunstprosa* (Leipzig, 1901).

BOWIE, ANGUS M., *The Poetic Dialect of Sappho and Alcaeus* (Salem, 1981).

BREITENBACH, W., *Untersuchungen zur Sprache der euripideischen Lyrik* (Stuttgart, 1934; repr. Darmstadt, 1967).

BROADHEAD, H. D., 'Prose-Rhythm and Prose-Metre', *CQ* 26 (1932), 35–44.

BRUHN, EWALD, 'Anhang' to the edition of Sophocles by F. W. Schneidewin and A. Nauck (Berlin, 1899; repr. 1963).

BUCK, C. D., 'Interstate Use of the Greek Dialects', *CPh* 8 (1913), 133–59.

—— 'Epigraphical Notes', *CPh* 20 (1925), 133–44.

CASSIO, A., and MUSTI, D. (eds.), *Tra Sicilia e Magna Grecia* (Naples, 1989).

CEG = P. A. Hansen (ed.), *Carmina Epigraphica Graeca*, i (Berlin and New York, 1983).

CHANTRAINE, PIERRE, *La Formation des noms en grec ancien* (Paris, 1933).

—— *Grammaire homérique*, 2 vols. (Paris, 1948–53).

CHATMAN, SEYMOUR, (ed.), *Literary Style: A Symposium* (London and New York, 1971).

CHING, MARVIN K. L., HALEY, MICHAEL C., and LUNSFORD, RONALD E. (eds.), *Linguistic Perspectives on Literature* (London, 1980).

CHRIST, MATTHEW, 'The Authenticity of Thucydides 3. 84', *TAPhA* 119 (1989), 137–48.

CODE, ALAN, 'Reply to Michael Frede's "Being and Becoming in Plato"', *OSAP*, Suppl. 1 (1988), 53–60.

CONOMIS, N. C., 'The Dochmiacs of Greek Drama', *Hermes*, 92 (1964), 23–50.

COUGHANOWR, E., 'On the Meaning of δίστομος in Euripides', *CQ*, NS 34 (1984), 235–6.

COX, D. R., and BRANDWOOD, LEONARD, 'On a Discriminatory Problem Connected with the Works of Plato', *Journal of the Royal Statistical Society*, Series B, 21 (1959), 195–200.

CRAIK, E. M. (ed.), *'Owls to Athens': Essays on Classical Subjects Presented to Sir Kenneth Dover* (Oxford, 1990).

CRYSTAL, DAVID, and DAVY, DEREK, *Investigating English Style* (Harlow, 1969).

CUCUEL, CHARLES, *Essai sur la langue et le style de l'orateur Antiphon* (Paris, 1886).

CUMMING, ROBERT, *Working with Colour: Recent Paintings and Studies by Bridget Riley* (London, 1984).

DALE, A. M., *The Lyric Metres of Greek Drama*, 2nd edn. (Cambridge, 1968).

xiv

Bibliography and Abbreviations

DAMON, CYNTHIA, 'Aesthetic Responses and Technical Analysis in the Rhetorical Writings of Dionysius of Halicarnassus', *MH* 48 (1991), 33–58.

DEBRUNNER, ALBERT, *Griechische Wortbildungslehre* (Heidelberg, 1917).

DEICHGRÄBER, KARL, 'Rhythmische Elemente im Logos des Heraklit', *AAWM* 1962, 481–551.

—— *Die Epidemien und das Corpus Hippocraticum* (Berlin and New York, 1971).

DELBRÜCK, BERTHOLD, *Vergleichende Syntax der indogermanischen Sprachen* (Strasburg, 1893).

DE MARTINO, F., and SOMMERSTEIN, A. H. (eds.), *Lo spettacolo delle voci* (Bari, 1995).

DENNISTON, J. D., *The Greek Particles*, 2nd edn. (Oxford, 1954).

—— [see also *GPS*, *SPG*].

DGE=P. Cauer (ed.), *Dialectorum Graecarum Exempla Epigraphica Potiora*, 3rd edn., rev. E. Schwyzer (Leipzig, 1923).

DIJK, TEUN VAN (ed.), *Discourse and Literature* (Amsterdam and Philadelphia, 1985).

DILLON, GEORGE L., *Language-Processing and the Reading of Literature* (Bloomington, Ind., 1978).

DODDS, E. R. (ed.), *Plato: Gorgias* (Oxford, 1959).

DONAT, MISHA, 'Records', *The Listener*, 4 Oct. 1973, 462–3.

DONINI, GUIDO, 'Erodoto, II, 17, 4: Osservazioni sulla variazione di tempo a scopo stilistico in Erodoto', *AAT* Cl. II, 118 (1983/4), 94–103.

DOVER, K. J. (ed., comm.), *Thucydides, Book VI* (Oxford, 1965).

—— *Greek Word Order*, 2nd edn. (Cambridge, 1968) ('1968a').

—— (ed., comm.) *Aristophanes: Clouds* (Oxford, 1968) ('1968b').

—— *Lysias and the Corpus Lysiacum* (Berkeley and Los Angeles, 1968) ('1968c').

—— *Greek Popular Morality in the Time of Plato and Aristotle* (Oxford, 1974).

—— (with M. L. West, Jasper Griffin, and E. L. Bowie), *Ancient Greek Literature* (Oxford, 1980).

—— *Greek and the Greeks* (Oxford, 1987).

—— *The Greeks and their Legacy* (Oxford, 1988).

—— *Greek Homosexuality*, 2nd edn. (Cambridge, Mass., 1989).

—— (ed., comm.), *Aristophanes: Frogs* (Oxford, 1993).

—— 'Style, Genre and Author', *ICS* 19 (1994), 83–7.

EARP, F. R., *The Style of Sophocles* (Cambridge, 1944).

—— *The Style of Aeschylus* (Cambridge, 1948).

EGIDI, P. M. V., 'Mythes et légendes des Kuni, British New Guinea', *Anthropos*, 9 (1914), 81–97, 393–401.

ELDH = A. López Eire, *Estudios de lingüística, dialectología e historia de la lengua griega* (Salamanca, 1986).

ELLENDT, FRIEDRICH, *Lexicon Sophocleum*, 2nd edn. rev. Hermann Genthe (Berlin, 1872; repr. Hildesheim, 1958).

ENKVIST, N. E., *Linguistic Stylistics* (The Hague and Paris, 1973).

EULENBURG, KURT, 'Zur Vokalkontraktion im ionisch-attischen Dialekt', *IF* 15 (1903/4), 129–211.

FARRINGDON, JILL, with A. Q. Morton, Michael Farringdon, and M. D. Baker, *Analysing for Authorship* (Cardiff, 1996).

FAURE, PAUL, 'Les Dioscures à Delphes', *AC* 54 (1985), 56–65.

FEHLING, DETLEV, review of Lilja (q.v.), *Gnomon*, 41 (1969), 134–9.

—— [see also *Wf*].

FGrHist = Felix Jacoby (ed.), *Die Fragmente der griechischen Historiker* (Berlin, 1923–9, Leiden, 1943–).

FIRTH, J. B., *Papers in Linguistics 1934–51* (London, 1957).

FISHMAN, JOSHUA A. (ed.), *Readings in the Sociology of Language* (The Hague and Paris, 1970).

FOLEY, WILLIAM A., *The Papuan Languages of New Guinea* (Cambridge, 1986).

FOWLER, R. L., 'Aristotle on the Period (Rhet. 3.9)', *CQ*, NS 32 (1982), 89–99.

FOWLER, ROGER, 'Style and the Concept of Deep Structure', *Journal of Literary Semantics*, 1 (1972), 5–24.

FRAENKEL, EDUARD, *Kleine Beiträge zur klassischen Philologie*, 2 vols. (Rome, 1964).

FRAENKEL, ERNST, *Geschichte der griechischen Nomina agentis auf -τήρ, -τωρ, -της (-τ-)*, i (Strasburg, 1910).

FREEMAN, DONALD C. (ed.), *Linguistics and Literary Style* (New York, 1970).

—— (ed.), *Essays in Modern Stylistics* (London, 1981).

FRIEDMAN, TERRY, *The Hyde Park Atrocity* (Leeds, 1988).

FUKS, ALEKSANDER, 'Thucydides and the Stasis in Corcyra', *AJPh* 92 (1971), 48–55.

GAUTHIER, LEOPOLD, *La Langue de Xénophon* (Geneva, 1911).

GG = Eduard Schwyzer, *Griechische Grammatik*, 2 vols. and 2 index vols. (Munich, 1939–71).

GOLLA, VICTOR, and SILVER, SHIRLEY (eds.), *Northern California Texts* (Chicago, 1977).

GOMBRICH, ERNST, *The Story of Art*, 14th edn. (Oxford, 1984).

GPS = J. D. Denniston, *Greek Prose Style* (Oxford, 1952) [see also *SPG*].

GRAY, BENNISON, *Style: The Problem and its Solution* (The Hague and Paris, 1969).

GREEN, GEORGIA M., *Pragmatics and Natural Language Understanding* (Hillsdale, NJ, 1989).

GRONINGEN, B. A. VAN, *La Composition littéraire archaïque grecque* (Amsterdam, 1958).

GROOT, A. W. DE, *Der antike Prosarhythmus*, i (Groningen, 1921).

GROSS, R., 'Found Poetry', *New York Times Book Review*, 11 June 1967, 2.

GRUBE, G. M. A., *A Greek Critic: Demetrius on Style* (Toronto, 1961).

GYGLI-WYSS, B., *Das nominale Polyptoton im älteren Griechisch* (Göttingen, 1966).

HABERLE, JAKOB, *Untersuchungen über den ionischen Prosastil* (Munich, 1938).

HALLIWELL, S., *Aristotle's Poetics* (London, 1986).

—— 'Style and Sense in Aristotle, Rhet. III', *RIPh* 47 (1993), 50–69.

HARRIS, ROY, *Synonymy and Linguistic Analysis* (Oxford, 1973).

HARTMANN, FELIX, 'Über die Grundlagen für die Beurteilung von Herodots Dialekt', *ZVF*, NF 60 (1933), 89–113.

HAVELOCK, ERIC, 'Pre-literacy and the Pre-Socratics', *BICS* 13 (1966), 44–67.

HCT = A. W. Gomme, A. Andrewes, and K. J. Dover, *Historical Commentary on Thucydides*, 5 vols. (Oxford, 1945–81).

HENRY, A. S. 'The Language of Attic Inscriptions 323–146 B.C.' (St Andrews dissertation, 1964).

HEYWARD, MICHAEL, *The Ern Malley Affair* (London, 1993).

HILL, ARCHIBALD A., 'A Program for the Definition of Literature', *University of Texas English Studies*, 37 (1958) 46–52.

HILTON, ISOBEL, article on Lady Thatcher, *The Independent*, 26 Nov. 1990, 16.

HIRT, HERMANN, *Indogermanische Grammatik*, 7 vols. (Heidelberg, 1921–34).

HOLLINGSWORTH J. E. *Antithesis in the Attic Orators from Antiphon to Isaeus* (Menasha, Wis., 1915).

HORNBLOWER, SIMON (ed.), *Greek Historiography* (Oxford, 1994).

HOUGH, GRAHAM, *Style and Stylistics* (London, 1969).

IEG = M. L. West (ed.), *Iambi et Elegi Graeci*, 2 vols., 2nd edn. (Oxford, 1989–92).

IG = *Inscriptiones Graecae*, 3rd edn. of vol. i by D. M. Lewis (Berlin and New York, 1981, 1994).

INGARDEN, ROMAN, 'Das Form-Inhalt-Problem im literarischen Kunstwerk', *Helicon* (Amsterdam and Leipzig), 1 (1938), 53–67.

—— *Das literarische Kunstwerk*, 2nd edn. (Tübingen, 1960).

ITALIE, GABRIEL, *Index Aeschyleus* (Leiden, 1955).

ITSUMI, K., 'The "Choriambic Dimeter" of Euripides', *CQ*, NS 32 (1982), 59–74.

JACKSON, JOHN, *Marginalia Scaenica* (Oxford, 1955).

JAKOBSON, ROMAN, *Language in Literature* (Cambridge, Mass., and London, 1987).

JEFFERY, L. H., *The Local Scripts of Archaic Greece*, 2nd edn., rev. Alan Johnston (Oxford, 1983).

KALE, M. R., *A Higher Sanskrit Grammar for the Use of Schools and Colleges*, 4th edn. (Bombay, 1912).

KAPSOMENOS, A. S., 'Aspects of the Vocabulary of Aeschylus' (St Andrews dissertation, 1975).

KENNEDY, GEORGE A. (ed.), *The Cambridge History of Literary Criticism*, i. *Classical Criticism* (Cambridge, 1989).

KENNY, ANTHONY, *The Computation of Style* (Oxford, 1982).

KG = Raphael Kühner, *Ausführliche Grammatik der griechischen Sprache*, part ii, rev. Bernhard Gerth, 2 vols. (Hanover, 1898–1904).

LAMB, W. R. M., *Clio Enthroned* (Cambridge, 1914).

LANHAM, RICHARD A., *Style: An Anti-Textbook* (New Haven and London, 1974).

LEDGER, G. R., *Re-counting Plato: A Computer Analysis of Plato's Style* (Oxford, 1989).

LEO, ULRICH, *Stilforschung und dichterische Einheit* (Munich, 1966).

LEUMANN, MANU, *Homerische Wörter* (Basle, 1950).

LEVIN, SAMUEL R., 'Deviation—Statistical and Determinate—in Poetic Language', *Lingua*, 12 (1963) 276–90.

LILJA, SAARA, *On the Style of the Earliest Greek Prose* (Helsinki, 1968).

LLOYD, G. E. R., *Polarity and Analogy* (Cambridge, 1966).

—— *The Revolutions of Wisdom* (Berkeley and Los Angeles, 1987).

LLOYD-JONES, HUGH, and WILSON, N. G., *Sophoclea: Studies on the Text of Sophocles* (Oxford, 1990).

LONG, TIMOTHY, *Repetition and Variation in the Short Stories of Herodotus* (Frankfurt am Main, 1987).

LÓPEZ EIRE, A., 'Géographie interdialectale de l'ionien-attique', *Verbum*, 10 (1987), 155–78.

—— [see also *ELDH*].

LOUIS, PIERRE, *Les Métaphores de Platon* (Paris, 1945).

LSJ = H. G. Liddell and R. Scott, *A Greek–English Lexicon*, 9th edn., rev. H. Stuart-Jones and R. Mackenzie (Oxford, 1940).

LUBBOCK, TOM, 'After You, Master, after You', *The Independent*, 1 Aug. 1995, Section 2, pp. 8–9.

LYONS, JOHN, *Structural Semantics* (Oxford, 1963).

—— *Semantics*, 2 vols. (Cambridge, 1977).

MCCABE, DONALD F., *The Prose-Rhythm of Demosthenes* (New York, 1981).

MACDONNELL, A. A., *A Sanskrit Grammar for Students*, 3rd edn. (London, 1927).

MACLEOD, COLIN, *Collected Essays* (Oxford, 1983).

MARCADÉ, JEAN, *Recueil des signatures des sculpteurs grecs*, 2 vols. (Paris, 1953–7).

MARSHALL, M. H. B., *Verbs, Nouns and Postpositives in Attic Prose* (Edinburgh, 1987).

MARTIN, J., *Antike Rhetorik* (Munich, 1974).

MEISTERHANS, K., *Grammatik der attischen Inschriften*, 3rd edn., rev. Eduard Schwyzer (Berlin, 1900).

MEYER, GUSTAV, *Die stilistische Verwendung der Nominalkomposition im Griechischen* (*Philologus*, Suppl. 16/3; Leipzig, 1923).

ML = R. Meiggs and D. M. Lewis, *A Selection of Greek Historical Inscriptions*, 2nd edn. (Oxford, 1989).

MUKAŘOVSKY, JAN, *On Poetic Language*, trans. John Burbank and Peter Steiner (New Haven, 1976).

NAVARRE, OCTAVE, *Essai sur la rhétorique grecque avant Aristote* (Paris, 1900).

NEWIGER, H.-J., *Metapher und Allegorie: Studien zu Aristophanes* (Munich, 1957).

NEWTON, BRIAN, *Cypriot Greek* (The Hague and Paris, 1972).

NORDEN, EDUARD, *Agnostos Theos* (Leipzig, 1913; repr. Darmstadt, 1956).

—— *Die antike Kunstprosa*, 2 vols. (Leipzig, 1898; repr. Darmstadt, 1958).

NUSSBAUM, MARTHA, '*Ψυχή* in Heraclitus, I', *Phronesis*, 17 (1972), 1–16.

OHMANN, RICHARD M., 'Generative Grammar and the Concept of Literary Style', *Word*, 20 (1964), 423–39.

PAGE, D. L., 'Thucydides' Description of the Great Plague at Athens', *CQ*, NS 3 (1953), 97–119.

PALMER, F. R., *Semantics*, 2nd edn. (Cambridge, 1981).

PARRY, ADAM M., *The Language of Achilles and Other Papers* (Oxford, 1989).

PCG = R. Kassel and C. Austin (eds.), *Poetae Comici Graeci* (Berlin and New York, 1983–).

PEARSON, LIONEL, 'Hiatus and its Purpose in Attic Oratory', *AJPh* 96 (1975), 138–58.

—— 'Hiatus and its Effects in the Attic Speech-Writers', *TAPhA* 109 (1978), 131–45.

PFEIFFER, RUDOLF (ed.), *Callimachus*, 2 vols. (Oxford, 1949–51).

PMG = D. L. Page (ed.), *Poetae Melici Graeci* (Oxford, 1962).

POUILLOUX, JEAN, *Recherches sur l'histoire et les cultes de Thasos*, 2 vols. (Paris, 1954–8).

POWELL, J. ENOCH, *A Lexicon to Herodotus* (Cambridge, 1938).

PUHVEL, JAAN, *Homer and Hittite* (Innsbruck, 1991).

RADFORD, R. S., *Personification and the Use of Abstract Subjects in the Attic Orators and Thucydides* (Baltimore, 1901).

RAU, PETER, *Paratragodia* (Munich, 1967).

REDARD, C., *Les Noms grecs en -της, -τις* (Paris, 1949).

REHDANTZ, C. (ed.), *Demosthenes, Neun philosophische Reden*, rev. F. Blass, 4th edn., index volume (ii/2) (Leipzig, 1886).

RHODES, P. J., *A Commentary on the Aristotelian* Athenaion Politeia (Oxford, 1981).

RIFFATERRE, M., 'Criteria for Style Analysis', *Word*, 15 (1959), 154–74.

—— 'Stylistic Context', *Word*, 16 (1960), 207–18.

RITTER, C., *Platon* (Munich, 1910).

RODEMEYER, K. T., *Das Präsens historicum bei Herodot und Thukydides* (Basle, 1889).

RONNET, GILBERTE, *Étude sur le style de Démosthène* (Paris, 1951).

ROS, JAN, *Die μεταβολή (variatio) als Stilprinzip des Thukydides* (Nijmegen, 1938; repr. Amsterdam, 1968).

ROSCHATT, A., *Die Metaphern bei den attischen Rednern* (Strasburg, 1886).

ROSÉN, HAIIM B., *Eine Laut- und Formenlehre der herodotischen Sprachform* (Heidelberg, 1962).

—— 'Early Greek Grammar and Thought in Heraclitus', *Proceedings of the Israel Academy of Sciences and Humanities*, 7 (1988), 23–62.

ROSENKRANZ, B., 'Der lokale Grundton und die persönliche Eigenart in der Sprache des Thukydides und der älteren attischen Redner', *IF* 48 (1930), 127–78.

RUSSELL, D. A. (ed., comm.), *'Longinus' On the Sublime* (Oxford, 1964).

—— *Criticism in Antiquity* (London, 1981).

—— *An Anthology of Greek Prose* (Oxford, 1991).

SAKALIS, D. TH., *Ιωνικὸ λεκτικὸ στὸν Πλάτωνα*, 2 vols. (Ioannina, 1978–80).

SANSONE, DAVID, 'The Computer and the *Historia Augusta*: A Note on Marriott', *JRS* 80 (1990), 174–7.

—— 'Observations on the Definite Article in Plato', *CPh* 88 (1993), 191–205.

SAPIR, EDWARD, *Language* (London, 1970).

SARTRE, J.-P., *What is Literature?*, trans. Bernard Frechtman (New York, 1949; Cambridge, Mass., 1988).

SCHMID, WALTER, *Über die klassische Theorie und Praxis des antiken Prosarhythmus* (*Hermes*, Einzelschrift 12; Wiesbaden, 1959).

SCHMID, WILHELM, *Geschichte der griechischen Literatur*, part i, 5 vols. (Munich, 1929–58).

SCHWYZER, EDUARD, 'Die Parenthese im engeren und im weiteren Sinn', *ADAW*, Phil.-hist. Klasse, 1939, no. 6.

—— [see also *GG*].

SEBEOK, THOMAS A. (ed.), *Style in Language* (Cambridge, Mass., 1960).

SEG = *Supplementum Epigraphicum Graecum.*

SEIDENADEL, CARL W., *The First Grammar of the Language Spoken by the Bontoc Igorot* (Chicago, 1909).

SELDEN, RAMAN (ed.), *The Cambridge History of Literary Criticism*, viii (Cambridge, 1995).

SERRAO, GREGORIO, *Problemi di poesia alessandrina*, i. *Studi su Teocrito* (Rome, 1971).

SGDI = H. Collitz and O. Hoffmann, *Sammlung der griechischen Dialekt-Inschriften* (Göttingen, 1884–1915).

SHEWRING, W. H., 'Prose Rhythm and the Comparative Method', *CQ* 24 (1930), 164–73 and 25 (1931), 12–22.

SILK, M. S., *Interaction in Poetic Imagery* (Cambridge, 1974).

SLATER, WILLIAM J., *Lexicon to Pindar* (Berlin, 1969).

SLINGS, S. R., 'Written and Spoken Language: An Exercise in the Pragmatics of the Greek Language', *CPh* 87 (1992), 95–109.

SMYTH, H. WEIR, *The Sounds and Inflections of the Greek Dialects: Ionic* (Oxford, 1894).

SOLMSEN, FELIX, 'Zur griechischen Wortforschung', *IF* 31 (1912/13), 448–506.

SPENCER, J. (ed.), *Linguistics and Style* (London, 1964).

SPG = *Lo stile della prosa greca*, Ital. trans. by Enrico Renna of *GPS*, with the addition of indexes (Bari, 1993).

SPORMANN, C., *De Ellipsis Brachylogiaeque apud Herodotum et Thucydidem Usu* (Halle, 1888).

STAHL, J. M., *Kritisch-historische Syntax des griechischen Verbums der klassischen Zeit* (Heidelberg, 1907).

STANFORD, W. BEDELL, *Greek Metaphor* (Oxford, 1936).

STEVENS, P. T., *Colloquial Expressions in Euripides* (*Hermes*, Einzelschrift 38; Wiesbaden, 1976).

SVENSSON, ARVID, *Zum Gebrauch der erzählenden Tempora im Griechischen* (Lund, 1930).

TARRANT, DOROTHY, 'Colloquialisms, Semi-Proverbs and Word-Play in Plato', *CQ* 40 (1946), 109–17 and NS 8 (1958), 158–60.

TAYLOR, TALBOT J., *Linguistic Theory and Structural Stylistics* (Oxford, 1981).

THESLEFF, H., 'Scientific and Technical Style in Early Greek Prose', *Arctos*, NS 4 (1966), 89–113.

—— *Studies in the Styles of Plato* (Helsinki, 1967).

THREATTE, LESLIE, *The Grammar of Attic Inscriptions*, i. *Phonology* (Berlin and New York, 1980).

THUMB, ALBERT, *Handbook of the Modern Greek Vernacular*, 2nd edn., trans. S. Angus (Edinburgh, 1912).

THUMB, *Handbuch der griechischen Dialekte*, i, 2nd edn., rev. E. Kieckers (Heidelberg, 1932); ii, 2nd edn., rev. A. Scherer (Heidelberg, 1959).

TOD, M. N., *A Selection of Greek Historical Inscriptions*, ii (Oxford, 1948).

TOLSTOY, LEV, *Diaries*, ed. and trans. R. F. Christian (London, 1994).

TRENKNER, SOPHIE, *Le Style καί dans le récit attique oral* (Brussels, 1948; repr. Assen, 1960).

TURNER, G. W., *Stylistics* (Harmondsworth, 1973).

ULLMANN, STEPHEN, *Language and Style* (Oxford, 1966).

UNTERSTEINER, MARIO, *La lingua di Erodoto* (Bari, 1948).

VERDENIUS, W. J., 'The Principles of Literary Criticism', *Mnemosyne*, 4th ser. 36 (1983), 14–59.

VOGEL, V., 'Die Kürzenmeidung in der griechischen Prosa des IV. Jahrhunderts', *Hermes*, 58 (1923), 87–108.

WACKERNAGEL, J., *Vorlesungen über Syntax*, 2 vols., 2nd edn. (Basle, 1926–8).

WALES, KATIE, *A Dictionary of Stylistics* (Harlow, 1989).

WANKEL, HERMANN, *Demosthenes' Rede für Ktesiphon über den Kranz*, 2 vols. (Heidelberg, 1976).

WEBSTER, T. B. L., 'A Study of Greek Sentence Construction', *AJPh* 62 (1941), 385–415.

WELLEK, RENÉ, and WARREN, AUSTIN, *Theory of Literature*, 3rd edn. (New York, 1962).

WERNER, A., *The Language-Families of Africa* (London, 1923).

WEST, MARTIN, *Studies in Greek Elegy and Iambus* (Berlin and New York, 1974).

Wf = Detlev Fehling, *Die Wiederholungsfiguren und ihr Gebrauch bei den Griechen vor Gorgias* (Berlin, 1969).

WHEELER, G. C., *Mono-Alu Folklore* (London, 1926).

WILAMOWITZ-MOELLENDORFF, ULRICH VON, *Aristoteles und Athen*, 2 vols, (Berlin, 1893).

WILLIAMS, C. B., *Style and Vocabulary: Numerical Studies* (London, 1970).

WILLIGER, EDUARD, *Sprachliche Untersuchungen zu den Komposita der griechischen Dichter des 5. Jahrhunderts* (Göttingen, 1928).

WINTERSON, JEANETTE, *Art Objects* (London, 1995).

WISHART, D., and LEACH, S. V., 'A Multivariate Analysis of Platonic Prose Rhythm', *Computer Studies*, 3/2 (1970), 90–9.

WYSE, WILLIAM (ed., comm.), *The Speeches of Isaeus* (Cambridge, 1904).

ZARNCKE, EDUARD, *Die Entstehung der griechischen Literatursprachen* (Leipzig, 1890).

ZARRAFTIS, JACOB, *Forty-five Stories from the Dodekanese*, ed. and trans. R. M. Dawkins (Cambridge, 1950).

ZEHETMEIER, JOS., 'Die Periodenlehre des Aristoteles', *Ph* 85 (1930), 192–208, 255–84, 414–36.

ZINN, T. L., 'An Emendation in Isocrates', *CR*, NS 1 (1951), 74–5.

Names and works of ancient authors are mostly abbreviated as in LSJ or more explicitly, but note 'And.' = Andocides, 'Ant.' = Antiphon the orator; Dionysius of Halicarnassus ('D.H.' in LSJ) is abbreviated as 'Dion.' and cited by volume, page, and line of the Teubner edition of his rhetorical works by Usener and Radermacher. Hermogenes is cited by page and line of the Teubner edition by Rabe. Pseudo-Xenophon on the Athenian democracy is cited as 'Anon. *Ath.*'. The titles of periodicals are abbreviated as in *L'Année philologique* or more explicitly. Dates are BC unless indicated otherwise; in the case of papyri and inscriptions a superscript 'P' = AD. Thirds of a century are indicated by 'pr.' = early, 'm.' = middle, and 'ex.' = late.

I

FORM AND CONTENT

A. LEVELS OF STYLE

IT is generally, though not universally, agreed that if I am asked about the style of your performance of a certain act, I am being asked not *what* you did but *how* you did it.[1] If, however, I am to give a truly informative answer to the question and not take refuge in some jocular adverb such as 'reluctantly' or 'superbly', I must specify in more detail, and in temporal sequence, what you did. That is to say, I give a 'what' answer to a 'how' question. Yet the details given in my answer are not an exhaustive catalogue; I select only those items in which I think you had a choice between alternatives, so that your choice may be compared with the choices made by others.[2] Choice and comparison are implicit in any question about style; asked about your style of playing a Chopin prelude, I do not include among my answers the datum that you sat on a piano-stool—though that could naturally be part of the answer to the different question, 'How is a piano played?'

Applied to the written or spoken word, the distinction between

[1] Hough 2–5, 8; Leo 30 (but Leo's 'how' goes beyond language to the structure of a work as a whole); Ohmann in Freeman (1970) 259, 263–5; Osgood in Sebeok 293; Sartre 39; Turner 22, 97.

[2] Hough 9; Lyons (1977) ii. 615; Palmer 65; Turner 238; Ullmann 102. Enkvist (1973) 21–5 and Spencer and Gregory in Spencer 102–4 emphasize the indispensability of comparison, but Enkvist in Spencer 16–20 and (1973) 74–6 makes difficulties over the limitation of choice to style, pointing to 'grammatical choice' and 'pragmatic choice' where I would speak rather of 'constraints'. It should be noted that Enkvist consistently treats style from the standpoint of the critic (e.g. (1973) 145), not from that of the writer; but it is actually our own experience of choosing which tells us most about choice. Gray 104–7 argues that we cannot know what range of choices the writer believed to be available to hrm, but only what s/he actually wrote. In demanding 'knowledge' Gray is perhaps misled by the use of *science* in French works on style (e.g. 12, 93, 97–9). In English usage I recommend classifying stylistics with history, not science, bearing in mind that enquiry into what happened last year is just as much a historical activity as enquiring into what happened in ancient Egypt. Since we know what words were in use at a given point in time and space, and know also that an individual is normally familiar with more words than s/he actually uses in a particular work, we are entitled to rational historical presumption in speaking of an author's choice.

'what' and 'how' immediately raises the problem of the dichotomy between 'content' and 'form'. It will be easier to tackle that problem if we can first decide how far actions (including the composition of texts) are commensurable. For that purpose it is necessary to construct a 'hierarchy'[3] of levels.

Suppose, for example, that I am the chairman of a committee and it matters to me very much that at its next meeting the committee should vote in favour of a certain proposal. How do I set about getting what I want? Do I spring the question on the committee towards the end of the meeting, when everyone is rather tired, and hope to push it through? I would say, 'No, that's not my style.' Do I prepare a memorandum and circulate it in good time? Or talk with each member of the committee separately before the meeting? Let us say, for the sake of argument, the latter. We have now answered a question about my *style of committee management*. When I see the members separately, the three main courses open to me are: reason, bribery, and threats. By 'bribery' I mean, conveying the impression that voting the way I want is likely to have desirable consequences for the member in question, and by 'threats' I mean the converse. Let us say that I choose bribery; we have answered the question, 'What is my *style of persuasion?*', and we can proceed to the next question, 'What is my *style of bribery?*' This involves us before long in consideration of the mechanism of communication: volume, speed, and tone of voice; stance, gesture, facial expression; and the choice and ordering of words, pauses, and syntactical constructions. We have finally arrived at the level of *linguistic style*. At each stage of the journey from one level to the next a 'how' question elicited a 'what' answer, which in turn generated a new 'how' question.

Let us apply that principle to a passage of contemporary literature. David Lodge, in *The British Museum is Falling Down*, imitates in successive chapters a number of different authors. In ch. 3 the protagonist of the book, Adam by name, becomes 'A'. He is trying to renew his reader's ticket at the British Museum, but he is overcome by fatigue, debilitated by hunger, and driven to despair by the obstacles which the tranquil lunacy of the officials to whom he applies puts in the way of the renewal. He faints. 'A' in itself signals Kafka, whose protagonist in *Der Prozeß* is 'K', and A's faint reminds us of K's wave of faintness in the oppressive air of the

---

[3] I do not use this term as Ingarden (1960) does (54, 97; cf. Golub in Selden 295–7 on Ingarden's 'layers' or 'strata'), nor quite as it is used by Enkvist in Spencer 36.

tribunal offices. K is spotted by a girl secretary, who summons a dignified and elegantly dressed man. The man suggests that K is adversely affected by the close atmosphere of the offices. K eagerly agrees, and expects to be helped outside into the fresh air, but the man stands there with his hands in his pockets and laughs loudly. 'You see?' says the man to the girl, 'This gentleman isn't really ill. It's just that he feels ill *here*.' K fervently agrees, and they do help him to go outside. On the way the girl says to K, 'Don't let his laugh worry you. We try to give a good impression here—that's why we dress so elegantly—but he spoils it with that laugh of his. It scares people off.' She does not whisper this, but says it aloud, and the man responds jocularly, 'I don't know why you insist on telling this gentleman all our secrets. He's got enough to worry about as it is.' Now, if the man had frowned fiercely at K, annoyed at a disturbance of the smooth routine of the office, and if the girl had whispered her reassuring words to K, the incident would have been banal, but Kafka (as so often) invests the scene with a character familiar to us in dreams, though luckily rare in our waking lives. This is equally true of the behaviour of Lodge's officials in the library. Kafka's narrative and Lodge's therefore share the same (unusual) *style at the level of invention*.[4]

The importance of distinguishing between levels in Greek literature can be shown by comparing the speeches in Herodotus with those in Thucydides. In Herodotus long speeches are comparatively rare, in Thucydides abundant; there is much conversation in the former, none in the latter. In a Thucydidean speech we often find that a generalization is derived from a factual datum and leads into another factual statement, which in turn generates another generalization (e.g. ii. 60, vi. 16; contrast Hdt. vii. 8–11, where all the generalizations are heaped together in 10. δ. 2, ε–ζ, η. 2). In Thucydidean generalizations we are struck by his fondness for treating the neuter singular adjective with the article as a noun (six examples in ii. 62. 5–63. 3; none at all in Artabanus' three-page speech, Hdt. vii. 10). If all these contrasts were brought together under the rubric 'style' without discrimination, nothing but confusion could result. The presence or absence of speeches and of conversation are matters of *historiographical style*; argument from

[4] Auerbach often uses 'style' in this sense (e.g. 106, 215, 223–6), but sometimes also of what I call 'linguistic style' (e.g. 121, 159–60), without discrimination.

4 *Form and Content*

generalization, of *oratorical style*; and constructions with the neuter adjective, of *linguistic style*.[5]

Some degree of interaction between levels is to be expected. The more generalization there is in a speech, the more numerous the *opportunities* for the substantivized neuter adjective and infinitive; but the opportunities do not have to be taken, because there are linguistic alternatives, e.g. the creation of abstract nouns in -ια. An interesting exercise in the disentangling of philosophical style from linguistic style is afforded by the extant citations from Heraclitus. No Greek prose writer is so readily recognized—or so easily parodied, as he is by Lucian in *Vit.* 14, whose Heraclitus says:

καὶ ἔστι τωὐτὸ τέρψις ἀτερπίη, γνῶσις ἀγνωσίη, μέγα μικρόν, ἄνω κάτω κτλ.

And delight and disgust are the same thing, knowledge, ignorance, great, small, up, down . . .,

reminding us of (among much else) DK 22 B 10:

συλλάψιες[6] ὅλα καὶ οὐχ ὅλα, συμφερόμενον διαφερόμενον, συνᾷδον διᾷδον, καὶ ἐκ πάντων ἓν καὶ ἐξ ἑνὸς πάντα.

Takings of things together (sc. are) wholes and not wholes, being brought together, being brought apart, in tune, out of tune. From all (sc. comes) one and from one all.

(With each of the four items from 'being brought together' to 'out of tune' we presumably have to understand 'something'.) The citations include several other examples of '*a*, opposite-of-*a*' (e.g. B 62) and 'not-*a* and *a*' (e.g. B 32 οὐκ ἐθέλει καὶ ἐθέλει). Propositions of this kind, inadequately or enigmatically explained, are one (only one) feature of Heraclitus' style of philosophical argument. All the features of the citations are to be found in one chapter of the Hippocratic *De Victu* (i. 5), which at all levels of style differs from the rest of the *De Victu*, and they naturally tend to be expressed in short clauses, often of just two adjectives or verbs. It is not, however, inevitable that asyndeton should be so common within such a pair or between successive pairs, or that the grammatical relation of a pair to its wider context should be as obscure as it sometimes is in Hera-

---

[5] Van Groningen 224 draws a distinction between the 'style' of a work and its 'composition'. Cf. Enkvist in Chatman 52, 64, Hasan ibid. 327. What I have said about 'levels' seems to be implied by Doležel in Chatman 95–106, Wellek ibid. 70, and Hough 105; but Hough 10, in speaking of scientific papers, runs two levels together, one of them being the organization of a paper.

[6] V.l. συνάψιες, but that does not affect my point.

clitus. There we see features of linguistic style which are distinct from the author's style of philosophical exposition and argument. Let us now consider an example in which two authors' treatment of the same topic can be compared step by step. In the funeral speech traditionally ascribed to Lysias (Lys. ii; and for present purposes the validity of the ascription does not matter)[7] the author uses at §§48–53 a narrative passage of Thucydides, i. 105, describing the Corinthian invasion of the Megarid in or about 459, thus:

	Thuc.	Lys.
1	πολέμου δὲ καταστάντος πρὸς Αἰγινήτας Ἀθηναίοις μετὰ ταῦτα	ὑστέρῳ δὲ χρόνῳ Ἑλληνικοῦ πολέμου καταστάντος
2		διὰ ζῆλον τῶν γεγενημένων καὶ φθόνον τῶν πεπραγμένων,
3		μέγα μὲν ἅπαντες φρονοῦντες, μικρῶν δ' ἐγκλημάτων ἕκαστοι δεόμενοι,
4	ναυμαχία γίγνεται ἐπ' Αἰγίνῃ μεγάλη Ἀθηναίων καὶ Αἰγινητῶν, καὶ οἱ ξύμμαχοι ἑκατέροις παρῆσαν,	ναυμαχίας Ἀθηναίοις πρὸς Αἰγινήτας καὶ τοὺς ἐκείνων συμμάχους γενομένης
5	καὶ ἐνίκων Ἀθηναῖοι, καὶ ναῦς ἑβδομήκοντα λαβόντες αὐτῶν	ἑβδομήκοντα τριήρεις αὐτῶν ἐλάμβανον.
6	ἐς τὴν γῆν ἀπέβησαν καὶ ἐπολιόρκουν,	πολιορκούντων δὲ
7		κατὰ τὸν αὐτὸν χρόνον Αἴγυπτόν τε καὶ Αἴγιναν,
8	Λεωκράτους τοῦ Στροίβου στρατηγοῦντος.	
9	ἔπειτα Πελοποννήσιοι ἀμύνειν βουλόμενοι Αἰγινήταις ἐς μὲν τὴν Αἴγιναν τριακοσίους ὁπλίτας πρότερον Κορινθίων καὶ Ἐπιδαυρίων ἐπικούρους διεβίβασαν,	
10		καὶ τῆς ἡλικίας ἀπούσης ἔν τε ταῖς ναυσὶ καὶ ἐν τῷ πεζῷ στρατεύματι,
11	τὰ δὲ ἄκρα τῆς Γερανείας κατέλαβον	
12	καὶ ἐς τὴν Μεγαρίδα κατέβησαν	

[7] It must have been among the speeches attributed to Lysias in Callimachus' catalogue, and may safely be assigned to the 4th c. BC. We have no epideictic works of Lysias with which to compare it except the short citation (50–60 lines of modern text) of his *Olympikos* in Dion. i. 46–8. Cf. Dover (1968c) 25 f., 60–7.

13	Κορίνθιοι μετὰ τῶν ξυμμάχων,	Κορίνθιοι καὶ οἱ σύμμαχοι
14	νομίζοντες	ἡγούμενοι
15	ἀδυνάτους ἔσεσθαι Ἀθηναίους βο-ηθεῖν τοῖς Μεγαρεῦσιν	ἢ εἰς ἔρημον τὴν χώραν ἐμβαλεῖν
10	ἔν τε Αἰγίνῃ ἀπούσης στρατιᾶς πολ-λῆς καὶ ἐν Αἰγύπτῳ·	
16	ἦν δὲ καὶ βοηθῶσιν, ἀπ᾽ Αἰγίνης ἀναστήσεσθαι αὐτούς.	ἢ ἐξ Αἰγίνης ἄξειν τὸ στρατόπεδον,
17		ἐξελθόντες πανδημεὶ
11		Γεράνειαν κατέλαβον.
18	οἱ δὲ Ἀθηναῖοι	Ἀθηναῖοι δὲ
19		τῶν μὲν ἀπόντων, τῶν δ᾽ ἐγγὺς ὄν-των,
20	τὸ μὲν πρὸς Αἰγίνῃ στράτευμα οὐκ ἐκίνησαν,	οὐδένα ἐτόλμησαν μεταπέμψασθαι·
21		ταῖς δ᾽ αὑτῶν ψυχαῖς πιστεύσαντες καὶ τῶν ἐπιόντων καταφρονήσαντες
22	τῶν δ᾽ ἐκ τῆς πόλεως ὑπολοίπων οἵ τε πρεσβύτατοι καὶ οἱ νεώτατοι	οἱ γεραίτεροι καὶ οἱ τῆς ἡλικίας ἐν-τὸς γεγονότες
23		ἠξίουν αὐτοὶ μόνοι τὸν κίνδυνον ποι-ήσασθαι, οἱ μὲν ἐμπειρίᾳ τὴν ἀρε-τήν, οἱ δὲ φύσει κεκτημένοι,
24		καὶ οἱ μὲν αὐτοὶ πολλαχοῦ ἀγαθοὶ γεγενημένοι, οἱ δ᾽ ἐκείνους μιμού-μενοι, τῶν μὲν πρεσβυτέρων ἄρχειν ἐπισταμένων, τῶν δὲ νεωτέρων τὸ ἐπιταττόμενον ποιεῖν δυναμένων.
25	ἀφικνοῦνται ἐς τὰ Μέγαρα	
26	Μυρωνίδου στρατηγοῦντος.	Μυρωνίδου ⟨οὖν⟩ στρατηγοῦντος
25		ἀπαντήσαντες αὐτοὶ ἐς τὴν Μεγα-ρίδα
27	καὶ μάχης γενομένης ἰσορρόπου πρὸς Κορινθίους διεκρίθησαν ἀπ᾽ ἀλλήλων, καὶ ἐνόμισαν αὐτοὶ ἑκάτε-ροι οὐκ ἔλασσον ἔχειν ἐν τῷ ἔργῳ.	ἐνίκων μαχόμενοι
28		ἅπασαν τὴν δύναμιν τὴν ἐκείνων τοῖς ἤδη ἀπειρηκόσι καὶ τοῖς οὔπω δυναμένοις, τοὺς εἰς τὴν σφετέραν ἐμβαλεῖν ἀξιώσαντας, εἰς τὴν ἀλλο-τρίαν ἀπαντήσαντες,

29   καὶ οἱ μὲν Ἀθηναῖοι (ἐκράτησαν γὰρ   τροπαῖον δὲ στήσαντες
      ὅμως μᾶλλον) ἀπελθόντων τῶν Κο-
      ρινθίων τροπαῖον ἔστησαν·

30   καλλίστου μὲν αὐτοῖς ἔργου,

31   οἱ δὲ Κορίνθιοι κακιζόμενοι ὑπὸ τῶν   αἰσχίστου δὲ τοῖς πολεμίοις.
      ἐν τῇ πόλει πρεσβυτέρων

32   καὶ παρασκευασάμενοι, ἡμέραις
      ὕστερον δώδεκα μάλιστα ἐλθόντες
      ἀνθίστασαν τροπαῖον καὶ αὐτοὶ ὡς
      νικήσαντες. καὶ οἱ Ἀθηναῖοι ἐκβο-
      ηθήσαντες ἐκ τῶν Μεγάρων τούς τε
      τὸ τροπαῖον ἱστάντας διαφθείρουσι
      καὶ τοῖς ἄλλοις ξυμβαλόντες ἐκρά-
      τησαν.

33   οἱ μὲν οὐκέτι τοῖς σώμασιν, οἱ δ'
      οὔπω δυνάμενοι, ταῖς δὲ ψυχαῖς ἀμ-
      φότεροι κρείττους γενόμενοι, μετὰ
      καλλίστης δόξης εἰς τὴν αὐτῶν ἀπ-
      ελθόντες οἱ μὲν πάλιν ἐπαιδεύοντο,
      οἱ δὲ περὶ τῶν λοιπῶν ἐβουλεύοντο.

34   οἱ δὲ νικώμενοι ὑπεχώρουν κτλ.
      (ch. 106: vivid tactical details of
      destruction of Corinthian force
      on its retreat)

After that the Athenians became involved in war against the Aeginetans, and there was a great sea-battle off Aegina between Athenians and Aeginetans, allies being present on both sides. The Athenians won, captured seventy ships of the Aeginetans, landed, and laid siege to Aegina, under the command of Leocrates, son of Stroibos. Then the Peloponnesians, wishing to help the Aeginetans, first sent three hundred Corinthian hoplites, with Epidaurian support, across to Aegina, and now the Corinthians and their allies occupied the heights of Geraneia and came

Later, a war between Greek states broke out, through emulation of what had been done and envy of past achievements, all with high ambition and each city needing only slight excuse. There was a sea-battle between the Athenians and the Aeginetans and their allies, and the Athenians captured seventy Aeginetan triremes; and as they were laying siege at the same time to Aegina and Egypt and their men of military age were away in the fleet and the land forces, the Corinthians and their allies, believing that they would be invading a country empty of defenders or that they would down into the Megarid, believing that the Athenians would be unable to help the Megarians, having large forces away both on Aegina and in Egypt, and, if they did intervene, that they would lift the siege.

But the Athenians did not move their force from Aegina. The oldest and youngest of those who remained in the city arrived at Megara under the command of Myronides.

cause the Athenian force to come back from Aegina, came out in full strength and occupied Geraneia.

But the Athenians, with their own forces away and their enemies close at hand, were bold enough not to recall anyone; trusting in their own spirit, and despising their attackers, the older men and those below military age judged that they should face the danger on their own; the older men possessed valour through experience, the younger by nature, for the former had often themselves fought bravely, and the latter followed their example, the older men knowing how to command and the younger being capable of doing what they were told.

So under the command of Myronides they, by themselves, met the enemy in the Megarid and defeated in battle the entire enemy force, with those who had by now given up active service and those who were not yet qualified for it—defeated the enemy who had thought he could invade their territory, encountering him on foreign soil.

An indecisive battle was fought against the Corinthians, and they parted with both sides thinking that they had given as good as they got.

And the Athenians—for they in fact had the best of it—set up a trophy when the Corinthians had gone, while the Corinthians, being vilified by the older people in the city, made fresh preparation, and about twelve days later

And having set up a trophy of an achievement most creditable to themselves and most shameful for their enemies,

came and tried to set up a trophy of their own, as if they had
won. But the Athenians, arriving
on the scene from Megara, killed
those who were setting up the
trophy, fell upon the rest of the
Corinthian force, and worsted it.

the older men no longer at the
peak of bodily strength and the
younger not yet, but both superior in spirit, they returned to
their own land with glory, and
while the younger returned to
their education the older delibe-
rated on the future.

The defeated force withdrew . . .

At two points the authors are in conflict: were Athenian allies present at the sea-battle (4), and did the Athenians defeat the whole
strength of Corinth (17, 27–8) or the Corinthian hoplite force mi-
nus the 300 hoplites despatched to Aegina (9)? Whatever the truth
of the matter, they cannot both be telling it. Item 28 in Lysias,
profoundly misleading if Thucydides is right in 27, 29, 32, could
perhaps be defended by Lysias as an abbreviation, a justifiable dis-
regard of details in order to bring out the essential point. Such
differences in the relation between narrative and fact, if they are to
be brought into the category of stylistic difference, are differences
not in *historiographical* style but the style of the activity which we
call *history*.[8] Lysias omits the name of Leocrates (8) while mention-
ing Myronides (26); Myronides was enshrined in popular tradition
(e.g. Ar. *Eccl.* 304), but Leocrates was not. Thucydides says nothing of the sentiments, discipline, and courage of the 'oldest and
youngest'; Lysias insistently enlarges on those aspects of the story,
and this is a matter of historiographical style, for the orator becomes
a historiographer to the extent to which he narrates past events. On
the level of linguistic style the most striking contrasts lie in the
co-ordination of phrases and sentences: rhyme and assonance are
ubiquitous in Lysias (2, 19, 21, 24 (*bis*), 30–1, 33) and antithesis
with μέν and δέ abundant (3, 19, 23, 24 (*bis*), 30–1, 33 (*bis*)), to
which we should add two pairs of symmetrical phrases with καί

---

[8] What came to be called the 'history' of Herodotus is called by him (i proem.)
the 'exposition' (ἀπόδεξις) of his 'enquiry' (ἱστορίη).

(2, 10). Thucydides has no assonance or rhyme; he uses μέν and δέ only three times, always asymmetrically (9–11, 20–2, 29–31), and co-ordination with τε and καί twice (10, 32). It will also be observed that there are in Thucydides 14 finite verbs, of which no less than 9 are co-ordinated with the previous finite verb by καί. In Lysias, on the other hand, we find only 8 finite verbs, and none of them is linked to another by καί.

In Aeschines' reuse (ii. 172–6) of material composed by Andocides fifty years earlier (iii. 3–9) the adherence to the wording of the original is closer and modification of the content much more subtle, e.g.

	And. iii. 8	Aeschines ii. 175
1	πάλιν δὲ διὰ Μεγαρέας πολεμήσαντες	πάλιν δὲ εἰς πόλεμον διὰ Μεγαρέας πεισθέντες καταστῆναι
2	καὶ τὴν χώραν τμηθῆναι προέμενοι	καὶ τὴν χώραν τμηθῆναι προέμενοι
3	πολλῶν ἀγαθῶν στερηθέντες	καὶ πολλῶν ἀγαθῶν στερηθέντες
4		εἰρήνης ἐδεήθημεν,
5	αὖθις τὴν εἰρήνην ἐποιησάμεθα, ἣν Νικίας ὁ Νικηράτου κατηργάσατο.	καὶ ἐποιησάμεθα διὰ Νικίου τοῦ Νικηράτου.
6	οἶμαι δ' ὑμᾶς ἅπαντας εἰδέναι τοῦτο,	
7		καὶ πάλιν ἐν τῷ χρόνῳ τούτῳ
8	ὅτι διὰ ταύτην τὴν εἰρήνην	
9	ἑπτακισχίλια μὲν τάλαντα νομίσματος εἰς τὴν ἀκρόπολιν ἀνηνέγκαμεν,	ἑπτακισχίλια τάλαντα ἀνηνέγκαμεν εἰς τὴν ἀκρόπολιν
8		διὰ τὴν εἰρήνην ταύτην
10	ναῦς δὲ πλείους ἢ τριακόσια ἐκτησάμεθα κτλ.	τριήρεις δὲ ἐκτησάμεθα πλωΐμους καὶ ἐντελεῖς οὐκ ἐλάττους ἢ τριακοσίας κτλ.

We went to war again because of the Megarians, and having sacrificed our land for ravaging, deprived of many benefits, we again made peace, which Nikias son of Nikeratos brought about.

And I think you all know that because of that peace we put 7,000 talents in coinage up on to the

We were again persuaded to go to war because of the Megarians, and having sacrificed our land for ravaging, and being deprived of many benefits, we desired peace, and we made peace through Nikias son of Nikeratos.

And again in that period we put 7,000 talents up on to the Acropolis because of that peace, and

Acropolis, and we acquired more than 300 triremes.	we acquired no fewer than 300 triremes, seaworthy and fully equipped.

The thrust of the argument is not the same in both speeches; Andocides had argued, 'There's *no harm* in making peace now', but Aeschines wants to argue that peace has always been positively beneficial to Athens. Hence (item 1) his 'persuaded to go to war' instead of simply 'going to war',[9] (items 4–5) 'we wanted peace, and we made it . . .' instead of 'we made peace', and the expansion (item 10) of '300 triremes' to 'no fewer than 300 seaworthy, completely fitted-out triremes'. The purely linguistic differences are of a trivial kind, though they *might* prove on investigation to exemplify syntactical preferences characteristic of Andocides and Aeschines respectively.

From now on I propose to use the term 'style' in the sense 'linguistic style'. It is reasonable to suspect that the adoption of different styles by Thucydides and by Lysias is at least in part determined by the different purposes for which they are composing: Thucydides for the reader who 'wants to know what actually happened' (i. 22. 4), Lysias for an audience[10] attending a ceremonial occasion and wishing to be reassured of the unique worth of its city and the valour of its ancestors. Linguistic difference between 'epideictic' oratory and 'forensic' oratory is recognized by Arist. *Rhet.* 1414ᵃ18–28, and Dionysius i. 86. 8–92. 4, ii. 120. 5–8, illuminates the difference by scrutiny of Isoc. xvii (the *Trapezitikos*), observing that the sentence (§9)

. . . in the belief that if I attempted (ἐπιχειροίην) to stay here, I would be extradited (ἐκδοθήσεσθαι) by Athens to Satyros, and if I took refuge

[9] Andocides himself said 'persuaded by Argos' (iii. 9) in connection with hostilities between 421 and 414, and Aeschines ii. 176 naturally repeats that. Andocides' words are in keeping with his resistance (iii. 24 ff., especially 31–2) to Argive pressure at the time of the speech.

[10] Greek writers in general designed their work more for the ear than for the eye (note the implications of Pl. *Tht.* 142 D–143 C and *Prm.* 127 B–E). Cf. de Groot 11 f. and Deichgräber (1962) 481 f. (following Wilamowitz). I therefore refer to 'audiences' and 'hearers' rather than to 'readers'. Modern writers on style tend to think more readily in terms of readership, e.g. Dillon 46–9 on 'hypotheses which are generated by expectation of an imminent clause-boundary but are "disappointed"'. The prosodic features of a sentence spoken aloud may normally be expected to preclude disappointment. What Mukařovský 54–8 says about 'semantic accumulation' applies to hearers and readers alike.

(τραποίην) anywhere else, he would take no notice of my plea, and if I sailed (εἰσπλευσοίμην) to Pontus I would be executed (ἀποθανεῖσθαι) with my father

exceeds the 'forensic manner' in length and makes use of symmetries and assonances which are characteristic of epideictic oratory (91. 8–15, 19–92. 1)—precisely the features which we have observed in the Lysian funeral speech.

Expectations may be so torpidly constant, and satisfied so fully by speaker, writer, artist, or composer, as virtually to preclude any significant change of style over a long period, as has happened from time to time in religious iconography.[11] S/he may, on the other hand, broaden these expectations by tactful innovation; but the tact is indispensable for success, because blatant incongruity provokes a laughter or revulsion neither intended nor welcomed by the author. This matter will be discussed further on pp. 53–6.

B. ALTERNATIVE FORMULATIONS

Dogmatic answers have sometimes been given to the unhelpful question 'Can form and content be separated?', when the question which matters is, 'To what extent, and in what circumstances, is it useful to separate form from content?'[12] The question is applicable to all activities, and in the arts it does not apply only to the written or spoken word. Do two portraits of A depict the same 'content' in different 'forms'? They certainly share something important which neither of them shares with a portrait of B. What is the right term for that 'of'-relationship which they share? More pertinently, Frank Auerbach's pictures 'after' Rembrandt and Rubens[13] *extract* the 'form' from paintings, discard the 'subjects' of the original, and

---

[11] Much of the public, including churchmen, reacted against Epstein's *Risen Christ* with a ferocity which now seems insane (Friedman 30–9). Joyce's *Ulysses*, which did not give the general public what was expected of a novel, provoked equal shock but less fury.

[12] Puck's speech at the end of *Midsummer Night's Dream* and the Clown's song at the end of *Twelfth Night* differ greatly in respect of the extent to which they could be paraphrased. Roger Fowler 6 f. justly regrets the uncompromising polarization of views on form and content, and Barthes in Chatman 4 observes that the dichotomy 'has an irreducible grain of truth'; cf. Starobinski ibid. 286–8 and Wells in Sebeok 422. Wales 91 f., 134 f., 184 f., 305 defines the issues lucidly, as always. Ingarden's approach (1938) to the question is somewhat metaphysical. It may well be thought that the fact of translation from one language into another settles the matter (cf. Hasan in Chatman 302 f.), and translation from one register into another within the same language (cf. pp. 53 f.) is no different in principle.

[13] Illustrated in Lubbock's article.

present us with an abstract pattern of line and colour. In music, theme and variations find a more appropriate analogy in evolutionary genetics than in language, but what about a transcription? After Beethoven had composed his violin concerto, it was suggested to him that it would go rather well as a piano concerto. He agreed, and transcribed it accordingly. The orchestral part remained intact from beginning to end, and the violin part became the right-hand part on the piano. A left-hand part had to be added, which (I am told by musicians) is somewhat banal and mechanical. The sound of a violin and the sound of a piano being rather different, one can hardly refuse to treat the sound as part of the content, but the left-hand part in Beethoven's concerto could fairly be compared to the empty 'ornamental' epithets which Aristotle *Rhet.* 1406^{a}10–35 criticizes as inappropriate in speech, however acceptable they may be in poetry (γάλα λευκόν is his first and clearest example).

However disputable separation of form from content may be in such cases, it becomes a great deal easier when the function of an utterance is clearly discernible and precisely definable. Practically all utterance is 'goal-directed',[14] designed to cause a change in the hearer: a cognitive change, when information is being communicated, and in other cases the movements entailed by physical action or the reinforcement or debilitation of an emotion or attitude.[15] Just as I may choose for the tightening of a screw a red-handled screwdriver in preference to one which has identical length, weight, and blade but a green handle, so I may choose between different verbal means to the attainment of the goal of my utterance.

The simplest illustrations can be drawn from administrative documents. An Attic decree normally contains a provision that 'the secretary of the council is to inscribe this decree on a stone stele and set it up on the Acropolis'. Here are six instances of that formula from the first half of the fourth century BC:

[14] Jakobson 64.
[15] Green 3 f., Turner 146 f., Wellek in Sebeok 415. It will be obvious by now that my approach to all utterance is pragmatic and resolutely intentionalist. The problems and limitations of intentionalism are helpfully discussed by Rabinowitz in Selden 347–74, but it seems to me that intentionalism is fundamental to all translation. Without a defensible hypothesis about what Greeks *intended* to cause in the mind of a hearer by uttering the disyllable ἄνδρα we cannot translate even the first word of the *Odyssey*, and therefore cannot say anything about the line except as a succession of vocal sounds.

(a) *IG* ii² 24b. 6–8 (390/389): ἀν]αγράψ[αι δὲ τόδε τὸ] ψήφισμα ἐν στήληι
λ[ιθίν]ηι τὸν [γραμματέα τ]ῆς βολῆς καὶ στῆσαι [ἐμ πό]ληι

(b) Ibid. 31. 12–14 (386/5): κ]α[ὶ στῆσ]αι [ἐ]ς στήλην ἀναγ[ράψαντ]α τὸν
γραμ[μ]ατέ[α] τῆς βολῆς τὰ ἐψ[ηφισμ]ένα ⟨ἐν ἀ⟩[κ]ροπό]λ[ει

(c) Ibid. 76. 17–20 (c.380): ὁ] δὲ γ[ραμ]ματεὺς ὁ τῆς βολῆς ἀν[αγρ]αψάτω¹⁶ ἐν
στήληι λιθ[ίνηι] καὶ θέτω ἐν ἀκροπόλε[ι

(d) Ibid. 81. 7–10 (c.380): τὸ] δὲ ψήφισμα τόδε ἀ[ναγραψάτω ὁ γραμμ]ατεὺς ὁ
τῆς βολῆ[ς ἐν στήληι λιθίν]ηι καὶ καταθέτω ἐ[ν ἀκροπόλει

(e) Ibid. 106. 15–17 (367): τὸ δὲ [ψήφισμα τόδε ἀναγραψ]άτω ὁ [γ]ραμματεὺς
τῆς βολ[ῆς ἐν στήληι λιθίνηι κ]αὶ στ[η]σάτω ἐν ἀκροπόλη[ι

(f) Ibid. 107. 18–20 (367): ἀναγράψαι δ[ὲ τ]όδ[ε τὸ ψ]ή[φι]σμα τὸν γραμματέα
τῆς [βου]λῆ[ς] ἐν στήληι λιθίνη[ι καὶ στ]ῆσαι ἐν ἀκροπόλει

The provision may be expressed either in the imperative, with a
nominative subject as in (c), (d), and (e), or in the infinitive, with
an accusative subject as in (a), (b), and (f). Example (b) is peculiar
in beginning with 'set', separating that from 'on the Acropolis',
and putting 'inscribe' into participial form. As a normal rule, the
provision may begin with any of the three ingredients 'secretary'
as in (c), 'this decree' as in (d) and (e), and 'inscribe' as in (a)
and (f). 'This' may either precede 'decree' or follow it. 'Set' is
usually στῆσαι, but may be θεῖναι as in (c) or καταθεῖναι as in (d).
'Acropolis' may be either πόλις or ἀκρόπολις. In 'the secretary of the
council' the masculine article may be repeated as in (c) and (d). If
we ignore the five singularities contained in (b)—καί instead of δέ,
ἐς στήλην instead of ἐν στήληι, the omission of 'stone', the participial
construction, and τὰ ἐψηφισμένα—we have so far reached 288 different ways of saying 'and let the secretary . . . etc.'. Include the
oddities of (b), and we go into the thousands. Yet every one of these
ways has an absolutely identical function,¹⁷ to cause the secretary to
perform a certain closely defined action; the differences of wording
allow him no latitude of interpretation, and it is hard to see how
any one of them could have affected him emotionally more or less
than the others—except, of course, for the enjoyment which Neon
of Halai, secretary in one prytany of 386/5, must have derived from
his highly original manipulation of the formula in (b). Let us hope

---

¹⁶ There is no accidental omission of 'this decree' here, because the decree is
honorific and the understood object of 'inscribe' is 'him', i.e. 'his name'; cf. *IG* ii²
51. 9, 95. 6 f. (. . . ἀναγράψαι τὸν γραμματέα τῆς βουλῆ]ς Ἀπολλω[νίδην), although there
is no objection (cf. 82. 13 f.) to 'this decree' in such a case.

¹⁷ Cf. Jakobson 66, Enkvist 21.

that his ghost rejoices that he is mentioned in a book about prose style 2,400 years later.

The variability of the formula 'And let the secretary . . .' is matched by variability in other inscribed formulae, e.g. boundary-markers:[18]

IG i³ 1111: ἄχρι τê[s] hοδô τêσδε τὸ ἄστυ τêιδε νενέμêται
Ibid. 1113: [ἄ]χρι τ[έσ]δε τês hοδô τêιδε hē Μονιχίας ἐστὶ νέμησις (η sic)

and

Ibid. 1129: . . . Περαιὸν δὲ τριττὺς ἄρχεται
Ibid. 1127: . . . ἄρχεται δὲ Μυρρινοσίον̣ τριτ[τύς]
Ibid. 1128: . . . Θριασίων δὲ ἄρχεται τριττύς.

An honorific decree often has occasion to say that the honorand has proved himself a good friend of Athens 'both now and earlier'. The communication of this fact may take many forms,[19] e.g.:

IG ii² 26. 10 f. (c.390): καὶ ν[υνὶ] καὶ ἐν τῶι προτέρωι χρόνωι
Ibid. 96. 9 f. (375): [κ]αὶ νῦν καὶ ἐν τῶι πρόσθ[εν χρόνωι
Ibid. 207. 5–7 (348): καὶ νῦ]ν καὶ ἐν τῶι ἔμπροσθεν χρόνωι
Ibid. 347. 14 f. (331): κα]ὶ νῦν καὶ ἐν τῶ (sic) παρ[εληλυθό]τι χρόνωι
Ibid. 400. 10 (c.320): καὶ ἐν] τῶι πρόσθεν χρ[όνωι καὶ νῦν
Ibid. 401. 5 f. (c.320): ἔν τ[ε τ]ῶι ἔμπροσθεν χρόνωι καὶ νῦ[ν

It is not only administrators and clerks who have recourse to formulae; they are inescapable also for people who write books on scientific, medical, geographical, or genealogical topics, and we may often observe an individual writer using alternative formulations in the same context, for the avoidance of monotony, as in Hdt. ii. 17. 3–5, on the outflow of the Nile:[20]

μέχρι μὲν νυν Κερκασώρου πόλιος ῥέει εἰς ἐὼν ὁ Νεῖλος, τὸ δὲ ἀπὸ ταύτης τῆς πόλιος σχίζεται τριφασίας ὁδούς. καὶ ἡ μὲν πρὸς ἠῶ τρέπεται, τὸ καλέεται Πηλούσιον στόμα, ἡ δὲ ἑτέρη τῶν ὁδῶν πρὸς ἑσπέρην ἔχει· τοῦτο δὲ Κανωβικὸν στόμα κέκληται. ἡ δὲ δὴ ἰθέα τῶν ὁδῶν τῷ Νείλῳ ἐστὶ ἥδε· ἄνωθεν φερόμενος ἐς τὸ ὀξὺ τοῦ Δέλτα ἀπικνέεται, τὸ δὲ ἀπὸ τούτου σχίζων μέσον τὸ Δέλτα ἐς θάλασσαν ἐξίει, οὔτε ἐλαχίστην μοῖραν τοῦ ὕδατος παρεχόμενος ταύτῃ οὔτε ἥκιστα ὀνομαστήν, τὸ καλέεται Σεβεννυτικὸν στόμα. ἔστι δὲ καὶ ἕτερα διφάσια στόματα ἀπὸ τοῦ Σεβεννυτικοῦ ἀποσχισθέντα φέροντα ἐς θάλασσαν, τοῖσι οὐνόματα κεῖται τάδε, τῷ μὲν Σαϊτικὸν αὐτῶν, τῷ δὲ Μενδήσιον.

---

[18] Dover (1968a) 53.
[19] Dover (1987) 35.
[20] Donini, esp. 97–9.

As far as the city of Kerkasoros the Nile flows as one stream, but after that city it splits into three paths; one of them turns to the east, which is called the Pelusian mouth, and the other path holds to the west; this has been named the Canobic mouth. That path of the Nile which goes straight on is this: coming from the south to the apex of the Delta, from there onwards it discharges into the sea by cutting the Delta in half, producing by this route a proportion of the water which is neither the smallest in quantity nor the least renowned, which is called the Sebennytic mouth. There are two further mouths split off from the Sebennytic and bearing to the sea, to which the names which have been given are: to one of them, the Saïtic, and to the other, the Mendesian.

Absolute synonyms, a pair of words of which either can be substituted for the other *in any context* without any perceptible impairment of information-content, affect, or relation between speaker and hearer, may not exist in any language; but *in a given context*, as we are aware from our own practice in writing, alternative lexemes, morphemes, tenses, and syntactical constructions, of identical function and association, are often available to us.[21] In the case of Greek, alternative orderings of words may be identical in communicative function (cf. the trittys-boundaries cited above), but the principles of Greek word-order are such that in a given context some of the theoretically possible orders are ruled out (the 'given' element is subordinated and the 'new' element brought into prominence).[22]

Ancient literary critics take for granted the distinction between content and form,[23] ἃ δεῖ λέγειν and ὡς δεῖ λέγειν (Arist. *Rhet.* 1403ᵇ16), τὰ λεγόμενα and πῶς λέγεται (Demetr. 75), a distinction expressed by a variety of antitheses, e.g. διάνοια/λέξις (Arist. *Rhet.* 1410ᵇ27, Demetr. 115, 184, Dion. ii. 32. 13–15), διάνοια/

---

[21] Harris 8, 123, 159; Lyons (1963) 74–8; Palmer 89; Riffaterre (1959) 118 n. 20; Taylor 30. Here are some modern examples (my italics throughout): (i) 'Avoid *mowing* the lawn for three days before treatment, and do not *cut* again for at least four days after' (instructions on a packet of mosskiller), (ii) 'Whatever she did, it was the more fascinating because of her *gender* . . . but she could never be allowed, because of her *sex*, to become an insider' (Hilton 16), (iii) 'scaduto ormai a puro elemento erudito e *decorativo*, il motivo del *letto* di foglie . . . la presenza . . . del *giaciglio* di foglie, scaduto ormai a puro elemento erudito ed *esornativo* . . .' (Serrao 134). See further p. 138.

[22] Dover (1968a) 34–43.

[23] Cf. Russell (1981) 4–7, Kennedy 185 f., 192 f. Halliwell (1993) 64–6, however, points out that since antithesis is treated by Aristotle as a σχῆμα of λέξις (*Rhet.* 1410ᵇ28–31) and at the same time it appears from Aristotle's examples (1409ᵇ33–10ᵃ 23) that meaning is crucial to antithesis, his distinction between form and content is to that extent blurred.

ὀνομασία (ibid. 9. 11–13), διάνοια/ὀνόματα (Demetr. 2), νοήματα/ ὀνόματα (Dion. ii. 4. 7 f., 14. 14 f.), νόησις/λέξις (ibid. 8. 20 f.), πράγματα/ἑρμηνεία (Demetr. 119, 132), πράγματα/λέξις (Arist. *Rhet.* 1408ᵃ19 f., Demetr. 114, 133, Dion. ii. 4. 12–20), πράγματα/ὀνομασία (Demetr. 304), πράγματα/ὀνόματα (Dion. ii. 14. 9–12), ὑποκείμενα/ ὀνόματα (ibid. 62. 1). In conformity with this distinction, the critics often illustrate their arguments by rewriting sentences from the classical authors to show how the same διάνοια can be expressed in different λέξεις. Their point, however, is not to show that alternative λέξεις are a matter of indifference, but quite the opposite, to show how a passage would lose its χάρις and πάθος by linguistic change (e.g. Dion. ii. 31. 9–17, on the closing words of Thuc. iii. 57. 4)[24] or to suggest that an author has used in one genre stylistic features which are more appropriate to another (cf. pp. 53–6).

There are, however, instances from which we can infer an author's own view of synonymy. Antiphon uses in v. 14 and 87–9 material which he had used earlier[25] in vi. 2–6, e.g.:

vi. 2	v. 14
ὁ χρόνος γὰρ καὶ ἡ ἐμπειρία τὰ μὴ καλῶς ἔχοντα διδάσκει τοὺς ἀνθρώπους, ὥστ' οὐ δεῖ ὑμᾶς ἐκ τῶν λόγων τοῦ κατηγοροῦντος τοὺς νόμους μαθεῖν εἰ καλῶς ἔχουσιν ἢ μή, ἀλλ' ἐκ τῶν νόμων τοὺς τούτων λόγους, εἰ ὀρθῶς ὑμᾶς καὶ νομίμως διδάσκουσιν ἢ οὔ.	ὁ γὰρ χρόνος καὶ ἡ ἐμπειρία τὰ μὴ καλῶς ἔχοντα ἐκδιδάσκει τοὺς ἀνθρώπους. ὥστ' οὐ δεῖ ὑμᾶς ἐκ τῶν τοῦ κατηγόρου λόγων τοὺς νόμους καταμανθάνειν εἰ καλῶς ὑμῖν κεῖνται ἢ μή, ἀλλ' ἐκ τῶν νόμων τοὺς τοῦ κατηγόρου λόγους, εἰ ὀρθῶς καὶ νομίμως ὑμᾶς διδάσκουσι τὸ πρᾶγμα ἢ οὔ.

For time and experience teach men what is not satisfactory; so that you ought not to learn from the arguments of the accuser whether the laws are satisfactory or not, but learn from the laws whether the arguments of my adversaries } instruct you { in the case } rightly and lawfully or not. of the accuser

Two simple verbs (διδάσκει, μαθεῖν) are replaced by compound verbs (ἐκδιδάσκει, καταμανθάνειν) and in the second case the aspect is changed (after 'do not ...', 'cannot ...', 'must not ...', etc., the aspect of the infinitive is semantically immaterial); the positions of

---

[24] e.g. Demetrius 6, 28, 31.
[25] There are reasons (Dover (1988) 13–25) for dating vi before v, but those who think otherwise may substitute 'vi. 2–6 ... v. 14 and 87–9' without impairing the argument.

two postpositives (γάρ, ὑμᾶς)[26] are changed; καλῶς . . . κεῖνται replaces καλῶς ἔχουσιν, διδάσκουσι τὸ πρᾶγμα replaces διδάσκουσι, and 'the argument(s) of my accuser(s)' is expressed differently. It is not possible to demonstrate that the prefixes ἐκ- and κατα- here fortify or modify the message transmitted from speaker to hearer (though no doubt, if we started from the axiom that somehow they must, we would try to translate accordingly). The changes may be phonaesthetic, perhaps rhythmical.[27] That, at least, must be the explanation of a change made by Demosthenes when he reuses in xxiv. 160–86, attacking Timocrates, material which he used in xxii. 47–78, attacking Androtion. He is, of course, compelled by his argument to change the singular verbs, referring to Androtion, into plural verbs, incriminating Timocrates and Androtion together, but in addition we find:

xxii. 53	xxiv. 165
ὃν οὐδ' ὑπὲρ αὐτοῦ δίκην λαμβάνειν ἐᾷ	ὃν οὐδ' ὑπὲρ αὐτοῦ δίκην ἐᾷ λαβεῖν τὰ
τὰ πεπραγμένα καὶ βεβιωμένα	πεπραγμένα καὶ βεβιωμένα

. . . who is not permitted, because of what he has done and the way he has lived, to get legal satisfaction even on his own behalf

where his reason must be either a preference for the iambic rhythm of δίκην ἐᾷ λαβεῖν over the (*Flying Dutchman*) rhythm δίκην λαμβάνειν ἐᾷ or an aversion to -νειν ἐ- in close company with πεπραγ- and βεβι-.[28]

There is, however, one area of Greek prose writing where the recognition of synonymy of lexemes and equivalence of constructions is absolutely necessary if the argument is to hold together.[29] A passage of the following form appears prima facie nonsensical:

*It seems, then, that every A is B.
It does seem so.
But we agreed, did we not, that every B is C?
We agreed.

---

[26] On 'postpositives' see p. 27.

[27] Changes which I make in rewriting what I have written myself are nearly always phonaesthetic; cf. also Dover (1988) 215 on revisions made by modern authors, the reasons for which are not always apparent to audience or readers.

[28] Given the negative 'does *not* allow him to . . .', any attempt to distinguish semantically between the imperfective and aorist aspects of the infinitive would be a waste of effort.

[29] Cf. Lyons (1963), part ii, *passim*.

So the argument compels us to acknowledge that every A must be D?
Yes, Socrates, it does.

It is not nonsensical, though, if (*a*) it has already been taken for
granted that every C is D or (*b*) 'C' and 'D' are synonymous in the
context of the argument. In Plato condition (*b*) is quite commonly
fulfilled, as in the following passage of *Lysis* (207 D 5–208 A 1). Let
us take the opportunity to mark not only the points at which lexemic
synonymy is required by the argument but also those at which a
stylistic choice between options is made. There are 56 such points
in all, and 17 pairs or sets of options.

ἦ πού, ἦν δ' ἐγώ,[1] ὦ Λύσι,[2] σφόδρα φιλεῖ σε[3] ὁ πατὴρ καὶ[4] ἡ μήτηρ;
πάνυ γε,[5] ἦ δ' ὅς.[6]
οὐκοῦν[7] βούλοιντο[8] ἄν σε ὡς εὐδαιμονέστατον[9] εἶναι;[10]
πῶς γὰρ οὔ;[11]
δοκεῖ δέ σοι[12] εὐδαίμων[13] εἶναι[14] ἄνθρωπος δουλεύων[15] τε[16] καὶ ᾧ[17] μηδὲν[18]
ἐξείη ποιεῖν[19] ὧν[20] ἐπιθυμοῖ;[21]
μὰ Δί'[22] οὐκ ἔμοιγε, ἔφη.[23]
οὐκοῦν[24] εἴ σε[25] φιλεῖ ὁ πατὴρ καὶ[26] ἡ μήτηρ καὶ εὐδαιμονά[27] σ'[28] ἐπιθυμοῦσι[29]
γενέσθαι,[30] τοῦτο[31] παντὶ τρόπῳ δῆλον, ὅτι προθυμοῦνται ὅπως ἄν εὐδαιμονοίης;[32]
πῶς γὰρ οὐχί;[33] ἔφη.[34]
ἐῶσιν ἄρα σε[35] ἃ[36] βούλει[37] ποιεῖν,[38] καὶ οὐδὲν ἐπιπλήττουσιν οὐδὲ διακωλύουσι[39] ποιεῖν[40] ὧν[41] ἄν ἐπιθυμῇς;[42]
ναὶ μὰ Δί'[43] ἐμέ γε,[44] ὦ Σώκρατες,[45] καὶ μάλα γε πολλὰ κωλύουσιν.[46]
πῶς λέγεις;[47] ἦν δ' ἐγώ.[48] βουλόμενοί[49] σε μακάριον[50] εἶναι[51] διακωλύουσι[52]
τοῦτο[53] ποιεῖν[54] ὅ[55] ἄν βούλῃ;[56]

'I imagine, Lysis', I said, 'that your father is very fond of you, and so is
your mother?'
'Very much so,' he said.
'Would they, then, wish you to be as happy as possible?'
'Of course.'
'Do you think that a man is happy if he were enslaved and not permitted
to do any of the things he desired to do?'
'No, indeed I don't,' he said.
'So, if your father loves you, and your mother does too, and they desire
that you should become happy, isn't it absolutely clear that they do all they
can for your happiness?'
'Of course,' he said.
'Do they, then, allow you to do what you wish, and don't correct you or
prevent you from doing whatever you desire?'
'They do indeed prevent me, Socrates, from doing a great many things.'

'Why!' I said, 'wishing you to be enviable, they prevent you from doing whatever you wish?'

   (i) 'said': (a) ἦν δ᾽ ἐγώ, ἦ δ᾽ ὅς: 1, 6, 48; (b) ἔφη: 23, 34; (c) nothing: 7, 11, 12, 24, 35, 43.

   (ii) assent: (a) πάνυ γε: 5; (b) πῶς γὰρ οὔ;: 11, 33; (c) an oath: 43 (cf. negative oath at 22); (d) personal pronoun with γε: 44.

   (iii) vocative: (a) present: 2, 45; (b) absent: 5, 7, 11, 12, 22, 24, 33, 35, 47.

   (iv) position of σε: (a) after prepositive:³⁰ 25; (b) after first mobile word of clause: 28, 35, 49; (c) after second mobile word: 3.

   (v) 'A and B': (a) καί: 4, 26; (b) τε . . . καί: 16.

   (vi) 'wish/desire' (you to be enviable): (a) βούλεσθαι: 8, 49; (b) ἐπιθυμεῖν: 29.

   (vii) 'enviable'/'happy': (a) εὐδαίμων: 9, 13, 27; (b) μακάριος: 50.

   (viii) 'be'/'become' enviable: (a) . . . εἶναι: 10, 14, 51; (b) . . . γενέσθαι: 30; (c) εὐδαιμονεῖν: 32.

   (ix) forms of negative: (a) οὐ: 11; (b) οὐχί: 33.

   (x) conditional constructions: (a) participle: 15; (b) relative clause: 17.

   (xi) antecedent of relative: (a) demonstrative: 31, 53; (b) none: 18, 36, 41.

   (xii) relative pronoun: (a) singular: 55; (b) plural: 20, 36, 41.

   (xiii) generalizing relative: (a) with indicative: 37; (b) with ἄν and subjunctive: 41, 55.

   (xiv) position of ποιεῖν: (a) before relative clause: 19, 40, 54; (b) after relative clause: 38.

   (xv) 'wish'/'desire' (to do): (a) βούλεσθαι: 37, 56; (b) ἐπιθυμεῖν: 42.

   (xvi) 'prevent': (a) διακωλύειν: 39, 52; (b) κωλύειν: 46.

   (xvii) optative of verbs in -ε-: (a) -οῖ(-): 21; (b) -οίη(-): 32.

And the argument continues in the same strain: 208 D 3: ἐκείνη σε ἐᾷ ποιεῖν ὅτι ἂν βούλῃ, ἵν᾽ αὐτῇ μακάριος ᾖς . . . 208 E 4 εὐδαίμονα εἶναι καὶ ποιεῖν ὅτι ἂν βούλῃ . . . E 6 ὧν ἐπιθυμεῖς οὐδὲν ποιοῦντα . . . 209 A 3 οὐδὲ ποιεῖς οὐδὲν ὧν ἐπιθυμεῖς, and so on.

This passage of *Lysis* contributes the beginnings of an answer to a disturbing question which besets all consideration of style at the linguistic level: if we were to construct a complete inventory of the idiolects of two or more authors and observe all the differences between them, would there be anything left to say about their 'style' as distinct from their 'language'? Or would we be moved to discard 'style' altogether as a superfluous concept serving no useful purpose? I think not. Suppose that an author, confronted with a choice

---

³⁰ On 'prepositives' and 'mobiles' see p. 27.

between formulations a_1 and a_2, always chooses a_1, and a second author uses both even-handedly; that difference between them is revealed by an inventory. But if a third author, also using both formulations, regularly alternates blocks of a_1 with blocks of a_2, so that the hearer receives (except at block-boundaries) an impression of monotony and repetition, that is something—very different from what we observe in the *Lysis* passage—which, although it can be discovered from concordances or (more painstakingly) from complete word-indexes, would not normally be regarded as part of a linguistic inventory.[31] This may seem to suggest that style is an epiphenomenon of language. However, the distribution and concentration of choices are much less important than the extent to which the writer combines lexemes and constructions which belong to different registers[32] and are associated with different purposes and occasions of utterance, in conflict (even, on occasion, shockingly) with our assumptions and tantalizing to our expectations. This is an aspect of style (to be discussed more fully on pp. 54–6) which can never emerge solely from the linguistic inventory of a text. It necessarily involves us in examination of the relation between speaker and hearer and of the appropriateness of an utterance to its purpose and occasion. There is no sharp boundary between stylistics and sociolinguistics,[33] because assumptions and expectations depend on our awareness of a non-linguistic datum, the context of utterance.[34] Texts differ *stylistically*—and their difference is reconcilable with *linguistic* homogeneity—by virtue of the relation between the linguistic and the non-linguistic.

APPENDIX: ART AND LITERATURE

Books and articles about style seldom pay much attention to boundary-stones, by-laws, dispatches, insurance policies, recipes, or any of the numerous categories of written utterance which are not clas-

[31] Dover (1987) 73 f., and Halliday, McIntosh, and Strevens in Fishman 149–59.

[32] On 'register' see Wales 397–9, and Halliday, McIntosh, and Strevens in Fishman 149–59. I appreciate the argument of Crystal and Davy 61 f. that the term is insufficiently discriminating, but for the description of ancient Greek prose I find it adequate.

[33] Lanham 123 f., 132 f.; Lyons (1977) 580–4; Spencer xi and Spencer and Gregory in Spencer 6–8, 85–91; Turner 168, 194.

[34] Cf. Wellek in Sebeok 417, Levin 281 f. on 'macrocontext', Bickerton in Ching 47–9, and Mukařovsky 55–6.

sified as 'literature'. Since most of us have discovered for ourselves
that the formal characteristics of a 'non-literary' work sometimes
evoke in us a stronger and more favourable aesthetic response than
much of what is published as poetry or fiction, it is not surprising
that some critics agonize over the question[35] 'What is literature?'
The question cannot be translated into Greek, because Greek has
no term with the same denotation as 'literature'; nor has it any
term with which to distinguish 'creative' prose from any other kind
of written utterance in prose. We can agree that literature is an
art-form, only to be beset by the even more forbidding question—
also impossible to translate satisfactorily into Greek—'What is art?'
This question, however, becomes much less forbidding once we
have succeeded in shaking free of the common notion that art is
always and necessarily good, a notion that leads to the dismissal of
some literature, painting, and music as 'not art'.[36] It is preferable
to begin with the acknowledgement that a very great number of
works of art are trivial, incompetent, worthless, of such a kind that
our emotional response to them is much less favourable than our
response to natural phenomena or even to patterns and sequences
of sounds and sights which result from an accident.[37] After that we
can start to think about what makes *good* art.

I propose to treat art as an activity which constitutes an ingredient of a wide range of complex activities: it is the activity of

[35] Cf. Wellek in Chatman 65 f. Saporta in Sebeok 98 f. is not hopeful of finding any satisfactory criterion for distinguishing literature from non-literature; Jen-
kins ibid. 99 makes a start on a process of elimination by suggesting that a tele-
phone directory is not literature. One could say that also of an archon-list, but
there are not enough of such things in the Greek world to cause us any real
trouble. Hill 47 f. argues that literature is that which bears a formal resemblance
to what is already regarded as literature in the tradition of a given society, and
(51 f.) 'triviality should not alarm us'. Hollander in Sebeok 399 makes it a matter of the author's declared intention (cf. Riffaterre (1959) 156 f.), and I accept
that if 'declared' is expanded to 'declared or plausibly inferred'. So far as concerns ancient Greek literature, I repent of my ill-considered words on 'literature'
in Dover (1980) 106, 120. Quite recently the denotation of 'literature' has become
broader, as in 'Please read the enclosed literature carefully before connecting the
appliance.'
[36] In the same way, religious people tend to treat only their own preferred form
of religion as 'real' religion, dismissing Elmer Gantry, Aztec priests, etc., as a 'per-
version' of religion.
[37] Hill 46 f.; Beardsley in Sebeok 431 and Richards ibid. 433 agree, while Hollander ibid. 402 and Wimsatt ibid. 424 do not find it easy to come to terms with the
concept 'bad literature'. I applaud the no-nonsense opening (8) of Adams's preface:
'the bulk of English poetry is bad'.

caring about the look or sound of what we bring into being.[38] This is an omnipresent ingredient of fiction and drama, a predominant ingredient of poetry and the visual arts, and in music excludes others.[39] In daily life we constantly perform artistic acts,[40] for example, in choosing a tie or straightening a picture which is hanging askew.

This definition is open to two obvious objections, both of which are mistaken.

In the first place, it may be thought to imply that art is 'mere décor'; but there is no such implication. This may be illustrated by consideration of a passage from Wolsey's exhortation to Cromwell in *Henry the Eighth*:

> Had I but served my God with half the zeal
> I served my King, He would not in mine age
> have left me naked to mine enemies.

The effect of the rhythm is (to me) overpowering: a sombre procession of monosyllables for two and a half lines, broken by the disyllable 'naked' and ending with the liquid patter of 'enemies'. It might be thought that this effect could equally be achieved by:

> *Had I but swerved my dog with half the wheel
> I swerved my pin, she would not in my rage
> have wished me crated to my symmories.

Unfortunately, the content there is drivel.[41] The content of the original could be expressed as:

*If I'd put half the energy into getting right with God that I put into my work in the King's office, now that I'm an old man he wouldn't have left me exposed to the people who want to get at me.

[38] Jakobson in Sebeok 356, and van Dijk 41. Cf. Gombrich 3: 'There really is no such thing as art; there are only artists.'

[39] Cf. Sartre 27 f.

[40] This seems to be implied by Enkvist in Van Dijk 19, Mukařovsky in Freeman (1970) 49, and Richards in Sebeok 433.

[41] It is, of course, possible to construct poetry in a wholly artificial language, manipulating articulated sound as a kind of music, or as an abstract painter uses colour and two-dimensional shape. If the syntax of a natural language is used and the individual lexemes all belong to that language, e.g.

> *O Bill! Repair the hayloft, lest I sing
> of plaques, and emus' bums, and regicide . . .,

the affinities of the poem are with surrealism.

A grumble in the corner of a pub;[42] but it communicates what Wolsey wishes Cromwell to understand. What makes the original great art is the *combination* of powerful form with powerful content.[43]

The second objection to my definition is that we cannot observe and assess directly how much the author of a written text cared;[44] that is to say, the author of a text other than our own, because we each have the experience of revising what has been composed and changing ingredients which we do not like, replacing them with something which 'sounds better' or 'looks better'. It is prudent to assume that no utterance is such that its author *cannot* care what it sounds like.[45] In the spoken language there are, of course, utterances in which such care is minimal (e.g. 'Help!', 'Oh, shit!', and 'I love you'), but since all those who once spoke ancient Greek are dead, we are concerned in the present enquiry only with what was expressed in the conscious and deliberate activity of writing. We should therefore consider any Greek utterance in writing *as if* the author cared how it sounded; that is to say, as if the activity which I label 'art' were always present. If we are sometimes wrong, it does not matter, because we are not a jury awarding prizes for artistic intention, and no sense of injustice can be felt by victims of our errors; we are exploring the history of phenomena in extant texts.

In certain circumstances it is useful, without prejudice to the working principle just advocated, to classify some Greek texts as

[42] A good actor could make something of it, certainly; but it does not pack the Shakespearian punch.

[43] It is sometimes demanded of a work of art nowadays that it should 'make a statement'. Some of the 'statements' made, however, are rather banal, e.g. 'You can make yellow shapes by pissing on snow', and in any case there are more effective ways of making 'statements': statements, for instance. An *objet trouvé* placed in an art gallery as a 'subversive gesture' no more becomes a work of art than a car becomes a cow if you turn the cow out of her byre and keep the car there instead. The currently fashionable notion that 'true' art is 'aesthetic terrorism' can safely be voiced so long as the terrorized do not believe it.

[44] Hill 47; Taylor 103 (on the receiver's processing of the sender's message), 'a theory which takes as its criterion of verification an unobservable mental operation is not falsifiable'.

[45] Green 11, Ingarden (1960) 5 f., Jakobson 69 f., Wellek in Sebeok 417, Wellek and Warren 178. Cf. *Wf* 70 f. and Sapir 225 f., 231 on language as a 'collective art'.

'documentary' and the rest as 'literary'. With reference to the archaic and classical periods, I use 'documentary' to mean 'incised or painted on hard material', and 'literary' to mean 'presumed to have been written in ink on soft material'. In dealing with the Hellenistic period the distinction would need to be qualified in a number of ways.

2

UNITS OF UTTERANCE

A. WORDS

A TEXT composed of very long sentences and a text composed of very short sentences differ greatly in their aesthetic effect, and length is normally regarded as a function of the number of words. For those of us who are accustomed to alphabetic scripts (of which Greek script is one) and also to the graphic conventions of the last few centuries, 'word' is implicitly defined as 'continuous succession of letters bounded at each end by at least one letter-space'. For Greek, that definition is wholly unsatisfactory, but before attempting to improve on it let us remove an ambiguity which is inherent in 'word', however defined. The usual disambiguation is to replace 'word' in some contexts by 'type' and in others by 'token'.[1] The famous Shakespearian line:

Never never never never never

is treated as consisting of five 'tokens' but containing only one 'type'. 'Token' is useful, but 'type' unfortunate, because we so often need it in its common denotation 'sort', 'kind', 'category', etc.; I shall therefore use 'lexeme' instead, and 'lexeme' and 'token' together will make it possible to abjure 'word' altogether, except in such established terms as 'word-order', 'word-group', etc. Being concerned with the sound of an utterance rather than the treatment of its ingredients in a reference grammar, I treat suppletive forms as distinct lexemes, so that λέγειν, εἰπεῖν, ἐρεῖν are three lexemes but ἐρεῖν and εἰρηκέναι are the same lexeme; πολύς, πλείων, and πλεῖστος are treated as one, but ἀγαθός, κρείσσων, ἄριστος, and βελτίων/βέλτιστος as four.[2] Some of my decisions in this area are disputable, but never enough to make a difference.

Morphologically, every Greek lexeme belongs to one or other of four categories: (*a*) declinables, inflected for case, number, and

---

[1] Lyons (1977) 6 f., 13–18.

[2] This practice is normally followed by LSJ for verbs but not for degrees of comparison.

sometimes gender; (*b*) conjugables, inflected for person, number, tense, and mood; (*c*) infinitives; (*d*) uninflected lexemes (adverbs, prepositions, particles). I include, however, regular adverbs in -ως/ -ῶς in category (*a*). Syntactically, almost every Greek lexeme is either mobile or appositive. If mobile, it can occur immediately after pause, immediately before pause, or anywhere else. Appositives are subdivided into 'prepositives' and 'postpositives'. Prepositives (e.g. εἰ, καί) cannot occur immediately before pause, and postpositives (e.g. γάρ, με, ἄν) cannot come immediately after pause.[3] Some lexemes, however, may be mobile in some contexts and appositive in others, according to what they mean. Thus αὐτ- is mobile when it means 'self' or 'same', but postpositive when it is anaphoric ('her', 'them', etc.); ὁ (all forms) is prepositive in the sense 'the' but mobile when it is an anaphoric pronoun (e.g. ὁ δέ 'and/but he . . .') or distributive, e.g. Anon. *Ath.* 2. 12 ἀλλὰ τὸ μὲν τῇ, τὸ δὲ τῇ); πρός . . . 'in addition to . . .' is prepositive, but πρός 'in addition', mobile; and so on. I treat the simple negatives οὐ and μή as prepositive except where they bear antithetical stress,[4] e.g. Antiphon Soph. DK 87 B 44 A3. 12–18 ἐφ᾿ ἅ τε δεῖ . . . ἰέναι καὶ ἐφ᾿ ἃ οὐ δεῖ· καὶ . . . ὧν τε δεῖ . . . ἐπιθυμεῖν καὶ ὧν μή. The least tractable problem of classification is presented by the oblique cases of σύ, ἡμεῖς, ὑμεῖς, and σφεῖς (presence or absence of accent on σε, σου, σοι is of course a matter of post-classical convention, dependent on interpretation).[5] I have treated those pronouns as postpositive unless they bear antithetical stress.

B. SENTENCES

The definition of 'sentence' commonly implied in the presentation of statistics of sentence-length is 'continuous succession of tokens bounded at each end by a full-stop, colon, or question-mark in the modern edition which the investigator has chosen to use'. There is a fair degree of consistency in editors' use of those marks of punctuation, but also on occasion significant differences. Whereas certain particles, such as καίτοι, καὶ μὲν δή, or (postpositive) τοίνυν, signal a fresh start after pause, difficulties are caused by the connective relative (e.g. οἵ . . . 'and/but they . . .') and causal ἐπεί (ἐπεί x . . .

---

[3] Dover (1968*a*) 12–14.
[4] I have changed my mind about that since 1968.
[5] On the accentuation of personal pronouns in the plural see Barrett 425.

often=x γάρ . . .). For example, in Thuc. vi. 10.2 (see below) Stuart Jones prints a comma at . . . βέβαιον, αἳ κτλ., creating a sentence of 34 mobile tokens, but de Romilly a colon, giving two sentences of 6 and 28 respectively; and it is hard to see why de Romilly does not print a second colon at . . . ποιήσονται, οἷς κτλ., which would make a sequence of three sentences: 6, 15, and 13 mobile tokens. In Isoc. vii. 33 Mathieu's colon at οὐ γὰρ ἐδέδισαν μή . . .· ἀλλ' ὁμοίως ἐθάρρουν κτλ. contrasts with his comma at 35 . . . οὐδεὶς οὔτ' ἀπεκρύπτετο . . . οὔτ' ὤκνει . . ., ἀλλ' ἥδιον ἑώρων κτλ. It is often the longest sentences which are the most affected by disagreements of this kind. I propose to replace 'sentence' by 'main-clause–finite-verb unit' (MCF for short). On this principle, Thuc. vi. 10. 2 is resolved into six MCFs, thus:

καὶ οἴεσθε ἴσως τὰς γενομένας ὑμῖν σπονδὰς ἔχειν τι βέβαιον ||

And perhaps you think that there is some stability in the peace-treaty you have made.

αἳ ἡσυχαζόντων μὲν ὑμῶν ὀνόματι σπονδαὶ ἔσονται ||

If you remain inactive, it will be a nominal peace.

οὕτω γὰρ ἐνθένδε τε ἄνδρες ἔπραξαν αὐτὰ καὶ ἐκ τῶν ἐναντίων ||

That is the effect of the actions of men from here and from the other side.[6]

σφαλέντων δέ που ἀξιόχρεῳ δυνάμει ταχεῖαν τὴν ἐπιχείρησιν ἡμῖν οἱ ἐχθροὶ ποιήσονται ||

But if we meet with a reverse on a significant scale, our enemies will be quick to make their attack on us.

οἷς πρῶτον μὲν διὰ ξυμφορῶν ἡ ξύμβασις καὶ ἐκ τοῦ αἰσχίονος ἢ ἡμῖν κατ' ἀνάγκην ἐγένετο ||

In the first place, they came to the agreement by necessity, in consequence of misfortunes and from a position less creditable than ours.

ἔπειτα ἐν αὐτῇ ταύτῃ πολλὰ τὰ ἀμφισβητούμενα ἔχομεν ||

Secondly, the disputed points in the agreement itself are numerous.

The definition of MCF, however, needs a good deal of refining by exclusions and inclusions.

1. Parentheses,[7] whether or not they contain a mark of punctua-

---

[6] This clause is bracketed as parenthetical by editors; see below.
[7] On parenthesis see KG ii. 353 f., 602, Schwyzer (1939), *GG* ii. 705 f., Wilhelm Schmid v. 184 f.

tion normally indicating major pause, must be excluded and given subordinate status if they postpone the syntactical completion of a clause already begun, e.g. Thuc. vii. 70. 4:

ξυμπεσουσῶν δὲ ἐν ὀλίγῳ πολλῶν νεῶν (πλεῖσται γάρ . . . ἐναυμάχησαν· βραχὺ γὰρ ἀπέλιπον . . .) αἱ μὲν ἐμβολαί . . . ὀλίγαι ἐγίγνοντο . . .

Since many ships were forced into contact in a small space (for this was the greatest number . . . for they fell not far short . . .) ramming attacks . . . were few.

Not all sequences enclosed in brackets by editors need be classified as parentheses, e.g. Thuc. i. 9. 2 τυγχάνειν δέ . . . θάνατον. Parenthetical 'I/he said' and (e.g.) 'said Polemarchus' are ignored entirely.

2. An infinitive used in an imperatival sense must be accorded 'honorary' MCF status, e.g. Hdt. i. 32. 7:

πρὶν δ' ἂν τελευτήσῃ, ἐπισχεῖν μηδὲ καλέειν πω ὄλβιον.

But before he is dead, hold back and do not yet call him fortunate.

3. The ghost of the verb 'be' with ἀνάγκη, εἰκός, ῥᾴδιον, etc., must be recognized as MCF.

4. As well as causal ἐπεί, consequential ὥστε 'and so . . .' with finite verbs should be treated as introducing an MCF, except when οὕτως, τοι-, τοσ-, and the like look forward to it. I choose also to treat 'until' = 'but then/eventually . . .' in the same way, and so too connective or parenthetic relative clauses whenever possible, e.g. Hdt. i. 6. 1:

. . . ἐντὸς Ἅλυος ποταμοῦ, ὃς ῥέων . . . ἐξίει . . .

. . . east of the river Halys. It flows . . . and discharges . . .

5. While the first infinitive dependent on φασί, λέγουσι, λέγεται, and the like should be treated as dependent, it is essential—if we are not to posit MCFs of extreme and unrealistic complexity—to treat all the subsequent narrative infinitives dependent on the same 'say' as MCF, e.g. Hdt. i. 1–5, 24, vi. 52, Pl. *Rep.* 359 C–360 B. Such narrative sequences may also be rounded off with a λέγουσι (Hdt. i. 5. 3, 24. 8, vi. 53. 1) and intermittently reinforced by a reminder (λέγουσι in Hdt. i. 2. 1, 3. 1, 4. 3). The writer's freedom to choose between direct and indirect narration is clear from the instances in which the direct option is chosen, e.g. Hdt. i. 31. 2–5 λέγεται . . .· ἐούσης . . . ἔδεε κτλ., iv. 150. 1–154. 1 (framed between Θηραῖοι

ὧδε γενέσθαι λέγουσι and ταῦτα δὲ Θηραῖοι λέγουσι). The distinction
between (e.g.) ἔχειν σέ φασιν and ἔχεις, ὥς φασιν, . . . is formal rather
than semantic (cf. Pl. *Rep.* 363 D παῖδας . . . φασι . . . λείπεσθαι~
364 C τοὺς θεούς, ὥς φασι, πείθοντες), and the boundary between
'direct' and 'indirect' speech is sometimes hazy, e.g. Anon. *Ath.* 1.
6 εἴποι δ' ἄν τις ὡς ἐχρῆν κτλ.~1. 7 εἴποι τις ἄν, "τί ἂν οὖν γνοίη κτλ.",
above all when direct quotation is introduced by ὅτι,[8] making the
status of the ὅτι-clause as 'subordinate' questionable and strongly
suggesting that if the speaker uttered the Greek equivalent of 'er' or
'mm', that came after ὅτι, not before it. Similar uncertainties arise
with (e.g.) οἶμαι and δοκεῖ (cf. Pl. *Rep.* 359 B οἶμαι . . . οὐκ ὀλίγον
ἔργον αὐτὸ εἶναι~368 D ἕρμαιον ἂν οἶμαι ἐφάνη, Hdt. iii. 38. 4 ὀρθῶς
μοι δοκέει Πίνδαρος ποιῆσαι~5.2 ἐούσης, ὡς ἐμοὶ δοκέει, Σαρδίων οὐ
πολλῷ ἐλάσσονος, i. 172. 1 αὐτόχθονες δοκέειν ἐμοί εἰσι). In Thuc. i. 3.
2 δοκεῖ δέ μοι, οὐδὲ τοὔνομα τοῦτο ξύμπασά πω εἶχεν it seems at first
sight that the first four syllables are a self-contained phrase, like ὡς
ἐμοὶ δοκεῖ in 3. 3, but then δοκεῖ comes to life and a succession of
infinitives (εἶναι . . . παρέχεσθαι . . . καλεῖσθαι . . . ἐκνικῆσαι) depends
on it. Sometimes in a series of infinitives dependent on δεῖ, χρή, and
the like the subordinate character of all the infinitives after the
first quickly fades from the hearer's mind, and their imperatival
character[9] takes over. This is true, I think, of Thuc. vi. 13:

> ἀντιπαρακελεύομαι μὴ καταισχυνθῆναι . . .
> μηδέ . . . δυσέρωτας εἶναι . . .
> ἀλλά . . . ἀντιχειροτονεῖν,
> καὶ ψηφίζεσθαι
> τοὺς μὲν Σικελιώτας . . . ξυμφέρεσθαι,
> τοῖς δ' Ἐγεσταίοις . . . εἰπεῖν . . .[10]
> καὶ τὸ λοιπὸν . . . μὴ ποιεῖσθαι . . .

and of 22 δοκεῖ χρῆναι . . . ἄγειν . . . ναυσί τε . . . περιεῖναι . . .
τὸν δέ . . . ἄγειν . . . τά τε ἄλλα . . . ἑτοιμάσασθαι . . . καὶ μὴ . . .
γίγνεσθαι . . . μάλιστα δέ . . . ἔχειν.

More serious uncertainties are introduced by a pair or triad of
lexemes of which the first (most commonly appositive, e.g. μέν)
predicts the occurrence of the next, e.g.:

---

[8] KG ii. 367, *GG* ii. 638.
[9] Cf. p. 14 on the options—infinitive with accusative subject or third-person
imperative with nominative subject—open to the composer of an Attic decree.
[10] I have taken this clause to be dependent on ψηφίζεσθαι ('vote for telling Segesta . . .'), not as co-ordinated with it.

(*a*) Isoc. vii. 37 οὐκ ἐν μὲν ταῖς παιδείαις πολλοὺς τοὺς ἐπιστατοῦντας εἶχον, ἐπειδὴ δέ . . . δοκιμασθεῖεν, ἐξῆν αὐτοῖς . . ., ἀλλ' ἐν ταύταις ταῖς ἀκμαῖς . . . ἐτύγχανον κτλ.

It was not that they had many overseers during their education but permission . . . when they had come of age; it was actually in that age of maturity that . . .

(*b*) Ibid. 12 οὐδένα χρόνον τὰς εὐτυχίας κατασχεῖν ἠδυνήθημεν, ἀλλὰ ταχέως διεσκιραφησάμεθα[11] καὶ διελύσαμεν αὐτάς.

We were not able to preserve our good fortune for any length of time; we were quick to fritter it away and dissolve it.

(*c*) Xen. *HG* ii. 3. 29 τούτῳ οὔτε ἐσπείσατο πώποτε οὐδεὶς οὔτ' ἐπίστευσε τοῦ λοιποῦ.

No one ever yet exchanged pledges with that man or trusted him for the future.

(*d*) Ibid. vii. 1. 22 Θηβαῖοι δὲ καὶ πάντες οἱ ἀποστάντες . . . ὁμοθυμαδὸν ἔπραττον καὶ ἐστρατεύοντο ἡγουμένων Θηβαίων.

The Thebans and those who had revolted . . . acted in accord and took the field under Theban leadership.

In (*b*) the second verb has an ambiguous character, half explanatory gloss on the first and half consequential; we can, however, split ἀλλά . . . αὐτάς into two MCFs by understanding ⟨αὐτάς⟩ with the first verb. So too in (*c*) we *can* understand ⟨τούτῳ⟩ with the second verb; but analysis of the sentence as A B + C ⟨A⟩ rather than A {B + C} is ruinously counterintuitive. Example (*d*) could be heard by one person as meaning ὁμοθυμαδὸν {ἔπραττον καὶ ἐστρατεύοντο κτλ.}, by another as ὁμοθυμαδὸν ἔπραττον ‖ καὶ ἐστρατεύοντο κτλ. In (*a*) it is easy enough to treat οὐκ . . . and ἀλλ' . . . as two separate MCFs, but impossible so to treat ἐν μέν . . . εἶχον and ἐξῆν αὐτοῖς because the initial negative is crucial to the sense of ἐξῆν.

We have in fact to recognize a category of double or multiple MCFs, and in identifying instances of that category we cannot always rely on the formal criterion of connecting particles; there is no alternative to invoking semantic criteria, and that entails—literally, not metaphorically—'playing it by ear', humbly recognizing that in the placing of minor pauses within a narrative or argument we may

[11] Cj. Zinn: -σκαρι- codd. ('slur' LSJ).

not only differ individually but may also be insufficiently Hellenic even when we agree.[12]

C. SUBSTANTIVAL PHRASES

Thucydides' characterization (iii. 82 f.) of stasis is one of the passages which most readily spring to mind in response to the stimulus of the words 'Thucydidean style'. Hermogenes (249. 15–250. 5) treats it as an example of ὀνοματικὴ λέξις ('substantival language') which creates σεμνότης, 'solemnity', and Dion. i. 373. 22–381. 8 wrestles with its problems, castigates it (i. 379. 15 f., cf. i. 128. 17–130.1) as ἀσαφὴς καὶ πεπλεγμένη 'obscure and complicated', and rewrites much of it in simpler terms.[13] If we expected to find his rewriting ῥηματικώτερον ἢ ὀνοματικώτερον, we would be disappointed at least by the answer to the crude question 'What is the ratio of noun-tokens to other mobile tokens in Dionysius' "translations" compared with the ratio in the original?', because it is actually a little higher. But, of course, apart from the fact that Dionysius and Hermogenes are not talking about the same aspect of the text—Hermogenes is concerned with 'solemnity', Dionysius with the morass in which Thucydides is sometimes immersed by zeal for linguistic experiment—Hermogenes is speaking not just of nouns but also of noun-equivalents, substantival phrases; that is clear from 249. 13–15, where he refers to expressions constructed out of 'pronouns, participles, and the like'.

A substantival phrase (=S for short) may be constituted[14] by:

1. A noun, i.e. a declinable mobile variable for case but not for gender.

2. A pronoun, i.e. a declinable mobile with deictic reference.

3. An adjective, i.e. a declinable mobile variable for both case and gender,

    (*a*) without the definite article,

    (*b*) with the definite article.

4. A participle,

    (*a*) without the definite article,

[12] Cf. Sansone (1990), who gives references to other recent discussion of this problem.

[13] He gives up (378. 27–379. 14) on 82. 7 ῥᾷον δ᾽ . . . ἀγάλλονται. See Macleod 131–5 on what Dionysius' paraphrases miss.

[14] Every definition in this list is open to criticism for one reason or another, but all the criticisms seem to me peripheral.

(b) with the definite article.

5. An infinitive with the definite article.

6. An adverb, phrase, or genitive, with the definite article; e. g. Thuc. iii. 82. 3 τὰ τῶν πόλεων, on which Dion. i. 374. 7 f. remarks that αἱ πόλεις would have been ὑγιέστερον 'sounder'.

7. A combination of (1)–(6), e.g. Thuc. iii. 82. 3 τὴν ὑπερβολὴν τοῦ καινοῦσθαι τὰς διανοίας 'the extravagance of their novelty in revenge', where three =S go to make up a complex =S. I would treat τὰ τῶν πόλεων and τὸ καθ' ἡμέραν as =S each constituting two =S.

8. A clause containing a finite verb, substantivized by the article,[15] e.g. Lys. xxiii. 8 τὸν ὃς ἔφη δεσπότης τούτου εἶναι 'the man who claimed to be his master', Dem. iii. 2 περὶ τοῦ τίνα τιμωρήσεται τίς καὶ ὃν τρόπον 'on the question, who is to retaliate against whom, and in what way'.

9. A relative clause with the substantival sense 'he who . . .', 'those which . . .', etc. Since there are many circumstances in which it is impossible to draw a semantic distinction between (e.g.) ἐάν τις . . . and ὅστις ἄν . . ., there is necessarily a margin of error in the tally of =S in any text.

All these types (except 8) are attested at all periods, but their relative frequency varies strikingly between periods and genres. Scientific and philosophical argument and exposition naturally call for type 3b; first attested in Homer (*Il.* i. 106 τὸ κρήγυον 'good'), it occurs in a few citations from Heraclitus (B 1, B 3, B 8, B 32) and abounds in Anaxagoras,[16] e.g. B 12

καὶ ἀποκρίνεται ἀπό τε τοῦ ἀραιοῦ τὸ πυκνὸν καὶ ἀπὸ τοῦ ψυχροῦ τὸ θερμὸν καὶ ἀπὸ τοῦ ζοφεροῦ τὸ λαμπρὸν καὶ ἀπὸ τοῦ διεροῦ τὸ ξηρόν.[17]

And the dense is separated from the rarefied, and the hot from the cold, and the bright from the dark, and the dry from the moist.

Type 4b has a very similar history to 3b, but both types afford illustrations of two important aspects of the history of style: the extent to which subject-matter can affect linguistic constructions, and the way in which experiments can create short-lived linguistic fashions. All the examples of 3b and 4b in Anaxagoras are neuter (mostly singular, some plural), whereas Heraclitus exhibits eight mascu-

---

[15] KG i. 583 f., Rehdantz 51.
[16] Actually 10% of the total of mobile tokens in the citations from him.
[17] For the contrast between this passage and the opening passage of Hp. *VM* see p. 144.

lines and Democritus over seventy. The reason for the difference is that Anaxagoras writes about the constitution of the universe, but Democritus mainly, and Heraclitus sometimes, about human behaviour. And, not surprisingly, type 4*b* was well established in documentary language before the mid-fifth century, e.g. *IG* i³ 104. 14 (the Athenian homicide law)[18] τὸν κō[λύ]οντα, 20 τōι κτέναν[τι; ML 13. B. 2 (Ozolian Lokris, s. vi ex.) τὸν γεγραμένōν 'this text'; *DGE* 413.6 f. (Elis, s. vi/v) τοὶ καδελέμενοι (= οἱ ἀδικοῦντες), *DGE* 362. 31 (Ozolian Lokris, s. v in.) τὸ κατιϝόμενον 'the appropriate share'; ibid. 43 τōι ἐγκαλειμένōι 'the accused'; cf. *DGE* 744. 35 (Halikarnassos, s. v m.) τὰ ἐόντα αὐτō 'his property'. Not surprisingly—for law and didactic moralizing have something in common—at an even earlier date type 4*b* is found in Hesiod's *Works and Days*: 353 τὸν φιλέοντα φιλεῖν καὶ τῷ προσιόντι προσεῖναι, 342 τὸν φιλέοντα contrasted with τὸν ἐχθρόν.

What I have called an 'experiment' is the inclination of Antiphon and Thucydides[19] to assimilate types 3*b* and 4*b* fully to type 1 by attaching genitives or possessive adjectives to neuter adjectives and participles, e.g. Thuc. vi. 16. 2 τῷ ἐμῷ διαπρεπεῖ τῆς 'Ολυμπίαζε θεωρίας 'the conspicuous distinction of my participation in the Olympic Games', i. 36. 1 τὸ δεδιὸς αὐτοῦ 'his fear', cf. ii. 61. 2, iv. 87. 3, v. 98, i. 90. 2 τὸ βουλόμενον καὶ ὕποπτον τῆς γνώμης 'the suspicious intention they had in mind', Ant. v. 73 τὸ ὑμέτερον δυνάμενον ἐμὲ δικαίως σώζειν . . . τὸ τῶν ἐχθρῶν βουλόμενον ἀδίκως με ἀπολλύναι 'your power to save me, rightly, . . . my enemies' desire to destroy me, wrongfully', ii. γ. 3, iii. β. 10, v. 7, v. 96.

Type 5, the infinitive with the neuter article, has a history in which poetry and prose keep in step: one example in Homer (*Od.* xv. 52),[20] two in Hesiod (*Op.* 334, fr. 273. 1), and three in sixth-century poetry, but then eleven in Pindar[21] and nearly fifty in Aeschylus.[22] In prose: one in Heraclitus (B 113), but four in a single citation

---

[18] On the antiquity of the document see p. 58. Its language often figures in discussions of law, e.g. Ant. ii. γ. 1 τῷ παθόντι, iii. β. 8 τὸν δράσαντα, Dem. xxiii. 40 τῷ παθόντι . . . τὸν δεδρακότα, Pl. *Lg.* 879 A ὁ δράσας.

[19] KG i. 267 f., *GG* ii. 409, Cucuel 62, 119 f.

[20] Chantraine 160; I see no justification whatever for his remark (305) 'τό garde ici sa valeur demonstrative et annonce φυλάσσειν', because that 'announcement' is one of the things a definite article does. Other examples in archaic poetry are Alcman *PMG* 41, Alcaeus *PLF* 400, and (but is it archaic?) Theognis 256.

[21] Slater 371 f.

[22] Italie 201 f.

from Anaxagoras (B 17) and one in another (B 3);[23] in Democritus the score is up to 23. Readers who begin Herodotus from the beginning may infer from the impressive triad in i. 4. 2 that a feast of articular infinitives awaits them, but in fact they have to wait until 42. 1, over 3,000 mobile tokens later, for the next one. From Herodotus onwards, through Thucydides, then Xenophon and Plato, to Demosthenes, the construction increases spectacularly both in frequency[24] and in scale. A well-known example[25] is Dem. xix. 55:

τὸ γὰρ ⌜πρὸς ἄνδρα θνητὸν καὶ διὰ καιρούς τινας ἰσχύοντα γράφοντας εἰρήνην
　　　⌞ἀθάνατον συνθέσθαι τὴν κατὰ τῆς πόλεως αἰσχύνην
　　　⌜καὶ ἀποστερῆσαι μὴ μόνον τῶν ἄλλων
　　　⌞ἀλλὰ καὶ τῶν παρὰ τῆς τύχης εὐεργεσιῶν τὴν πόλιν
　　　⌜καὶ τοσαύτῃ περιουσίᾳ χρῆσθαι πονηρίας
　　　　ὥστε μὴ μόνον τοὺς ὄντας Ἀθηναίους
　　　　ἀλλὰ καὶ τοὺς ὕστερόν ποτε μέλλοντας ἔσεσθαι πάντας
　　　⌞　ἠδικηκέναι,
πῶς οὐχὶ πάνδεινόν ἐστι;

To have made our city's shame undying by a peace treaty with a man who is mortal and owes his strength to certain opportunities, and to have deprived the city not just of all else but of the benefits conferred by fortune, and to have gone so far in villainy as to injure not only those Athenians who are alive now but also all those who will live in after time, is surely *monstrous*!

The =S here consists of three parts, to all of which the initial τό belongs. It cannot rightly be broken down into three =S, τό . . . συνθέσθαι . . . καὶ (sc. τὸ) ἀποστερῆσαι . . . καὶ (sc. τὸ) . . . χρήσασθαι . . ., changing πάνδεινον into the plural, because the speaker is not listing three actions but an action and two of its aspects.[26] A similar consideration prevents us from breaking down one of the earliest instances of the articular infinitive in Attic prose, Anon. *Ath.* 1. 3:

---

[23] Anaxagoras also experiments with negative =S, ἐκ μὴ τριχός . . . θρὶξ καὶ σὰρξ ἐκ μὴ σαρκός (DK 59 B 10), which appealed to Thucydides (i. 137. 4, iii. 95. 2, v. 35. 2, 50. 4, vii. 34. 6). Cf. KG ii. 197, Wackernagel ii. 263–5. Ar. *Eccl.* 115 is undoubtedly parodic: Barrett 198, Rau 206.

[24] Stahl 668.

[25] KG ii. 38.

[26] Given the explosive indignation of πῶς οὐ κτλ., I am inclined to hear in the infinitives a tone associated with the exclamatory infinitive ('to think that . . .!'). Cf KG ii. 26, *GG* ii. 380.

(sc. ὁ δῆμος) πλείω ὠφελεῖται ἐν τῷ μὴ αὐτὸς ἄρχειν ταύτας τὰς ἀρχὰς ἀλλ᾽ ἐὰν τοὺς δυνατωτάτους ἄρχειν

It is benefited more by not holding those offices itself but allowing the richest men to hold them

—which is not semantically identical with 'not by holding . . . but by allowing . . .' (*οὐκ ἐν τῷ ἄρχειν . . . ἀλλ᾽ ἐν τῷ ἐᾶν . . .). When an article or a preposition or a combination of the two goes with a pair (or more) of =S, it is sometimes possible to justify its repetition or non-repetition semantically; one could say of Hom. *Il.* i. 70

δς ἤδη τά τ᾽ ἐόντα τά τ᾽ ἐσσόμενα πρό τ᾽ ἐόντα

who knew present, future, and past . . .,

that future and past, as being hidden from us, belong together in opposition to the visible present, so that 'the present' is a single =S and 'the future and past' a multiple =S. Unfortunately, this kind of explanation patently does not work for a large number of examples—notoriously, for Aesch. *Ag.* 324:

καὶ τῶν ἁλόντων καὶ κρατησάντων δίχα
φθογγὰς ἀκούειν ἔστι κτλ.

The voices of the vanquished and of (sc. the) victors are to be heard in different strains . . .

It is evident from instances found in close proximity that the author had considerable freedom to choose;[27] e.g. Anon. *Ath.* 1. 4 'the bad and poor and ordinary', but then 'the poor and the ordinary[28] and the inferior', and Aeschines iii. 24:

ἐπὶ τίνος ἄρχοντος, καὶ ποίου μηνὸς καὶ ἐν τίνι ἡμέρᾳ καὶ ἐν ποίᾳ ἐκκλησίᾳ κτλ.

In whose archonship and (sc. in) what month, and on (ἐν) what day and at (ἐν) what assembly . . .?

The fluidity of usage in this respect makes it hard to formulate worthwhile historical generalizations about the balance between multiple =S and pairs or chains of single =S.

---

[27] Cf. KG ii. 548.
[28] δημόται and δημοτικοί are close in denotation to 'ordinary people' and 'the man in the street'.

(37)

APPENDIX: PERIOD AND KOLON

Aristotle, *Rhet.* 1409ᵇ16 f. (cf. Demetr. 10 f.), speaks of a περίοδος as being composed of κῶλα;²⁹ cf. Dion. ii. 7. 14–18, where we are told that combination of the basic parts of utterance makes 'what are called κῶλα' and the fitting-together (ἁρμονία) of kola makes up periods (τὰς καλουμένας συμπληροῖ περιόδους). Demetrius 9 adds a unit intermediate between kolon and token, the κόμμα. From the examples they quote it is clear that those terms do not correspond to the distinction we draw on syntactical grounds between 'sentence',³⁰ 'clause', and 'phrase'. In citing Dem. xx. 1 as a period of three kola Demetrius 10 presumably divides it thus:

μάλιστα μὲν εἵνεκα τοῦ νομίζειν συμφέρειν τῇ πόλει λελύσθαι τὸν νόμον,

Chiefly because of my view that it is advantageous to our city that the law should be repealed,

εἶτα καὶ τοῦ παιδὸς εἵνεκα τοῦ Χαβρίου,

and secondly, because of Chabrias' son,

ὡμολόγησα τούτοις, ὡς ἂν οἷός τ᾽ ὦ, συνερεῖν.

I agreed that I would speak in support of the defendants to the best of my ability.

Moreover, Arist. *Rhet.* 1409ᵇ13–17 acknowledges that a 'simple' (ἀφελής) period may consist of a single kolon (cf. Demetr. 34; ctr. 16); and Demetr. 9 treats the self-standing command 'know thyself' as a komma, which suggests that size, not syntax, is the criterion. Size naturally has implications for the control of the breath, and Demetr. 1 makes the essential point when he says that kolon-division 'allows the speaker a pause' (cf. Arist. *Rhet.* 1409ᵇ15 εὐανάπνευστος), for utterance that lacked such divisions would completely deprive the speaker of breath (ἀτεχνῶς πνίγων τὸν λέγοντα). At the same time (Demetr. 2) the kolon 'completes ⟨a unit of⟩ sense (διάνοια)'. Certainly it is the articulation of a passage in terms of what it means

²⁹ So too Anaximenes Rhet. 27 f., with reference to symmetry and assonance, but without mention of περίοδοι.
³⁰ I cannot agree with R. L. Fowler's insistence (90, 98 n. 40) on translating λέξις as 'sentence' in *Rhet.* 1409ᵃ35 'by "period" I mean λέξις which has a beginning and an end' and 1409ᵇ14 'λέξις ἐν κώλοις is that which is completed . . .'; in those passages it means '⟨segment of⟩ utterance' or 'sequence of tokens', something for which English does not have a term.

which dictates the points of pause, and the pattern of intonation which relates major to minor pauses.

The articulation of periods constitutes the difference drawn by Aristotle (*Rhet.* 1409ª24–35) between λέξις which is κατεστραμμένη and λέξις which is εἰρομένη. Demetrius follows Aristotle in the use of the term κατεστραμμένη (12). καταστρέφειν has a peculiarly wide semantic field: 'overturn', 'subdue', 'direct', and (intransitive active) 'end', 'expire'. Since all utterance whatsoever must end at some time, we cannot translate κατεστραμμένη simply as 'ended'; the same consideration applies to Aristotle's characterization of the period (1409ª35–7) as 'having beginning and end *by itself* (αὐτὴν καθ' αὐτήν) and a size which makes it comprehensible as a unity (εὐσύνοπτον)', and to passages in which Demetrius speaks in similar terms of the period: 10 σύστημα . . . εὐκαταστρόφως . . . ἀπηρτισμένον and συστροφὴν ἔχει, 20 συνεστραμμένον τὸ εἶδος and συνεστραμμένον τι ἔχει. It appears, therefore, that λέξις κατεστραμμένη, which Arist. *Rhet.* 1409ª35 equates with λέξις ἐν περιόδοις, is utterance composed of periods which end in a certain way.

The opposite of κατεστραμμένη is εἰρομένη (Arist. *Rhet.* 1409ª24–31), 'being strung together' (imperfective participle). Oddly, Demetrius, while agreeing with Aristotle in the use of κατεστραμμένη, does not follow him in using εἰρομένη, preferring διῃρημένη (21) 'divided up' or ἀνειμένη (22) 'loose' (cf. 21 διαλελυμένος 'disjointed'). The use of διῃρημένη is at first sight surprising, because Aristotle *Rhet.* 1409ᵇ14 uses it of utterance ἐν κώλοις and ibid. 34 of one particular species of such utterance. But, of course, any whole which is made up of parts 'strung together' is 'divided up' in so far as those parts are discrete items, many of which could be detached without affecting the interrelation of the remainder.[31]

What qualifies a period for inclusion in the category 'ended' appears to be its formal structure and its sense in combination (*Rhet.* 1409ᵇ8). Demetrius' citation of Dem. xx. 1 as an example strongly suggests that it is the syntactical and semantic completion of the period at or very near its end which is the καταστροφή; syntactically, any finite verb coming immediately after Χαβρίου would complete the period, but given the sense of ὡμολόγησα we ask ourselves 'agreed to what?', and the very last token answers our question. This period explains why Arist. *Rhet.* 1409ª31–4 (cf. Demetr. 11) draws an analogy between the runner who is inspired by the sight

<hr/>

[31] Cf. Fowler 94.

of the finishing-line ahead of him[32] and the speaker who envisages the conclusion of a period and works towards it, whereas 'strung together utterance has no end by itself other than the completion of its subject-matter' (1409ᵃ29–31). Some fourth-century documents contain periods of great length and complexity, commonly beginning with an ἐπειδή-clause which may itself contain several subordinate clauses; *IG* ii² 111 (363/2) is the most striking example.[33] My own inclination would be to divide that period of 62 mobile tokens into seventeen kola. It is not the kind of thing that would have interested Aristotle or Demetrius, but there is no doubt about their interest in periods which build up and are not resolved, syntactically or semantically,[34] until the end. Demetr. 10 regards his example from Dem. xx. 1 as (lit.) 'having a sort of bend (καμπήν τινα) and gathering-in (συστροφήν; cf. 8) at the end'. It could certainly be said that the last token, συνερεῖν, 'gathers in' the sense of the whole period; it is the key-word. It is not so easy to see why 'bend' is appropriate, or indeed why the term περίοδος 'way round' came to be applied to style in the first place; Demetrius explains it (11) as analogous to 'ways which are circular and carried round (περιωδευμέναις)', and (20) treats the form of his Demosthenic example as κυκλικός. Presumably the point is that a period is a unit of utterance which begins from major pause and 'returns' to a state of rest by leading to a second pause. In so far as Aristotle thinks of a normal period as containing two kola (*Rhet.* 1409ᵇ16, cf. Demetr. 34), we might think of the second kolon as a 'return journey' to rest-position.

Period and KolonPeriod and ColonThat, at any rate, would help to explain Aristotle's comparison of λέξις κατεστραμμένη to poetic ἀντίστροφα (1409ᵃ26 f.; cf. 1409ᵇ27). He can hardly mean to say that the second half of a period responds metrically to the first half, because we can see from our reading of the orators that it does not,[35]

---

[32] It is clear from the terms in which Aristotle enlarges on the analogy (ἐπὶ τοῖς καμπτῆρσι ἐκπνέουσι καὶ ἐκλύονται· προορῶντες γὰρ τὸ πέρας οὐ κάμνουσι πρότερον, 'it is at the καμπτῆρες that they lose breath and strength, for when they see the finish ahead of them they do not weaken before it') that he thinks of the καμπτήρ not as the turning-point in the δίαυλος but as the finishing-point in the one-stade race. Demetr. 11 is commonly believed to have the δίαυλος in mind, but I think that his 'circularity' means 'from point of rest to point of rest'.

[33] Dover (1987) 37–9.

[34] Fowler's explanation (91 f.) of *Rhet.* 1409ᵇ8 καὶ τῇ διανοίᾳ (ἅμα τῇ διανοίᾳ tent. Kassel) τετελειῶσθαι seems to me conclusive.

[35] Walter Schmid's attempt (153–7) to demonstrate a kind of strophic responsion

even though a trace of responsion *between* periods is not unknown
(cf. p. 181). There is in fact no good reason to suppose that Aristotle
conceived a *definition* of 'period' in terms of rhythm,[36] whatever
his views on the merits of particular rhythms at the beginning
and end of periods or kola. In hearing a speech a Greek critic
would recognize a period, and judge its quality, by attending in
combination to sense, syntax, pause, intonation, volume, and (cf.
Demetr. 19) gesture. In reading, he had to supply in his imagination
what he could not see and hear, in effect 'producing' the 'script'
and exercising choices as a producer necessarily does.[37] This made
it impossible for him to offer a general definition of 'period' or
'kolon' which we could confidently apply to all particular cases.

in Dem. xviii. 251 is unconvincing; by introducing 'ictus' he treats a Demosthenic
text as if it were Plautine.

[36] Zehetmeier (esp. 424–6) argues that Aristotle conceives the 'period' in rhythmical terms, but Demetrius in 'logical' terms; see, however, Fowler 92–4, 97, for the
strong arguments against that differentiation.

[37] He would, of course, be greatly assisted by the location of postpositives, as
shown by Eduard Fraenkel 93–122, 131–7 (see also Marshall *passim* for the rules
governing their location).

3

QUANTIFICATION

A. CONSCIOUS AND UNCONSCIOUS

SOME years ago a music critic, reviewing a new recording of Bruckner's symphonies, remarked:

There is no composer whose style is more individual; Bruckner is recognisable from a single bar, whereas with Brahms one frequently needs eight.[1]

A listener who is enthusiastic and fairly knowledgeable, but neither performer nor musicologist nor professional critic, might well fail to identify Bruckner from a single bar and yet identify him (or Vivaldi, or Sibelius, or many another) from forty-eight bars—without necessarily being able to tell us why. Such a listener is *reminded* of familiar work by a piece previously unheard, and can say, 'this is like that passage in . . .', but the perception of *likeness* is notoriously subjective, because one person may treat as highly significant a similarity or difference which another person does not even notice.[2]

In identifying the author of a text we normally get a great deal of help from its content; characters in Jackie Collins behave differently from those in Jane Austen. Such help, however, is not indispensable; that is clear from the type of literary competition in which the setter composes a piece in the style of X on a topic unlike any which appears in the known works of X, and many competitors, challenged to identify X, get the answer right. The process which leads them to that answer may be intuitive and immediate, but even when it is the product of sustained contemplation it may not admit of articulation and communication. And yet they *agree* on the identification, because they have perceived, and recognized as distinctive features of author X, ingredients which the setter

[1] Donat 462.
[2] Hough 47, Anon. in Chatman 90. An aesthetically alert but unscientific gardener may sometimes classify together plants which a botanist knows to be genetically far apart.

perceived as such and fed into the parody.[3] What exactly is going on? Something, for sure, which counteracts the element of subjectivity in the selection of similarities and differences.

Ancient critics were aware that they could not expect to explain everything in a way which would silence disagreement. Dionysius claims (i. 19. 14–20. 6) that when he had no other grounds for deciding on the authenticity of a speech ascribed to Lysias he allowed the last word to the aesthetic impression which it made upon him. The virtue which Lysias possessed in greater measure than the other orators was a beauty ($\chi \acute{\alpha} \rho \iota \varsigma$) which (18. 11–14)

is very easily seen, apparent to everyone alike, layman or professional, but very difficult to expound in words, a problem even for the most articulate.

The constitution of this beauty cannot be understood by precept, but only by long experience of the Lysian corpus and subjection to the ἄλογον πάθος ('incommunicable emotional effect') which shapes one's ἄλογος αἴσθησις ('incommunicable perception') (19. 6–10).[4]

However experienced a critic one may be, to decide questions of authenticity by appeal to an indescribable 'beauty' begs a few questions; in particular, there is no reason why Lysias should not sometimes have fallen short of his usual standard, and no reason why someone else should not sometimes have attained it. Certainly, the authority of experience is not to be despised, and room should always be made for the intuitive reactions of people who know what they're doing and really care about it, but not at the expense of the intellectual process which Samuel Johnson had in mind when he said:

Why, Sir, I think every man whatever has a peculiar style, which may be discovered by nice examination and comparison with others.[5]

Johnson was guessing; he could not know, nor can we, whether *everyone* has a style which can be distinguished from everyone else's by a sufficiently 'nice examination'. All the same, the analogy of fingerprints and genomes gives us every encouragement to pursue the matter, and I offer some general principles to be kept in view throughout the pursuit.

---

[3] Ohmann in Freeman (1970) 259 draws attention to the importance of parody for stylistics. Among other things, the type of competition I have described refutes Gray 68 f.

[4] Damon 34 n. 7 and ibid. 49; cf. Ohmann 426 on 'naked intuitions'.

[5] Boswell on 13 Apr. 1778.

First, there is no such thing as an utterance which has 'no style'.[6] We use the word 'shapeless' (of things or people) to describe a shape for which we do not have a ready-made familiar term, but plainly no spatio-temporal continuum can literally be shapeless. In the same way, no text can be such that it cannot be seen to resemble stylistically at least one other text by contrast with a third.

Secondly, there is no a priori limit to the number of respects in which two or more texts can be compared and contrasted stylistically.[7] Nor is there any a priori principle which will tell us what parameters we should take first. If we wish neither to look simply for what we have been told to look for on previous occasions nor to start from scratch and possibly waste time on phenomena which turn out not to differ significantly from one text to another within the same corpus, we shall be wise to begin from those which *strike* us as unusual and to discover whether our impression is correct. To be struck, we must have a fair idea, whether explicitly formulated or not, of what is usual, and with every text that we examine we shall be in a better position to decide on the order in which to examine parameters in the next one.

Thirdly, while a recurrent expression or construction, always a gift to the glib parodist, does not constitute a style, any more than a tic constitutes a personality,[8] it may prove to be a clear, perhaps exaggerated, example of a more general phenomenon truly characteristic of the text in question. This can be tested only by extensive sampling, in which attention must be paid not only to the scale of the samples but also to the extent to which a statistical 'population' needs to be defined in terms of genre rather than of authorship (cf. pp. 47 f.).[9] The number of samples matters more than their size.[10]

---

[6] When Schoenberg said of his own *Five Orchestral Pieces* (1909) that they had 'absolutely no architecture, no construction', one can see what he meant, but his wording is regrettable. Turner 98 lapses in referring to 'loss of style' when he should have said 'change of style'. As the ancients knew, a 'plain' or 'simple' style was not achieved without conscious effort (Demetr. 190–208, Cic. *Orator* 76–8). Avoidance of 'rhetorical figures' is itself a rhetorical technique (Enkvist in Spencer 12 f., 32; id. in van Dijk 15, 19; Hough 25, 28), although some critics continue to treat 'style' as if it were a layer of icing added to a plain cake: cf. Bally 19, Ullmann 101 on 'purely referential and communicative' as opposed to 'expressive' elements (does not a rather narrow conception of 'communication' underlie that?), Riffaterre (1959) 160, (1960) 210 on 'stylistic devices'.

[7] Spencer and Gregory in Freeman (1970) 88, Enkvist (1973) 147.

[8] Ohmann in Freeman (1970) 261, Spencer and Gregory ibid. 87, Ullmann 124.

[9] Dover (1994) 83 f.

[10] Enkvist (1973) 135–7 considers samples of 10,000 tokens, and Williams 38 re-

Indeed, a consolidated figure for a very large sample may, like an 'average', hide what we seek; treating the whole of Plato's *Symposium* as a single sample in respect of poetic vocabulary and rhythm would not alert us to the peculiar features of Agathon's speech.[11] In the presentation of stylistic data a cumulative graph is sometimes more illuminating than a single sum total.

The problem is often to determine what general characteristic is exemplified by a particular case which arrests our attention. An 'objective' instance is Thuc. vi. 76. 4:

καὶ οὐ περὶ τῆς ἐλευθερίας ἄρα οὔτε οὗτοι τῶν Ἑλλήνων οὔθ' οἱ Ἕλληνες τῆς ἑαυτῶν τῷ Μήδῳ ἀντέστησαν, περὶ δὲ οἱ μὲν σφίσιν ἀλλὰ μὴ ἐκείνῳ καταδουλώσεως, οἱ δὲ ἐπὶ δεσπότου μεταβολῇ οὐκ ἀξυνετωτέρου, κακοξυνετωτέρου δέ.

And they (sc. the Athenians) did not resist the Persian for the freedom of the Greeks, nor did the Greeks resist him for their own freedom, but the Athenians (sc. did so) for enslavement (sc. of the Greeks) to themselves rather than to him, and the Greeks to change one master for another, not less intelligent but more maliciously so.

The separation of preposition from substantive in περὶ δὲ κτλ. has so few parallels in Greek[12] that it does not admit of any treatment in a statistical table. If, however, we subsume it under 'syntactical experiments' it contributes to a general characterization which distinguishes Thucydides' style[13] from that of, say, Xenophon. There are 'subjective' instances, too, e.g. Hdt. i. 11. 4:

οὐκ ὦν δὴ ἔπειθε, ἀλλ' ὥρα ἀναγκαίην ἀληθέως προκειμένην ἢ τὸν δεσπότεα ἀπολλύναι ἢ αὐτὸν ὑπ' ἄλλων ἀπόλλυσθαι· αἱρέεται αὐτὸς περιεῖναι.

He failed to persuade her, and saw that he really was confronted with the necessity of either killing his master or being killed himself. He chooses his own survival.

To me, the asyndeton in αἱρέεται κτλ. is inspired; and the narrative present tense heightens the drama, even though I know that there is another narrative present in the same context (12. 1 κατακρύπτει)

ports 'gigantic totals' of 200,000 and even 400,000. Much depends on what kind of question one is posing.

[11] Thesleff (1967) rightly entitled his book *Studies in the Styles of Plato*, not . . . *in the Style* . . . Enkvist's definition of style as 'the aggregate of significant differences between a text and a contextually related norm' ((1973) 136 f.) is acceptable provided we understand 'or portion of a text' after 'text'.

[12] KG i. 533, *GG* ii. 427.

[13] Cf. Dover (1965) pp. xiii–xvii, (1989) 9–13.

which does not strike me as dramatic. It is easy enough to compile statistics for asyndeta in Herodotus and to classify them,[14] but even quite large samples might well fail to exhibit even one instance of asyndeton with the emotional effect which I attribute, perhaps wrongly,[15] to αἱρέεται κτλ.

'Characteristic', 'distinctive', 'peculiar', together with 'more', 'less', 'often', 'rarely', and the like, are all imprecise statistical terms,[16] and they can all be translated into precise quantification. Otherwise, we shall remain at the mercy of subjective priorities largely determined in each individual by that individual's most recent or (for a variety of reasons, some of them irrelevant to the history of style) most significant experiences. When a verdict founded on impression is vindicated by precise quantification (which is not always the case)[17] an interesting question is raised: is there such a thing as subliminal quantification? Much of the time this psychological question does not matter, because there are so many stylistic phenomena which *can* be observed, defined, and communicated by an attentive reader that we do not need to dip into the unconscious to explain χάρις as a whole, no matter how greatly individuals may differ in penetrability of the unconscious mind. Authors, however, can be shown to differ consistently in respect of linguistic habits of a kind which not only passes unobserved by the reader but is also extremely unlikely to have been planned or deliberately modified by the author. The best-known example is the relation between the accumulating sum of the variations of the sentence-lengths of a passage from the mean sentence-length and the accumulating sum of the variations of some very common occurrence in each sentence (e.g. words of two or three letters) from the mean occurrence.[18] Linguistic habits of this kind have been compared to 'fingerprints',[19] because there are cases in which they remain unchanged even when

[14] As is done by Denniston, *SPG* 174 f., 179=*GPS* 113 f., 117 f., but he does not mention i. 11. 4.

[15] On my implicit intentionalism cf. Ch. 1 n. 15.

[16] Turner 25. Note also Slings's warning (107 n. 54) that a numerical statement about one text requires comparisons if it is to be meaningful (cf. the 'control group' indispensable for biological enquiry).

[17] I once entertained the belief that a participial clause following a main clause and beginning with 'thinking', 'hoping', 'fearing', and the like is significantly more frequent in Thuc. v. 27–83 than elsewhere in Thucydides, but sampling showed that it is not.

[18] For a full exposition of this technique see Farringdon *et al.*

[19] Kenny 12 f., Farringdon *et al.* 310. Quirk in Crystal and Davy pp. v f., Williams 2 f. The analogy is not quite perfect, because none of us by taking thought can add a

authors believe that they have changed their 'style'; that is to say, when style is changed at what might be called the 'macrostylistic' level, it may still remain constant at 'microstylometric' level. Microstylometric analysis is particularly valuable in the detection of interpolation, composite authorship, and forgery,[20] but as problems of that kind do not concern my present enquiry no further reference to it will be made. It should be noted, however, that there is no good reason why the macros, moved to rapture or revulsion by stylistic effects, and the micros, composing cumulative sum charts with the aid of a computer, should be antagonistic towards each other, *except*—and one glimpses this now and again—when the micros assume that there is nothing worth saying to be said about style outside their own field.[21]

B. AUTHOR, GENRE, AND EXPECTATIONS

Some comparisons between authors in respect of =S have been drawn (pp. 33–5), and it is profitable now to pursue the comparison in more detail (section A). A similar enquiry will be pursued in respect of sentence-structure (section B).

(A) In the Thucydidean passage (iii. 82 f.) which Hermogenes characterized as 'substantival' (cf. p. 32) we are inevitably struck by the remarkable number of abstract nouns, e.g. $\tau \hat{\omega} \nu$ τ' $\dot{\epsilon} \pi \iota \chi \epsilon \iota \rho \dot{\eta} \sigma \epsilon \omega \nu$ $\pi \epsilon \rho \iota \tau \epsilon \chi \nu \dot{\eta} \sigma \epsilon \iota$ $\kappa a \dot{\iota}$ $\tau \hat{\omega} \nu$ $\tau \iota \mu \omega \rho \iota \hat{\omega} \nu$ $\dot{a} \tau o \pi \dot{\iota} a$ 'elaboration of enterprises and extraordinary nature of reprisals', together with =S of types 3(*b*), 4(*b*), 5, and 6. Table 3.1 shows how the passage compares with two other passages of approximately the same length (their identity will be revealed later) for five parameters:

(*a*) Nouns ending in -$\iota \hat{a}$, -$\epsilon \iota a$, -$o \iota a$, -$\dot{\eta}$, -$\sigma \iota s$ or -$\tau \iota s$, -$\tau \eta s$ (stem -$\tau \eta \tau$-), and -$\sigma \mu \acute{o} s$. This category is largely coincident with the semantic

---

whorl to his thumb, but it is not impossible to change a deep-seated habit to which one's attention has been drawn.

[20] Farringdon *et al.* 292–5 (interpolation), 93–101 (composite authorship), 199–201 (forgery).

[21] I am not sure whether Ledger 208 f., referring to 'the great shift in [Plato's] style which is found to occur between the middle- and late-period dialogues' and a 'radical alteration of style', has in mind only his own orthographic parameters (maybe not; cf. 173). It is not necessary, as he proposes (164–7), to attribute the microstylometric peculiarities of Pl. *Parm.* 137 c–166 c to 'a Zenonian original', because the topic (the 'unity' of 'reality') causes the ratio of occurrence of $\epsilon \hat{\iota} \nu a \iota$, $\dot{\epsilon} \sigma \tau \iota$, $\ddot{\epsilon} \nu$, $\dot{\epsilon} \nu \acute{o} s$, $\ddot{\epsilon} \tau \epsilon \rho o \nu$, $\dot{\epsilon} \tau \acute{\epsilon} \rho o \upsilon$, $o \dot{\upsilon}(\kappa / \chi)$, $o \ddot{\upsilon}(\kappa)$, $o \dot{\upsilon} \kappa o \hat{\upsilon} \nu$, $o \ddot{\upsilon} \kappa o \upsilon \nu$, and $\tau \iota$ to be twice what it is in the previous part of the dialogue.

T ABLE 3.1. *Comparison of three texts*

	(*a*)	(*b*)	(*c*)	(*d*)	(*e*)	Total
Text I (Thuc. iii. 82 f.)	52	60	53	52	81	298
Text II	19	13	118	23	132	305
Text III	49	53	53	54	97	306

category 'abstract noun', though it omits some nouns which are certainly abstract (e.g. τύχη, φθόνος) and includes one or two which are not (e.g. φυλή 'tribal regiment').

(*b*) = S consisting of the definite article with an adjective, participle, infinitive, adverb, phrase, or genitive.

(*c*) Nouns other than (*a*), but excluding names of persons, nations, and places.

(*d*) Adjectives (except as in (*b*)), participles used adjectivally, neuter adjectives used adverbially, and regular adverbs in -ως/-ῶς.

(*e*) Finite verbs (except the copula εἶναι), participles (except as in (*b*) and (*d*)), and infinitives without the article.

The count is of tokens, not lexemes. Pronouns, including pronominal adjectives, are entirely left out of account; so are πᾶς and ἅπας, πρότερον and ὕστερον, and πολύς and ὀλίγος (with their comparatives and superlatives).[22] If we treat rows I and II as a contingency table,[23] the value of χ^2 is 89.854 for five 'degrees of freedom', implying that the probability that Texts I and II are samples drawn from the same population is not much more than $1 : 10^{12}$. Rows I and III, on the other hand, yield $\chi^2 = 1.648$, giving the extremely high probability of 0.8 that I and III are samples of the same population. It is thus disconcerting to learn that Text II is chs. 85–91 of Thuc. iii, immediately following the stasis chapters,[24] while Text III is from another author, Isoc. vii. 20–33.[25]

The explanation, of course, is that Thuc. iii. 85–91 is a narrative of military and naval operations, whereas Isoc. vii. 20–33, like the stasis chapters, is a generalizing description of moral and political

[22] There is a touch of arbitrariness in these exclusions, but no harm is done provided they are the same for all the samples being compared; cf. p. 33.

[23] On contingency tables and the calculation of χ^2 see e.g. Kenny 110–19 and McCabe 176–83. I have applied 'Yates' correction' (Kenny 118 f.) throughout.

[24] Chapter 84 intervenes, but its authenticity was suspected by ancient scholars; cf. Fuks, whose argument about the content does not seem to me adequately refuted by Christ.

[25] In Dover (1994) 83 f. what is now '*b*' was 'C', and '*c*' was 'B'.

behaviour. It appears, therefore, that 'population' should be defined in terms of genre and content rather than of author.

Nevertheless, Texts I and III make a profoundly different impression on the reader, for reasons which will be apparent on p. 154. In Table 3.1 figures for a very restricted set of parameters are presented, and there is no reason why the relation between Texts I and III should be the same for a different set. Had we begun from the Isocratean passage instead of the stasis chapters, we would probably have selected phenomena of antithesis and co-ordination. It is worth noting also that whereas I and III are quite close in column (*b*), great differences between them appear if we subdivide that column into its six main categories, thus:

(*b*1) article with masculine singular adjective or participle.
(*b*2) article with neuter singular adjective or participle.
(*b*3) article with masculine plural adjective or participle.
(*b*4) article with neuter plural adjective or participle.
(*b*5) article with infinitive.
(*b*6) article with adverb, phrase, or genitive.

In the following graph (Fig. 3. 1) 'Thuc. (1)' and 'Isoc. (1)' refer to 'Text I' and 'Text III', and to test whether the differences which appear between them appear equally elsewhere in Isocrates and generalizing passages of Thucydides I have added the figures for Isoc. vii. 1–19 + 34–7 ('Isoc. (2)') and Thuc. ii. 35–46 + 51–3 + 60–4 ('Thuc. (2)'). It will be observed that both portions of Thucydides peak in (*b*2) and both of Isocrates in (*b*3), and that the two authors are also differentiated, though less conspicuously, in (*b*4)–(*b*6).

Reference has been made (p. 43) to the hypothesis that a phenomenon concentrated in a striking passage is one which is more likely to occur in other, far less striking, passages of the author in question than in other authors. It is worthwhile to test this hypothesis on Thuc. iii. 82 f. in comparison with iii. 85–91 and two randomly chosen narrative passages of the same length, i. 44–51. 1 and vii. 78–81. 4. The passage of 82. 3 partially quoted on p. 33 exhibits four conjoined substantives of types (*a*) and (*b*): πύστει τῶν προγεγενημένων, τὴν ὑπερβολὴν τοῦ καινοῦσθαι, τῶν τ᾽ ἐπιχειρήσεων περιτεχνήσει, and τῶν τιμωριῶν ἀτοπίᾳ, and there are four more elsewhere: ἀποτροπῆς πρόφασις (82. 4), ἰσονομίας . . . καὶ ἀριστο-κρατίας . . . προτιμήσει (82. 8), τὸ ἀνέλπιστον τοῦ βεβαίου (83. 2), and τὸ τῶν ἐναντίων ξυνετόν (83. 3). The same phenomenon occurs twice

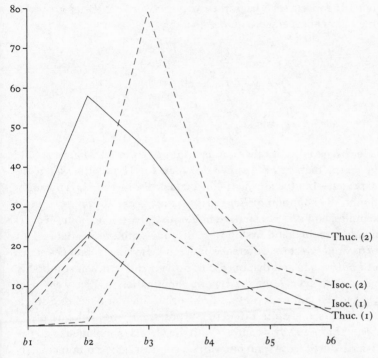

FIG. 3.1. Categories of =S with article

in 85–91, ἀπόγνοια . . . τοῦ ἄλλο τι ἢ κρατεῖν (85. 3) and οἰκειότητος
προφάσει (86. 4), and in vii. 80. 1 we have τῶν . . . ἐπιτηδείων . . .
ἀπορίᾳ. Three narrative passages of Xenophon, of the same length,
randomly chosen,[26] (*HG* iii. 1. 1–4 (λέγεται), v. 1. 1–15 (καρτερεῖν),
and vii. 1. 15–27 (ἔχων πολλά)), have no such examples. It should
also be observed that Thuc. iii. 82 f. contains no less than eleven
lexemes in -σις (ἀξίωσις, δικαίωσις, ἐπιχείρησις, κάκωσις, κατάγνωσις,
μέλλησις, περιτέχνησις, προτίμησις, πρόφασις, στάσις, φύσις). In the
three passages of Xenophon we find only αἴσθησις (v. 1. 8) and
στάσις (iii. 1. 1), but Thuc. i. 44–51. 1 yields διάγνωσις, δίωξις, and
πρόρρησις, iii. 85–91 ἐπαναχώρησις, ἐπίκλυσις, and πρόφασις, and vii.
78–81. 4 διάβασις and τάξις. These data suggest that concentrations
in striking passages may well be a pointer to general characteristics
of a writer.

(B) Defining 'sentence' as above (p. 27) and excluding some (but

[26] On the principle 'beginnings of odd-numbered books'.

not all) appositives[27] from the category 'word', Webster arrived at
the following average sentence-lengths:

Hdt.	16	Lycurg.	29
Xen.	19	Hyper.	30
Pl.	19	Aeschin.	31
Lys.	22.5	Dem.	32
Thuc.	25.4	Isoc.	34
Is.	27	Din.	43

The list is not entirely counter-intuitive—that the figure should
be much higher for Thucydides than for Herodotus was to be
expected—but the low figure for Plato is disquieting. It is no doubt
due to the adoption of *Rep.* 401 B–404 D as one of the three Plato
samples, and that is a stark reminder that there is no point in averaging as though authorship were the only significant variable. Few
of us would treat the difference between the average sentence-length
of *Epidemics* iii and that of *VM* as proving difference of authorship
or use the average of the two in combination as if it were relevant to the authorship of a third work. Different parts of a single
text may serve quite different purposes, e.g. the dialogue of Pl.
Smp. 201 D–207 A by contrast with the virtual monologue of 207 A–
212 A. Moreover, within one work a contrast between immediately
adjacent passages in respect of sentence-length may be designed
for stylistic effect. Consider e.g. the last thirty sentences (defined
as above) of Dem. xxi; quantifying sentence-length solely in terms
of mobile tokens (cf. p. 27), we observe the following sequence:[28]

7	20	16	20	7	11	2	5	1	27
10	8	9	3	3	4	7	34	3	5
1	5	2	6	5	22	15	10	34	15

The positions of the peaks and troughs would of course be entirely
veiled by averaging; indeed, there is no way of understanding them
stylistically except by examining them in context. However, in addition to substituting 'MCF' for 'sentence', we can improve on
averaging considerably by giving for each sample investigated the

---

[27] He says 'prepositions, articles and all but connective particles'.

[28] Note in particular the alternation of very short and very long sentences, a
feature of Demosthenes' style which contributes much to the vigour of his work.
It is well illustrated in ix. 15–20, which Russell (1991) xxvii f., 110–13 chooses as a
specimen. Cf. also Jeremy Trevett in De Martino and Sommerstein 133 f.

first and third quartiles, the median, and the five greatest. These data are given in Table 3.2 for the following samples:

Anon. *Ath.* i. 1–2. 12 (political exposition)
Hdt. i proem.–15 (mainly narrative, with some conversation)
Hdt. iii. 80–2 (the 'Persian Debate' on the constitution)
Hdt. vii. 8–11 (Xerxes' conference with his nobles)
Thuc. vi. 9–18 (speeches of Nicias and Alcibiades)
Thuc. vii. 69–75 (military narrative)
Xen. *HG* ii. 3. 24–49 (confrontation of Critias and Theramenes)
Xen. *HG* vii. 1. 2–14 (speeches of Procles and Cephisodotus)
Xen. *HG* vii. 1. 15–32 (military narrative)
Pl. *Smp.* 207 C 8–212 A 7 (Diotima's peroration)
Pl. *Rep.* 614 B 2–621 B 7 (the Myth of Er)
Isoc. vii. 1–49 (political exposition)

The samples from Anon. *Ath.*, Hdt. i, Xen. *HG* vii, and Isoc. vii were chosen at random,[29] Thuc. vi and vii to give maximum contrast with each other in subject-matter, and the remainder because they seemed likely to be interesting. The snatch of dialogue in *Smp.* 208 B 7–9 and the proclamation of Lachesis in *Rep.* 617 D 6–E 5 have been omitted. Of the two rows of figures entered against each sample, the upper row gives the number of mobile tokens in an MCF, and the lower row the number of subordinate finite verb-tokens, participles without the article, or infinitives without the article, in an MCF.

This table presents several noteworthy features. Clearly, there is no steady *chronological* progression towards longer or shorter MCFs; and, whereas the speeches in *HG* ii are composed in longer and more complex MCFs than the military narrative in *HG* vii, the contrast between speeches and narrative in Thuc. vi and vii is the reverse. Once in a while we may expect to encounter a monstrous MCF (here, Thuc. vii. 69. 2), and the samples suggest that the likelihood of such an encounter may prove to be quite high in Plato, but no safe predictions could be based simply on the third quartile, let alone the median. What is most important is the difference between the Persian Debate in Hdt. iii and the speeches at Xerxes' Council in Hdt. vii, and the even more striking difference between the two debates in Xen. *HG*; the samples from Hdt. iii and Xen.

[29] Cf. n. 26.

Quantification

TABLE 3.2. *MCF lengths in twelve samples*

Sample	1st quartile	Median	3rd quartile	Five greatest				
Anon. *Ath.*	5	7	10.5	17	17	20	21	25
	0	1	2.5	6	6	7	7	9
Hdt. i	4	6	9	17	18	24	25	25
	0	1	2	4	6	6	6	7
Hdt. iii	3	4	6	10	11	11	11	14
	0	1	2	2	3	3	3	3
Hdt. vii	4	6	10	19	21	24	24	32
	1	1	3	5	5	6	7	9
Thuc. vi	4.5	8	11	19	21	24	27	27
	1	1	3	7	7	7	9	10
Thuc. vii	6	8	12	28	30	34	43	74
	0	1	3	10	11	13	16	24
Xen. ii	5	9	12	17	18	26	28	33
	2	3	4	6	6	6	7	9
Xen. vii (1)	4	5	8	11	12	12	12	16
	0	1	3	2	2	3	3	3
Xen. vii (2)	4	7	10	19	19	20	23	24
	0	1	3	5	5	6	7	7
Pl. *Smp.*	4.5	7.5	15.5	37	38	42	46	51
	0	1.5	3.5	8	11	11	12	12
Pl. *Rep.*	5	7	10	26	28	40	47	59
	0	1	2	6	8	9	10	17
Isoc. vii	5	8	12	34	36	38	38	39
	0	1	3	9	9	11	11	13

HG vii (1) are in fact closer to each other than either of them is to any other of the samples. We can well understand that Herodotus chose for the theoretical generalizations of the Persian Debate a more gnomic, almost epigrammatic, style than for the discussion of practical issues in Xerxes' Council, and also that Xenophon judged it appropriate to elaborate the language of the eminent Athenians in *HG* ii far beyond that of less distinguished characters in *HG* vii.[30] This is not just a matter of genre in the broad sense, but of author's choice within the range of possibilities acceptable in a genre. The characterization of an author's style is not to be sought in the arithmetical mean of samples drawn from texts of differing

[30] Cf. *HCT* v. 443 f. on Thucydidean influence on the language of Xen. *HG* i–ii. 3. 10.

functions, but in observation of the way in which he chose to adapt language to function.

The demonstration in Table 3.1 that Thucydidean generalization and Thucydidean military narrative are, statistically speaking, different populations in respect of style has a very important bearing on our interpretation of the experience of being 'struck' by an 'unusual' or 'abnormal' phenomenon. In practice we measure abnormality against our expectations, and what we expect of a text depends on its function and the occasion for which it is composed. We have already seen (pp. 9 f.) how Thucydides' narrative of a sequence of military events and an orator's treatment of the same sequence in a ceremonial speech differ not only in expanding or suppressing different aspects of the events narrated—that is all at the level of content—but also in sentence-structure at linguistic level. The hearer of a ceremonial speech brings to the occasion expectations which are not the same as the expectations of a reader of history.

This point is illustrated by Dionysius' criticism (i. 91. 8–15) of Isoc. xvii. 9 as exceeding the 'forensic manner' in length and making use of the symmetries and assonances which are characteristic of epideictic oratory (cf. pp. 11 f.), phenomena conspicuous in the Lysian funeral speech.[31] Stylistic distinction between 'epideictic' and 'forensic' is assumed by Arist. *Rhet.* 1414^a18 f.

In some sectors of some cultures at some periods the recipient's expectations may be so rigidly defined that significant change of style is virtually precluded; cf. p. 12. The speaker, writer, artist, or composer may, on the other hand, extend those expectations by tactful innovation; but tact is indispensable for success, because blatant incongruity provokes a laughter neither intended nor welcomed by the author. Consider the following hypothetical English examples:

(*a*) *It has been established to the satisfaction of the court that the deceased formed this intention Septembery-time.

This is a simple mixture of 'registers' (cf. p. 21), the insertion of the dialectal expression 'Septembery-time', i.e. 'in or about September', in a context otherwise formal, even (in 'the deceased') a little pompous.

---

[31] Dion. i. 91. 15–92. 1 gives a further example, in which symmetry and assonance are less obtrusive.

(*b*) *If you eat all that, you'll be as ick as a bloody bow-wow.

This time, a more complicated mixture; baby-talk in 'ick' for 'sick', but the intensification 'sick as a dog' is a somewhat gross, adult expression; it can hardly be adapted to discourse with a small child by substituting 'bow-wow' for 'dog', with which 'bloody' is totally incongruous.

(*c*)   *Unhappy pupae, by dread hens devour'd!

The scientific term 'pupa' (most people, if they referred to a pupa at all, would call it a 'chrysalis') is incongruous with blank verse, the dramatic exclamation, the archaic adjective 'dread', the postponement of the participle, and the writing of disyllabic 'devoured' with an apostrophe. But here it is not so easy to separate form from content. We could quite correctly say that the 'contextual probability'[32] of 'unhappy' as an epithet of 'pupae' and of 'dread' as an epithet of 'hens' is low, but, of course, that is more than a bare statistical datum; the low probability rests on the extreme difficulty of responding to pathos in the misfortunes of half a cubic centimetre of yellow liquid encased in chitin, and on the obstinate fact that hens simply are not dread.[33]

Those hypothetical examples were meant to be funny; incongruity often is. However, contextual abnormality is not always or necessarily incongruous. Metaphors which are 'successful', i.e. attractive and memorable, often depend on it; and just as the effect of colour on the eye is an effect not in isolation but in combination and contrast with adjacent colours,[34] so an occurrence of stylistic import is a complex occurrence, the significance of which is to be sought in the relations between its elements. When the elements are drawn from more than one register, there is always a risk of bathos or absurdity.

Encountering 'Septembery-time' in a sentence otherwise so formal is rather like coming upon an anchovy in a wedding-cake. There are in fact strong analogies between cuisine and linguistic style. One

[32] Enkvist in Spencer 28, cf. id. (1973) 136 f.
[33] I modelled the verse on the coleopterological poetry of Edward Norman in Adams 97 f.
[34] Cf. Cumming 4 on Bridget Riley; and an analogy may be drawn from fashion design, since in recent years clothes designed by John Galliano have aggressively combined elements associated with entirely different historical periods. Thesleff (1967) 30 observes that a 'dynamic' author is 'more likely to put the traditional linguistic material in entirely new combinations'.

analogy may be seen in adjustment to occasion and function; for instance, the serving of bowls of custard at a stand-up reception for the launching of a new book would conflict very sharply with our expectations (unless the book was about custard). Nevertheless, culinary innovation is a continuous process, by which expectations are modified and enlarged; my parents would have been horrified at the idea of eating toast and marmalade with kippers or mixing orange juice with Worcester sauce to pour over fried cod, innovations which I have no difficulty in accepting. A second analogy is that the differences between alternative recipes for food judged appropriate for identical occasions are of two quite distinct kinds. Put the same ingredients at the disposal of a dozen cooks and ask each of them to make a batch of biscuits. The chances are that it will be possible to differentiate between some, at any rate, of the twelve resultant batches, because the proportions of the ingredients will not be the same in all of them, and the thoroughness of the mixing, the order of mixing, the temperature of the oven when they are put in, the time they stay in the oven—all such things affect the end-product. Comparable differences between stylistic 'recipes' can be identified and described by systematic, laborious counting and totalling.[35]

Some recipes are distinguished by deviations from the norm which may be very few in number but spectacular in effect, like the anchovy in the wedding-cake. A single instance of such a deviation in style may strike us so powerfully that we think of it as the very essence of the style of the author in question. We may be quite wrong about that, but we cannot know whether we are right or wrong until we have investigated the frequency with which the recipe recurs. Intuitive reactions of the type, 'Only Thucydides could have said that!' and 'Xenophon could never have said that!', though extravagantly expressed (how do we know, from what an author said, what he was *incapable* of saying?),[36] serve a good purpose as starting-points of investigation, but they are only starting-points.

Register is the medium in which the relations between composer

---

[35] I have not used a computer for any of the material presented in this book, because the preparation of an adequately 'enriched' (or 'flagged') machine-readable text and a program to answer my questions would have been more time-consuming than doing the whole job with pencil and paper. It is also my normal practice to read Greek texts aloud, and I find it distasteful to do that from a screen, especially when I want to glance up and down the page to remind myself of the wider context of a passage.

[36] Cf. Ch. 1 n. 2.

and recipient are fashioned, and those relations can be changed by an incongruity of register. In Greek a shift from the language of everyday discourse to the language of poetry may constitute an attempt to assume the didactic authority with which the Greeks were apt to invest the poet. Conversely, a shift from the formal to the colloquial may suddenly establish a relationship of familiarity and confidentiality. In modern usage, an account of a scientific experiment which moves from the passive (e.g. 'the temperature was raised . . .') to the active (e.g. 'I then removed . . .') may stimulate and gratify the reader. It does not take much to have an effect of this kind. Just as in a conversation a single ill-chosen word, a gesture, a smirk, a glance at the clock, may make an ineradicable impression on one of the participants, so in a text a single stylistic choice alienates or conciliates, patronizes or stimulates, and may not only affect reception from that moment onwards but also provoke revision of the attitude adopted by the recipient towards the previous portion of the text.[37]

[37] To take an actual example, in a recent television discussion in which a judge and two very eminent barristers did their best (looking grave and shocked) to rebut the allegation of an Assistant Chief Constable that the procedures of the lawcourts are essentially a *game*, one of the barristers used a sentence of the form, 'Whether . . ., I know not.' For some in the audience, that single pompous archaism engendered deep mistrust, because it was redolent of rhetorical debate and alien to the spirit of rationality expected in the discussion. ('Rhetorical' in the everyday sense of the word; I am aware that chattiness and earnest reasonableness are also rhetorical techniques; cf. n. 6.) We can make a similar experiment (in the reverse direction) by taking a passage of rather formal generalizing historical narrative, inserting a 'So,' at the start of one or two sentences, changing a couple of instances of 'not' to '-n't', and seeing how much difference that makes to us as readers.

4

SPEECHES, STORIES, AND TALK

LET us put ourselves in the position of the first Greek, whoever he was and wherever and whenever he lived, who committed a prose composition to papyrus,[1] whether he allowed it to go into circulation or retained it for his own recitation to friends. The second such writer could, if he wished, take the style of the first as a model, and at least is unlikely to have disregarded it altogether if he knew of it. The third could take the first two as models, and so on; but what about the very first?

The range of models available to him may be set out schematically thus:

I. Poetry
II. Prose
    A. Written
        (1) Laws, decrees, regulations, calendars, lists.
        (2) Letters and messages.
        (3) Graffiti and dipinti.
    B. Unwritten
        (1) Transmitted:
        Ritual formulae, prayers, curses, spells, proverbs.
        (2) Rehearsed:
        Political and forensic speeches.
        (3) Semi-rehearsed:
        (a) Stories.
        (b) Instructions and technical explanations.
        (4) Unrehearsed:
        Conversation.

[1] Or to leather. Cf. Hdt. v. 58. 3; and I learn from Professor Yu. G. Vinogradov that a recently discovered letter (on lead) from Olbia refers to letters and documents as διφθέρια.

For simplicity's sake I treat oracular responses as poetry, although some of them were not.

I. *Poetry*

At all periods available to our observation poetry and prose were strongly differentiated in rhythm and language. The extent to which prose authors adopted elements characteristic of poetry, and the reasons why they did so, will be discussed in Chapter 6, but one general consideration of the greatest importance must be kept in mind throughout any historical investigation of Greek prose. Because the sentence-structure of the earliest prose, to judge from the extant citations, appears to have been very much simpler (cf. p. 74) than what we repeatedly encounter in Thucydides, Isocrates, and Plato, we tend to forget that those early prose-writers had behind them not simply a long tradition of poetry but an exceptionally rich tradition of *great* poetry composed by people who needed no lessons in the art of language. If the first prose-writers seem unsophisticated, that was their choice—for reasons which are not mysterious (p. 60)— and should not be attributed to primitive or childlike incapacity.[2] Most of what can be said about phenomena such as word-order, repetition, antithesis, and asyndeton can be said of both poetry and prose; my present enquiry is concerned with those developments which were positively or negatively specific, in their scale if not in their essence, to prose.

II. *Prose*

A.1. Laws and decrees should not be underestimated as a model for early prose literature, because adequacy and accuracy of exposition matter even more in a law than in a cosmogonic theory. The Attic law of homicide, as reconstructed from *IG* i[3] 104 and citations in the orators, can fairly be regarded, as Aly recognized,[3] as our earliest Attic prose work, but we have nothing on a comparable scale among Ionian documents earlier than Hecataeus and Heraclitus.

   A.2. Letters and messages are valuable for the linguistic data they sometimes happen to provide, but they can hardly be taken

---

[2] Fehling 138, *Wf* 98–102, 105, 109 f. Cf. Navarre 92–111 on the rhetorical organization of speeches in archaic poetry and early tragedy.

[3] Aly (1929) 10–29; not everyone, though, shares his perception (178) of an *eigentümliche Schönheit* in the law.

into account as models for prose literature, because of the severe
constraints imposed by the dimensions of the objects on which they
were written. There are, however, one or two passages in early prose
which seem to show features characteristic of private documents.
Lys. i. 17

and everything came into my mind, and I was full of suspicion, when I
thought . . . All this came into my mind, and I was full of suspicion

is reminiscent of *SEG* xxvi. 845. 6–9 (Berezan', s. vi/v):

but he protests and denies that he has anything to do with Matasys, and
claims that he is a free man and has nothing to do with Matasys.

Anon. *Ath.* 2. 11 contains a comparable but more elaborate repetition (cf. p. 138). The threefold 'if they inhabited an island' (ibid. 2.
15) may be compared with Anaxagoras DK 59 B 12:

if it were not on its own but were mixed with something else, it would
participate in everything, if it were mixed with something else,[4]

for which the closest parallel is a semi-literate message (*P.Oxy.* 3070)
from the first century AD:

If you'll grant us buggery and it's all right with you, we won't beat you up
any more, if you grant us buggery.

A.3. The brevity of graffiti and dipinti makes them of little interest as models, but we can learn something (negatively; cf. p. 61)
from their style.

B.1. On the occasional utilization of formulae, proverbs, etc., see
p. 145.

B.2. Although we have no direct evidence at all for the stylistic
features of political and forensic speaking before the circulation of
written versions of speeches began in the last quarter of the fifth
century, it may well have been by far the most important single
model for the first prose-writer. The Greeks, like some preliterate
peoples in other parts of the world,[5] were connoisseurs of oratory,
as we can see from what the old Trojans say about the embassy
of Menelaus and Odysseus in *Il.* iii. 212–24, and we could have
inferred it from the epic phrases λιγὺς ἀγορητής and ἐσθλὸς ἀγορητής.
It is impossible to believe that litigants of the kind described in *Il.*

---

[4] *Wf* 149; Dover (1968*b*) 178–91; López Eire (1987) 15–17, 21.
[5] Dover (1987) 18–25; van Groningen 233 is one of the few to have emphasized
the importance of pre-literate oratory.

iii. 497–508 came before the elders without having given much careful thought to what they were going to say. There is a very high probability that by the time Antiphon wrote speeches every audience had stylistic expectations (different for different types of occasion) which were the product of evolution over many centuries. For the historian, the fact that data of the highest importance are irrecoverably hidden in darkness is extremely unsatisfactory; but we must never allow that patch of darkness to slip out of our field of vision, never treat what cannot be investigated as if for that reason it did not matter. Fortunately some inferences can be drawn from the earliest written speeches; see below, pp. 61–6.

B.3(*a*). Stories should be treated as straddling the 'rehearsed' and 'unrehearsed' categories; in any particular case, much depends on how often the teller has told the story and how much s/he cares about fidelity of reproduction. The assumption of the availability of stories as models for prose literature rests on the universality of story-telling in preliterate cultures and in the non-literate stratum of cultures in which literacy is the norm; it rests also on the occasional references in Classical literature to stories ascribed to Aesop (Ar. *V.* 566, 1259, 1446 f.), 'Sybarite' stories (*V.* 1259), and 'old wives' tales', e.g. Pl. *Rep.* 350 E 'and I'll chime in with "*Well!*", as they do to the old women who tell stories', and *Grg.* 527 A 'a story like an old woman's'.

B.3(*b*). The existence of technical instructions must be presumed, for there were plenty of techniques in the archaic period requiring exposition to the apprentice (e.g. in the surgery or the foundry) and the recruit (on the trireme or in the riding-school). We cannot form much idea of such instruction except by inference from existing written treatises ('Hippocrates', Xenophon on horses, Pseudo-Xenophon on hunting), but it should not be discounted as a model for early philosophic and scientific exposition. Cf. pp. 112–17.

B.4. Spoken dialogue is portrayed by tragedy, comedy, and Plato and Xenophon in their philosophical or quasi-philosophical works; it is also frequently portrayed in Herodotus and sporadically in narrative works of Xenophon and narrative passages of the orators.[6] If we find anywhere in such portrayals phenomena which occur in more than one author but do not occur when an author is speaking *in propria persona* or in public documents, we may suspect that

[6] For a very useful survey of reported direct speech in the orators see Trevett in De Martino and Sommerstein 123–45.

those phenomena are drawn from the colloquial register; and if they occur also in private documents (graffiti, dipinti, letters), the suspicion is greatly strengthened.[7]

We can distinguish 'non-colloquial' (or 'formal') from 'colloquial' (or 'informal') style negatively: by the absence from the former of phenomena which we have grounds for identifying as colloquial. In listing below phenomena which are rare or entirely avoided in formal style I put forward for serious consideration the hypothesis that these avoidances were not an innovation of the latter part of the fifth century but a long-standing feature of public speaking. In the absence of speeches from anywhere but Athens the contrasts must necessarily be drawn from Attic.

1. Obscenity. Comedy deploys a very large vocabulary of terms for the anatomy and physiology of sex and excretion (e.g. πέος, κύσθος, βινεῖν, λαικάζειν, πρωκτός, πέρδεσθαι, χέζειν), supplemented by many slang terms (e.g. σποδεῖν, παίειν) which are used in other contexts without obscene reference. Such terms cannot be regarded as confections peculiar to comedy, because they occur also in Attic private documents (e.g. καταπύγων, λαικάστρια) and indeed in the uninhibited verses of Archilochus and Hipponax. All such language is rigorously excluded from the formal style. The 'proper' words are admitted on the rare occasions when they are unavoidable (e.g. αἰδοῖα, 'genitals', in Thuc. ii. 49. 8 and Pl. *Smp.* 190 A, 191 B ('Aristophanes' is the speaker), *Ti.* 91 B), but euphemism is the rule. When the aged Sophocles is asked (Pl. *Rep.* 329 C) 'Can you still do it?', he is not offended by the question, but the verb is expressed by γυναικὶ συγγίγνεσθαι, 'be with a woman'. Xen. *Hi.* 1. 4 substitutes 'we all know what' for 'genitals'; Aeschines i. 52 makes heavy weather of uttering the word πεπορνευμένος (although it has occurred in the law which he cites in §29), and it appears from Polybius' report (xii. 13. 1) that Timaeus (*FGrHist* 566 F 35b) managed to accuse Demochares of fellation by means of a laboured circumlocution.[8] Obscenities are hardly the most important ingre-

[7] Dover (1989) 113 f., 142 f., 204 f.
[8] In Xen. *Smp.* 8. 23 Socrates, having spoken of the lover as begging for a kiss or caress from his boy (φιλήματος . . . ἢ ψηλαφήματος), pleads the effect of wine as his excuse for saying something λαμυρώτερον 'too saucy'; ψηλαφᾶν is used of stroking a horse (Xen. *Eq.* 2. 4), but also of groping in the dark (Pl. *Phd.* 99 B), and one thinks of the English sexual use of 'grope' and 'feel'. It should be noted that κίναιδος, which we would have expected to be a grossly obscene word, was evidently not so (Pl. *Grg.*

dient of human conversation, but their presence or absence affords
the starkest and simplest contrast between formal and informal.

2. Oaths. There are hundreds of occurrences of casual oaths (νὴ
Δία, μὰ τοὺς θεούς, etc.), serving as intensification or on occasion
almost as particles,[9] in comedy and in passages of dialogue in Plato
and Xenophon. In many cases the oath constitutes corroboration
or denial of the previous speaker's words, and we might not have
expected it to be any more conspicuous in narrative or sustained
exposition than 'Yes' in the *Cambridge Ancient History*, but even
when all such responses have been set aside there are plenty left, e.g.
(to cite from just one comedy and one Platonic work) Ar. *Ra.* 28,
288, 738, 937, 947, 1043, 1198, 1433, Pl. *Ap.* 17 B, 22 A, 24 E, 35 D,
39 C. In the earliest oratory, however, oaths are very rare indeed:
in Antiphon, only fr. 70 Thalheim (cited by the *Suda* as Ἀντιφῶν
ἐν προοιμίοις); in Lys. vi, three times (7, 32, 38; the speech is by
one of Andocides' accusers in 399, not by Lysias), and once in
Lys. viii (18; quite certainly not a forensic speech). No examples in
Andocides or Isocrates, and none in Thucydides or Anon. *Ath.* In
the historical works of Xenophon (including *Cyr.*, *Ages.*, and *Lac.*)
there are 86 occurrences in all, of which no less than 76 are in the
portrayal of dialogue; of the remaining ten, eight are in speeches and
only two (*HG* v. 1. 4, *Lac.* 14. 1) are the writer's intensification of
his own statement. Supporting evidence for the informal character
of oaths is furnished by their absence from tragedy (Eur. *Andr.*
934 μὰ τὴν ἄνασσαν is the nearest thing in tragedy to the casual
oath of prose dialogue) but presence in satyr-plays (six times in
Eur. *Cyclops*) and in dipinti (Θέογνις καλὸς νὴ Δία on a black-figure
cup from Palermo, *ABV* 675).[10] With Isaeus a marked change in
the orators' attitude to oaths becomes apparent, for he offers 14
instances. Five of these are in objections or suggestions attributed
hypothetically to the speaker's adversary (iii. 24, 73, iv. 20, 24, vii.
33) and four in the speaker's answer to a rhetorical question (iii. 25,
39, 49, viii. 29). Both categories have an obvious affinity with the
representation of dialogue. Two instances are the strong negative
formula οὐ μὰ Δί' οὐ (xi. 35 *bis*) familiar in comedy (e.g. Ar. *Nu.*
1066, *Ra.* 1043); that leaves three straightforward intensifications:

494 E). Chrysippus apparently (Diog. Laert. vii. 187 f.) used scandalously obscene
words.

[9] Dover (1987) 50.
[10] Ibid. 48.

vi. 61 'so that they don't deserve to be the target of resentment; it's much rather my opponents, νὴ τὸν Δία καὶ τὸν Ἀπόλλω, who deserve it', xi. 36 'that he has acted wrongly . . . I think that you too μὰ τοὺς θεούς are not unaware', fr. 23 Thalheim μὴ μὰ Δία ταῦτα ποιεῖν. Isaeus' innovation is greatly extended in Demosthenes: 52 instances in speeches i–xviii, three of them reproducing direct speech (vi. 23, viii. 17, ix. 68), nine with the objections of hypothetical speakers (vi. 13 accompanied by εἴποι τις ἄν, and viii. 7 and xvi. 6 somewhat disguised), sixteen answering rhetorical questions, three the strong negative formula, one (xviii. 261) a close approximation to that, and the remaining twenty various kinds of intensification. The history of oaths in oratory thus indicates a change towards informality, no doubt very carefully calculated, in the middle of the fourth century.

3. The demonstrative affix -ί. In Thuc. iii. 113. 4 there is a brief passage of dialogue which contains (τὰ ὅπλα ταυτί) the only instance of the demonstrative οὑτοσί in Thucydides. Since the suffix -ί is the verbal equivalent of a pointing finger, it is understandable that it should not occur in historical narrative (the narrator can 'point' figuratively but not literally), but the fact that it does not occur in Thucydidean speeches (except νυνί, mysteriously, in iv. 92. 2; the Boeotian Pagondas is speaking)[11] makes iii. 113. 4 a neat illustration of its informality. The contrast between the orators' use of the suffix and its use in Aristophanes and Platonic dialogue is shown in Table 4.1. 'Pl.' refers to 'early' Plato only (Brandwood's Group IA), and 'Isoc.' only to the forensic speeches, xvi–xxi. [And.] iv is excluded as spurious, and so are the Demosthenic prooemia and epistles. Lys. xiii is separated from the rest of Lysias, and 'Lys.' excludes speeches xi and xv as rhetorical exercises. After each figure I have added the ratio of the tokens with -ί to the corresponding tokens without -ί; 'c.' is a sign that very large numbers have been calculated from word-indexes and not counted meticulously.

The suffix, despite its usefulness as a metrical alternative, cannot be poetic (for otherwise we would encounter it in tragedy), nor can it be specifically comic (for there is no conceivable reason why the prosecutor of Agoratus in Lys. xiii should wish to leaven his passion with a touch of comedy).[12] When its extension in Demosthenes is

[11] There is one other νυνί in Thucydides, but it is in the verbatim quotation of a public document (v. 47. 11), where νυνί seems to have been at home, to judge from (e.g.) *IG* i³ 93. 3.

[12] Equally, there is no apparent reason for the solitary appearance in Plato of ὁτιή, a lexeme otherwise confined to comedy and satyr-drama, at *Phlb.* 58 A.

TABLE 4.1. *The suffix -ί*

	Ar.	Pl.	Ant.	And.	Lys. xiii	Lys.	Isoc.	Is.	Dem.
δευρί	18 (1:9)			1 (1:3)					6 (1:11)
ἐκεινοσί	10 (1:18)								1 (1:118)
ἐνθαδί	15 (1:3½)								1 (1:46)
ἐνθενδί	1 (1:10)								
ἐνταυθί	1 (1:43)	1 (1:26)							10 (1:7½)
ἐντευθενί	15 (1:1½)					1 (1:2)			1 (1:18)
νυνί	77 (1:3½)	15 (1:4)	1 (1:13)	11 (1:4)	4 (1:2½)	47 (1:2½)	4 (1:7)	20 (1:3½)	149 (c.1:6)
ὁδί	126 (1:2½)							3 (1:12)	16 (1:7)
οὑτοσί	340 (c.1:4)	35 (c.1:44½)	9 (c.1:56)	18 (c.1:12½)	16 (1:7)	24 (c.1:46)	7 (1:40)	46 (c.1:20)	c.1,560 (c.1:7)
οὑτωσί	7 (1:15)	12 (1:21)	3 (1:9)	1 (1:26)				2 (1:49)	47 (c.1:15)
τηλικουτοσί	2 (1:3)								2 (1:46½)
τοιοσδί	3 (1:2½)								1 (1:2)
τοιουτοσί	17 (1:4)				1 (1:14)				7 (c.1:118)
τοσουτοσί	10 (1:2½)								2 (c.1:200)
ὡδί	14 (1:1½)	1 (1:17)							12 (no ὡδε)
Total -ί lexemes	15	5	3	4	4	2	2	4	14
Total -ί tokens	656	64	13	31	22	71	11	71	c.1,815
Ratio -ί:not -ί tokens	c.1:4	c.1:30	c.1:4	1:10	1:6½	c.1:17	1:28	c.1:16	c.1:7½

taken in conjunction with the extension of the casual oath, there can be little doubt that the prima-facie inference from Thuc. iii. 113. 4 as to the informal character of that passage is correct. And from that I venture to draw the further inference that the formal style of fifth-century written oratory was not an innovation of that period, modelled on historical and scientific writing, but the product of a very long tradition of formality in unwritten speeches.

4. Miscellaneous colloquialisms. Tarrant lists 32 phenomena in Plato which she classifies as 'colloquial', and Stevens 116 of that character in Euripides (the two lists coincide in only five items). Tarrant's classification is distinctly subjective, whereas in the very few cases where Stevens appeals to intuition he makes it quite clear

that he is doing so; and for the great majority of his items he cites examples from Aristophanes and other comic poets, Herodas, and those poems of Theocritus (notably 4, 14, and 15) which portray the dialogue of uncultured characters. In the nature of the case, not everyone will agree with his classification in its entirety, but it is striking that of his 116 phenomena no less than 30 are attested in Demosthenes, but only 8 in the earlier orators:[13] Ant. iv. β. 3 and v. 58 εἶέν, v. 43 κακοδαίμων, And. i. 22 . . . ἢ οὔ; ἐγὼ μὲν οἶμαι, 41 ἀρά γε (reported conversation), 128 φέρε, Lys. i. 21 ὅπως . . . μηδείς . . . πεύσεται, 'mind that no one gets to hear of it' (reported conversation), xii. 50 ὅπως τοίνυν μὴ φανήσεται κτλ., i. 36 χαίρειν ἐᾶν, vii. 12 frequentative ἄν. Only eight of Stevens's phenomena are in Thucydides: i. 73. 2 δι' ὄχλου (speech), iii. 75. 4 οὐδέν . . . ὑγιές (summarized speech), and iv. 22. 2 τι ὑγιές (summarized thought), iii. 113. 4 οὐκ ἄρα . . .; (conversation), v. 59. 4 and 60. 2 ἐν καλῷ (both reported thought), 100 ἦ 'που ἄρα (Melian Dialogue), vi. 34. 9 ὅσον οὔπω (speech), vii. 71. 3 frequentative ἄν, viii. 78 ἄλλως ὄνομα (summarized thought). Tarrant rightly includes ληρεῖς ἔχων 'you keep on talking nonsense' (Ar. *Av.* 341, *Lys.* 945, *Ra.* 512), with which compare φλυαρεῖς ἔχων in Pl. *Euthd.* 295 C and *Grg.* 490 E; in the former Euthydemus, in the latter Callicles, is becoming angry and impatient[14] (Callicles couples his discourteous words with the informal ποῖα ὑποδήματα; 'What do you mean, *shoes?*'[15]). This intransitive ἔχων occurs with other verbs in Aristophanes and in Theocr. 14. 8 (a crude rustic is speaking); once again, it is Demosthenes (xxiii. 35 κακοῦν ἔχοντα 'keep on maltreating him') who is the first orator to use it.

The hypothesis that the language of early oratory was recognizably formal accords with the tradition that in the 'good old days' the gestures, stance, and tone of the speaker were severely restrained and dignified. We first encounter this belief in Aeschines i. 25:

What we are all now accustomed to do, speaking with the hand unconcealed, was in those days regarded as rather daring, and they took care not to do it,

and subsequently Cleon gets the blame for the deterioration in man-

---

[13] In Stevens 57 'Lys. fr. 1' refers to the comic poet Lysippos.

[14] On the textual problem which ἔχων ληρεῖς raises and solves in *Grg.* 497 AB see Dodds ad loc.

[15] Stevens 38; but Pl. *Chrm.* 174 B ἀλλὰ ποῖα μάλιστα, cited by Tarrant (1946) 110, is certainly not an instance of this idiom.

ners: [Arist.] *Ἀθ. π.* 28. 3, Plut. *Nic.* 8. 6. Unsatisfactory evidence for what people really did in the old days, but good evidence for the existence of an ideal by which the actual could be (polemically) judged.

Oral narrative generally is characterized by a great deal of dialogue. This is true of Herodotus; but it is also true of Homer, and it would be perverse to privilege folktales as a model for a man as familiar with Homer as Herodotus must have been. What is significant, though, is that subsequent historians, notably Thucydides (Xenophon is a little more eclectic), distanced themselves from this distinctive feature of oral narrative. There are other features of modern Greek story-telling which, so far as our evidence goes, even the earliest written prose narrative had outgrown. One of these is the question by which the teller hauls the listener into the situation of a character in the story, e.g. Zarraftis 31:

> But when he was sixteen, the old woman died, and he remained unprotected. Who is to look after him? His mother? But she needed someone to look after *her*. He leaves his books, then, and he seeks work, to support his mother and himself. But what work is he to take up? A craft? He needed to learn it first.

Cf. Thumb (1912) 301 (Macedonia), 'What is he to do? How is he to finish the job now?', Zarraftis 320 'And where will the old man catch up with them now?', shading into cases where the character's uncertainty is not conspicuous, e.g. Thumb (1912) 301 'This father had only one son. What did he say to him? "This son . . ."', etc. Their remote ancestor, *Il.* i. 8 'What god brought them into conflict? The son of Leto and Zeus', is a rhetorical device ('You may be wondering . . .').

Another feature of oral narrative is the interjections by which the teller enlivens his story and (again) thrusts the listener into the situation described, e.g. *e* and *ahá* in Thumb (1912) 301–3, 'O the wonder . . .!' (Thumb 291, Aegina), Zarraftis 320, 'and just behind them, *na* the old man, out of breath!' One is reminded of ἰδού in the Gospel narratives, e.g. Matt. 17. 3–5:

> καὶ ἰδού Moses became visible to them . . .
> ἰδού a bright cloud overshadowed them,
> καὶ ἰδού a voice out of the cloud, saying . . .

Something of the same dramatic effect is achieved by the historic present intermingled with past tenses, e.g. Zarraftis 184:

The tailor . . . goes and brings it all to him and leaves him by himself. The tailor-boy locks himself in his room, sets the wine and the fruit before him, put a piece of apple in his glass and drank at a leisurely pace.

Cf. Newton 164 'a few days pass, another man came . . . He went, he sees a giant, and he' (sc. the giant) 'was watching a pot . . .', and in the New Testament (e.g.) Matt. 17. 1 f. 'Jesus takes Peter and James . . . and leads them up . . . and he was transfigured . . . and his face shone . . .'. This phenomenon is familiar enough to us in the ancient historians, e.g. Thuc. vi. 57. 3 f.:

ὥρμησαν . . . καὶ περιέτυχον τῷ Ἱππάρχῳ . . . καὶ εὐθὺς ἀπερισκέπτως προσπεσόντες . . . ἔτυπτον καὶ ἀποκτείνουσιν αὐτόν. καὶ ὁ μὲν τοὺς δορυφόρους τὸ αὐτίκα διαφεύγει ὁ Ἀριστογείτων . . . καὶ ὕστερον ληφθεὶς οὐ ῥᾳδίως διετέθη· Ἁρμόδιος δὲ αὐτοῦ παραχρῆμα ἀπόλλυται.

They set forth . . . and encountered Hipparchus . . . and, falling on him straightway without further thought, struck him and kill him. And one of them, Aristogeiton, escapes for the moment . . . and captured afterwards was not mercifully handled; but Harmodius perishes immediately on the spot.

This phenomenon is common in Herodotus, where it is sometimes, but not always (cf. p. 44), explicable in terms of dramatic effect;[16] the same can be said of narrative in comedy, e.g. Ar. *Pl.* 653–759, where 676 'Looking up, I see the priest' may be compared with Hdt. i. 10. 2 'and the woman glimpses him going out' (both somewhat dramatic), and 683 'I stand up to get at the pot' with Hdt. i. 12. 1 'And, giving him a dagger, she hides him behind the same door' (where there is no touch of dramatic suddenness). When the early historians are dealing with genealogy, they constantly use γίγνεται and τίκτει (e.g. Acus. *FGrHist* 2 F1, Pherec. Ath. *FGrHist* 3 F 18),[17] but they also mix aorist, imperfect, and present in narrative (e.g. Acus. F 22, cited on p. 71) in such a way as to preclude explanation of the tense of any given verb-token in semantic or rhetorical terms.[18] It should also be noted that in modern folktales the most obtrusive narrative present is the banal 'says' = 'said'. We must always

---

[16] Rodemeyer 6–11, Wackernagel i. 164 f., Bruhn 58, Svensson 93.

[17] Lilja 101–19.

[18] Cf. Ros 283 f. on the difficulty of deciding on the relative 'importance' of elements in a narrative (ctr. Lilja 116 f.); Rodemeyer 17.

beware of postulating a single cause for a common phenomenon.[19] Allowance must be made for metrical convenience,[20] stylistic variation,[21] and association with particular verbs, notably those denoting birth, death, capture, and perception.[22] No explanation in terms of temporal relation between successive verb-tokens can account for the absence of the phenomenon from epic (strikingly shown by the contrast between ἔτεκε or ἔτικτε in Hesiodic genealogies and τίκτει in Euripidean prologues). 'Must have . . .' is a rash expression, but the contention that archaic Greek oral narrative must have made use of the historic present is hardly resistible.[23] This implies that the epic poets eschewed it deliberately, despite its metrical utility, and the hypothesis that they did so because of its prominence in vulgar story-telling[24] is only a half-answer, open to a logical objection: it was vulgar because they made it so by eschewing it, and that leaves us with the question, 'Why did they do that?' If in the indicative mood of the imperfective and aorist aspects temporal reference was stronger and less equivocal than some (in understandable anxiety not to seem linguistically naïve) have been inclined to suppose, the historic present in stories could very well have been a technique employed by the teller to impart dramatic vividness, bringing narrator and audience into the scene, while the epic poet, by contrast, was concerned with commemoration of a remote, ancestral past.[25] The historians chose the story-teller as one of their models in preference to the 'singer of tales'. Whether the ancient story-teller, like the modern, sustained the involvement of the hearer by the constant occurrence of 'says' = 'said', we cannot know,[26] but the historians do not avoid it: in Herodotus the ratio λέγει : εἶπε is 2 : 5, and ἀμείβεται is found 8 times (ἀμείβετο 30 times), while in Xenophon's *Cyropaedia* the ratio λέγει : εἶπε is 1 : 6 (neither author uses φησί = ἔφη). The attempt to discover precisely why the author uses 'says' rather than 'said' in any given case is no more likely to arrive at a persuasive conclusion than an attempt to account for the difference between

[19] Hirt vi. 1. 213–16, *GG* ii. 274.
[20] Rodemeyer 10 f.
[21] Ros 285–90.
[22] Ros 284 f., Lilja 105, 111.
[23] The historic present is unquestionably an Indo-European inheritance; Hirt loc. cit. (n. 19). On Sanskrit, Macdonell 205; and on *Il.* xviii. 386 (ctr. xiii. 228) Wackernagel i. 47; Lilja 102.
[24] *GG* 271.
[25] Svensson 101.
[26] This occurs in Sanskrit (Kale 519).

Zarraftis 185 ' "Good, good!" said (*ípan*) the men, and turned to go' and 186 ' "Good, master-tailor" say (*léun*) the King's men. They take the apprentice . . .'. but there can be no doubt that if a historian liberally seasons his narrative with 'says' in preference to 'said' he effects a certain shift in our relationship with him, in the direction of informality and intimacy.

There are languages which have no participles, infinitive, or subordinate clauses.[27] If Greek were such a language, Hdt. i. 8.1 f. (left-hand column below) would be cast in a form like that of the right-hand column.

οὗτος δὴ ὢν ὁ Κανδαύλης	*οὗτος δὴ ὢν ὁ Κανδαύλης
ἠράσθη τῆς ἑωυτοῦ γυναικός.	ἠράσθη τῆς ἑωυτοῦ γυναικός.
ἐρασθεὶς δὲ ἐνόμιζέ οἱ εἶναι γυναῖκα πολλὸν πασέων καλλίστην.	ἠράσθη. ἐνόμιζε δέ, "γυνή μοι ἐστὶ πολλὸν πασέων καλλίστη."
ὥστε δὲ ταῦτα νομίζων,	ταῦτ᾿ ἐνόμιζε.
ἦν γάρ οἱ τῶν αἰχμοφόρων Γύγης ὁ Δασκύλου ἀρεσκόμενος μάλιστα,	τῶν δ᾿ αἰχμοφόρων ἠρέσκετό οἱ μάλιστα Γύγης ὁ Δασκύλου.
τούτῳ τῷ Γύγῃ καὶ τὰ σπουδαιέστερα τῶν πρηγμάτων ὑπερετίθετο ὁ Κανδαύλης	τούτῳ τῷ Γύγῃ καὶ τὰ σπουδαιέστερα τῶν πρηγμάτων ὑπερετίθετο ὁ Κανδαύλης
καὶ δὴ καὶ τὸ εἶδος τῆς γυναικὸς ὑπερεπαινέων.	καὶ δὴ καὶ τὸ εἶδος τῆς γυναικὸς ὑπερεπαίνεε.
This Kandaules	*This Kandaules
fell in love with his own wife.	fell in love with his own wife.
Having fallen in love, he thought that he had a wife most beautiful of all women.	He fell in love.
Thinking that,	He thought 'I have a wife most beautiful of all women.'
since in his bodyguard	He thought that.
Gyges son of Daskylos pleased him more than anyone,	In his bodyguard
to this Gyges Kandaules communicated his most important concerns,	Gyges son of Daskylos pleased him more than anyone.
in particular, praising his own wife very highly.	To this Gyges Kandaules communicated his most important concerns,
	and in particular he praised his own wife very highly.

[27] e.g. Mono (Solomon Islands; texts in Wheeler), Kuni (Papua; texts in Egidi). Mono in fact has a prefix which converts a finite verb into 'those who . . .'.

This is not a world apart from recorded folktales in modern European languages (including Modern Greek), except that some languages which organize narrative as a sequence of short finite-verb clauses also introduce each clause with a word (sometimes quite a heavy word) meaning 'and', 'so', or 'then'.[28] Modern Greek storytellers vary their practice, sometimes alternating unpredictably sequences in asyndeton with sequences in which 'and' recurs half a dozen or more times in succession, e.g. Newton 165 (§12 *ékamnas . . . to dikón tu*), 167 (§35). The latter type is prominent in the New Testament,[29] e.g. Mark 4. 1–8:

> καί again he began to teach by the lakeside,
> καί a great crowd gathers round him,
>   so that he went into a boat on the lake and sat there,
> καί all the crowd was on the land down to the lake.
> καί he taught them much in parables,
> καί said to them in his teaching,
> 'Listen. ἰδού the sower went out to sow,
> καί it happened in the sowing,
> some seed fell beside the road,
> καί the birds came,
> καί they ate it,
> καί other seed fell on stony ground,
>   where there was not much earth,
> καί it sprouted straightway through having no depth of soil,
> καί when the sun rose it was scorched,
> καί through having no root it withered,
> καί other seed fell among thistles,
> καί the thistles grew up,
> καί suffocated it,
> καί it did not bear a crop,
> καί other seed fell on good land,
> καί rising up and growing it bore a crop,
> καί it yielded thirtyfold, or sixtyfold, or a hundredfold.

There are other types of language which make great use of participles; for example, a literal English translation of an Amharic version[30] of Hdt. i. 8 would be:

[28] On recurrent 'and' in folktales see Trenkner 74–8. Heavy connectives obtrude in Igorot (Philippines; texts in Seidenadel 485 ff.), Nyanja (Malawi; text in Werner 72 f.), and Karok (California; texts in Golla and Silver 3–7).

[29] Trenkner 10, 64 f.

[30] I am greatly indebted to Professor Edward Ullendorff for this information about Amharic. For an actual Amharic example see Armbruster 193.

This Kandaules having fallen in love with wife, thinking, 'I have the most beautiful of all wives', Gyges the son of Daskylos pleasing him most among his bodyguard, communicating his most important concerns to this Gyges, praising his wife very highly . . .

and continuing in this strain down to:

not a long time having passed, an evil fate being in store for Kandaules, he said to Gyges . . .

A comparable mechanism is found in the 'sentence-medial' tenses of many Papuan languages, where the tense-and-person affix of a verb varies according to (i) whether the subject is the same as that of the next verb, and (ii) the temporal or conditional relation of the verb to the next one. In a language of that type the speaker can prolong a chain of sentence-medial verbs indefinitely but can terminate it by a sentence-final tense at any moment and start a new chain.[31]

Ancient Greek authors had at their disposal a rich apparatus of participles, infinitives, and constructions for subordinate clauses, and those authors with whom we are most familiar seem to have been ready to use all of it all of the time. However, the few citations we have from the earliest prose narratives bring to mind the Parable of the Sower, e.g. the second half of Acus. *FGrHist* 2 F22 (= B 40a):

> καί he becomes king of the Lapiths
> καί made war on the Centaurs.
> ἔπειτα setting up a javelin in the market-place[32]
>   he commanded that it be counted a god.
> The gods δέ were not pleased,
> καί Zeus threatens him for doing that,
> καί incites the Centaurs against him.
> καί they hammer him down upright into the earth
> καί put a rock over him as a marker
> καί he dies.

Cf. the first half of Hecat. *FGrHist* 1 F 15:

> Orestheus son of Deucalion came to Aetolia to rule over it.
> καί a dog of his gave birth to a root-stem,
> καί he ordered it to be buried,

---

[31] Foley 175–98.
[32] The supplement is Boll's, from Σ *Il.* i. 264, where Acusilaus is not named as the source.

καί from it grew a vine laden with clusters;
for which reason he called his son Phytios.

We may feel that this is not the sort of thing to which we are
accustomed in Herodotus and Thucydides, but to check the validity
of our impression we need to take samples of narrative and answer
three questions: first, what proportion of verb-tokens in the sample
are MCFs; secondly, what proportion of MCFs are connected with
the previous MCF by simple καί; and thirdly, in both cases, is
the phenomenon evenly distributed or concentrated in blocks? To
eliminate incommensurables the samples are filleted, removing all
direct speech, future participles, and participles with the article. All
parentheses are demoted to subordinate-clause status (including
some, e.g. Hdt. i. 8. 1 ἦν γὰρ κτλ. and χρῆν γὰρ κτλ., which modern
editors do not normally enclose in brackets). A periphrastic perfect
is treated as a single verb-token. Some infinitives are classified as
MCF in accordance with the principles described on pp. 29 f.

In Fig. 4.1 the horizontal axis gives the number of verb-tokens,
the vertical axis the number of MCFs, for the first 150 verb-tokens.
In Fig. 4.2 we see, for the first 150 (or total) MCFs, how many are
linked to the previous MCF by καί. The samples are:

A Pherecydes Syr. DK B 2 col. 1 + Pherecydes Ath. *FGrHist* 3
   F 1a + 18a + 22a + 38 + 64a + 66 + 82a + 95 + 105 + 125a + Acusilaus
   FGrHist 2 F 22 (= DK 9 B 40a) + Hecataeus *FGrHist* 1 F 15 +
   Charon of Lampsacus *FGrHist* 262 F 1 + Anaxagoras DK 59
   B 1.

B Hdt. v. 92. α. 1 to (Fig. 4.1) 92. η. 1, (Fig. 4.2) 104. 1; the story
   of Cypselus.

C Hdt. vi. 1. 1 to (Fig. 4.1) 12. 4, (Fig. 4.2) 24. 2.

D Thuc. i. 1. 1 to (Fig. 4.1) 8.2, (Fig. 4.2) 17.

E Thuc. vii. 78. 1 to (Fig. 4.1) 81.3, (Fig. 4.2) the end of the book;
   the Athenian retreat from Syracuse.

P Pl. *Prt.* 320 c 8–323 A 3; the myth told by 'Protagoras'.[33]

S Pl. *Symp.* 219 E 5–221 C 1; 'Alcibiades'' story of Socrates at Poti-
   daea.

X Xen. *HG* vii. 1. 15 to (Fig. 4.1) 1. 28, (Fig. 4.2) 2. 3; military
   narrative.

The most striking features of Fig. 4.1 are:

[33] Norden (1913) 368, Thesleff (1967) 74.

(i) The immense separation of A from all the later texts;[34] its accumulation of MCFs, without plateaux, is steady. Any idea that the construction of an artificial sample by putting citations from different authors together may have affected its score is refutable by making up a similar composite text from the other authors; Hdt. v. 92. γ. 1 + vi. 3. 1 + Thuc. vii. 78. 2 + Xen. *HG* vii. 1. 18 + Hdt. v. 92. ε. 1 + vi. 6 + Thuc. vii. 80. 2 + Xen. *HG* vii. 1. 22 + Hdt. v. 92. η. 1 + vi. 9. 1 + Thuc. vii. 81. 2 + Xen. *HG* vii. 1. 26, strung together as a continuous text, yield 39 MCFs at the 100th verb-token, and the texts from which those random excerpts were made score between 39 and 44 at that point. The score for A at the 100th verb-token is 75 (off the top of the graph). One important affinity of the earliest narrative prose with oral narrative is thus demonstrated.

(ii) In keeping with that, the Cypselus story separates itself from Hdt. vi between verb-tokens 15 and 70, while the last part of Protagoras' myth stands out to the same extent from the story about Socrates (tokens 70–100).

(iii) Xenophon scores lowest most of the time.

(iv) Thucydides' narrative of the retreat from Syracuse scores higher than Herodotus most of the time.

(v) Not surprisingly, Thucydides' narrative of military movements scores higher than his generalizing narrative about the early Greek world, though the latter catches up by token 140.

A bigger surprise emerges from Fig. 4.2, because the difference between Thucydides and Herodotus is spectactular in respect of simple καί, and that is not due solely to the flying start (MCFs 0–30) and finishing spurt (MCFs 135–45) of sample E. It is clear that although the first half of the Cypselus story is ahead of Hdt. vi in its use of καί, Herodotus departed very markedly from the 'καί-style'. The chronological progression from the earliest historians to Xenophon is not straightforward. The recipe which an author chooses for narrative is not necessarily determined by his date of birth, nor was he bound to be consistent (consider the plateaux and leaps of Xenophon in Fig. 4.2). An author was always free to decide that a succession of MCFs linked by καί sounded better for one portion of a narrative than for another.

There is one more phenomenon which throws some light on the relations of literary prose with oral narrative, oratory, and in-

[34] Cf. Norden (1913) 368–72, Aly (1929) 70–3, Trenkner 16–22, 63 f.

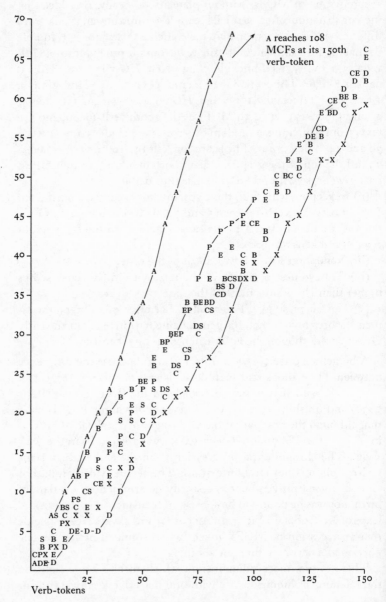

FIG. 4.1. MCFs within first 150 verb-tokens

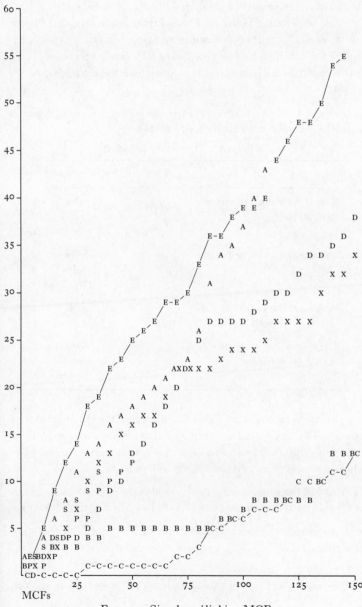

MCFs

FIG. 4.2. Simple *καί* linking MCFs

formal speech. The fragments which make up sample A contain six instances of ἔπειτα '(and) then' (Pherec. Ath. *FGrHist* 3 F 1a, 18a, 64a, 66, Acus. *FGrHist* 2 F 22 = DK 9 B 40a *bis*), and Pherec. Ath. F 21 adds another. A distinctive feature of narrative in comedy[35] is the frequency of εἶτα (δέ), κᾆτα (δέ), ἔπειτα (δέ), κἄπειτα, the equivalence of which appears from a non-narrative passage, Ar. *Pl.* 1103–6:

Run quick and call your master out, ἔπειτα his wife and children, ἔπειτα the slaves, εἶτα the dog, ἔπειτα yourself, εἶτα the pig!

TABLE 4.2. *'Then'-style in comedy*

	Total MCFs	εἶτα etc.	
Eq. 638–82 (omitting quoted words)	27	εἶτα	2
		κᾆτα	2
		ἔπειτα	1
Pax 605–48 (omitting the dialogue 615–18)	19	εἶτα	2
		κᾆτα	2
		κᾆτα δέ	1
Thesm. 476–89 (omitting dialogue in 483–5)	11	εἶτα	2
		κᾆτα	2
Pl. 653–759 (omitting dialogue exchanges)	53	εἶτα	2
		κᾆτα	1
		ἔπειτα	8

The narrative passages in Table 4.2 illustrate the phenomenon in comedy. The colloquial character of these words as connectives, not greatly differing from καί, δέ, and οὖν, is strongly suggested by a short passage of reported dialogue in Lys. i. 14:

When I asked her why the doors had creaked in the night, she said that the light beside the baby had gone out, εἶτα she had relit it at a neighbour's.

(In the immediately preceding section jocular words of the speaker's wife, "ἵνα σύ γε", ἔφη, κτλ., are reported directly).[36]

---

[35] Trenkner 8 f., 12 f. The phenomenon persists into New Comedy, e.g. Men. *Asp.* 80 (cf. 217–20), *Dysk.* 415, 529, 617, 627, *Epitr.* 487, 506.
[36] Dover (1987) 28, 233 f.

ἔπειτα (or -τε) in Herodotus (who does not use εἶτα)[37] sometimes (24 instances) functions as a temporal connective between MCFs in a past narrative sequence, mostly in the form καὶ ἔπειτα.[38] It is more frequent (40 examples) in the description of present customs or natural phenomena. In neither usage is there anything comparable with the concentrations found in comedy; the only passages in which one instance follows close on another are ii. 42. 6, iv. 26.1 f., 30. 2, 60. 2–61. 1, 62. 3 f., 70, 71. 4, 75. 1–3, v. 91. 2, vi. 83. 1 f., vii. 23. 3 f. In Thucydides and Xenophon even that minimal degree of concentration is confined to enumeration (Thuc. v. 67. 2) or the meaning is 'secondly . . ., thirdly . . .' in a series introduced by πρῶτον μέν (e.g. Xen. *Anab.* vi. 2. 1). Indeed, nearly half the examples of εἶτα and ἔπειτα used of past temporal succession in Thucydides and Xenophon respond to a preceding πρῶτον,[39] and in the remainder there is often an explicit temporal contrast, e.g. Thuc. vii. 41. 2 'as far μέν as the merchant ships they pressed the pursuit, ἔπειτα . . .', 78. 6 'for some time μέν they fought . . ., ἔπειτα . . .', 79. 6 'for some time μέν they held out . . ., ἔπειτα . . .' (cf. Xen. *HG* ii. 2. 17 'for a while μέν Lysander detained him, εἶτα told him . . .'). In the early orators the only examples of strictly temporal use (apart from Lys. i. 14, cited above) are And. i. 17, 112 (κᾷτα), iii. 5, 22, Lys. fr. 8 Thalheim (note also Ant. v. 38 in a present generalization). εἶτα and ἔπειτα in the orators[40] mostly mark argumentative points rather than temporal sequence, and are also common in indignant comments and questions. It thus appears that a phenomenon shared by rehearsed and unrehearsed oral narrative and so portrayed in comedy affected the earliest written historical narrative but was used very sparingly by historians from Herodotus onwards and by orators.

It is obvious that when a range of models (we could also call them 'sources') is available to writers, whether in poetry or in prose, the individual writer is likely to draw upon more than one model, and no two writers are likely to follow the same models in exactly

---

[37] εἶτα is not infrequent in the Hippocratic corpus, but does not appear in *VM*, *Aer.*, or *Morb. Sacr.*

[38] ἔπειτα in asyndeton linking past-tense MCFs in Herodotus is found only at ii. 56. 2, iv. 43. 2, and vi. 83. 1.

[39] This is true also of Ar. *Pax* 606 and *Pl.* 657, 718, 729, which are included in Table 4.2.

[40] There are no instances in the *Tetralogies* or early Isocrates.

the same proportions. The possibilities of mixture are virtually unlimited, and the effect varies according to whether the text brings elements from different models into close juxtaposition (cf. p. 53) or changes models a block of text at a time. Within each model there are differences of register—for example, within the category 'colloquial' or 'informal' we can distinguish between 'intimate', 'jocular', 'technical', and so on.

5

TIME AND PLACE

THE prosecutor of Theomnestus in 384/3 (Lys. x), having occasion to ridicule the defendant for a quibble over the wording of the law of slander, attempts to educate him by quoting from the 'old laws of Solon' (15–20) provisions containing words which are no longer in use at Athens (ποδοκάκκη, δρασκάζειν, ἀπίλλειν, πεφασμένως, πολεῖσθαι, οἰκεύς[1]) or have changed their meaning (ἐπιορκεῖν, στάσιμος). Similarly, the term ἀγορὰ ἐφορία in the Athenian homicide law (*IG* i³ 104. 27 ἀγορᾶ]c ἐφορί[ας) is explained to the jury by Dem. xxiii. 39. Exiguous though the available material is, we can compile a more extensive list of changes which occurred in the language of Attic prose between the sixth century and the mid-fourth, namely:

δάμαρ. The provision of the homicide law (cited by Dem. xxiii. 53) which exonerated the killer of an adulterer used the expression ἐπὶ δάμαρτι, but δάμαρ, 'wife', never occurs in Attic literary prose.

ἐπιόψασθαι in *IG* i³ 3. 14 appears[2] to mean 'select *for* . . .' and not, as in *IG* ii² 1933. 1 (*c*.330) and Pl. *Lg.* 947 c, 'select' or 'list'.

θωᾶν, θωά. The verb, 'penalize', is in *IG* i³ 4 B12 (cf. 7), securely dated to 485/4. That is also its last appearance, because from the mid-century ζημιοῦν takes over (ibid. 14. 8, 40. 7).[3] The noun ζημία appears at the same time (ibid. 21. 58, 76) and is common thereafter. In *IG* i³ 105 (s. v ex.) we find both ζημία (23) and θωά (41); this document is a prescription of the oath and duties of the Council, and

---

[1] The speaker explains that οἰκῆος (*sic*) = θεράποντος; but since the genitive of οἰκεύς (the nominative occurs in Soph. *OT* 756) would have been spelt ΟΙΚΕΟΣ in an Attic document of the sixth or fifth century, we should probably emend οἰκῆος (the reading of the sole primary MS, Palatinus gr. 88, adopted without comment by all modern editors) to οἰκέως. There is, however, a possibility that the speaker actually said οἰκῆος to make the word sound Homeric and venerable.

[2] If τὸν ἀγῶνα is its object; but see Lewis ad loc. for an alternative possibility.

[3] ζημιοῦν seems to have εὐθύνεσθαι as a suppletive passive. ἀθῷος continued to live with ἀζήμιος in Attic prose.

may reasonably be expected to incorporate parts of the foundation-document of the Cleisthenic Council.[4]

κάρτα. One of a range of intensifiers (the others are μάλα, πάνυ, and σφόδρα), it went out of use (with one exception; see below) in Attic prose literature at an early date in the Classical period. We meet it in acclamations on vases, e.g. Compiègne 978 (black-figure) Σώστρατος καλὸς κάρτα and New York 09.221.47 (red-figure) ὁ παῖς κάρτα κάρτα (where passion gets the better of coherence).

κιγχάνειν. Recorded by *Suda* κ 1586 in the sense 'prosecute', it occurs in *IG* i³ 2. 6 (χιγχάν[εν), but never (in any sense) in Attic prose thereafter.

μελεδαίνειν. *DGE* 731B. 8 (Sigeion, s. vi/v) is a text in the Ionic dialect of Proconnesus, followed by an Attic translation (in which ὑποκρητήριον becomes ἐπίστατον), and μελεδαίνειν, 'have a care for . . .', is in an extra clause added to the Attic version.

ὀλείζων. This word for 'less' is found in *IG* i³ 3. 9 (s. v in.), perhaps in 4B. 18 (485/4), and in a few other fifth-century inscriptions down to ibid. 85. 33 (418/17). In 78. 8 (about 420) it keeps very close company with its replacement ἐλάττων (6, 7); ἐλάττων ibid. 153. 8 may be a little earlier than that.[5] The only putative occurrence of ὀλείζων in literary prose is Anon. *Ath.* 2. 1, where the text has μείζους but the sense required is 'fewer' (hence ὀλείζους Wilamowitz, but Heinrich's μείους is a rival possibility).

-ᾱσι, -ησι. In the dative plural of the first declension, -ησι (-ᾱσι after iota) is the norm in the first half of the fifth century: e.g. *IG* i³ 4. B24 f. ταμίασι, 21. 36 δικαστέσιν. About 435 we find ibid. 256. 6 f. τῆσι Νύμ[φη]σι keeping company with τα[ῖ]ς Νύμφαις (13), and -ησι, -ᾱσι continue in the annual inventories of sacred treasure until after 420 (ibid. 303. 40, 325. 3, 353. 50).

-οισι. This form of the dative plural ending of the second declension coexists with -οις (e.g. *IG* i³ 4. B13 τοῖσι~B24 το[ῖ]ς, 6. B36 μυστερίοισιν~C12 f. μ]υστερίοις. -οισι dwindles away (without disappearing absolutely) after the mid-fifth century.

These data suffice to show that the language of Attic prose underwent changes in the Classical period, and it would have been a very unusual language, perhaps unique, if it had not done so.[6]

---

[4] Rhodes 196–8.

[5] In *IG* i³ 233. 6 (s. v pr.) Dow's supplement ἐλαττ]ον is printed, but why not ὀλειζ]ον (the spellings -λε- and -λει- both occur)?

[6] Aly (1927) 91 f., 102–4, Bowie 141; a simple enough point, but it bears repetition.

They remind us that archaism, whether or not it was ever actualized, remained a potential stylistic feature. That, however, is a minor matter compared with others which are raised by the data listed.

θωά is familiar to us in Ionic, in the form θωϊή: Amorgos (*IG* xii (7). 220. 3), Miletus (*DGE* 727. 12), and Thasos (*IG* xii Suppl. 347. II. 5), together with Hom. *Od.* ii. 192 (θωή).[7] μελεδαίνειν is also Ionic: once in Herodotus (viii. 115. 3), often in Hippocrates, plus Archil. 14. 1 (there in the sense 'care about'). It thus appears prima facie that both θωϊή/θωά and μελεδαίνειν were originally shared by Ionic and Attic but discarded in Attic. The abundance of κάρτα in Ionic makes a very strong contrast between Ionic and Attic prose; it occurs nearly eighty times in Herodotus, five times as often as μάλα, while πάνυ and σφόδρα occur only once each. In Ion of Chios *FGrHist* 392 F 6 there are three instances of κάρτα in only forty lines of printed text; two in Democritus, and one each in Anaxagoras and Protagoras. δάμαρ is different again; abundant in tragedy, but never in prose except in citing the phrase ἐπὶ δάμαρτι from the homicide law. If an Athenian used the word δάμαρ in any other context, it would strike the hearer as poetic. But what of θωά and κάρτα? Archaic, poetic, or alien? θωά might be recognized as archaic by a hearer learned in the law, or as poetic by someone steeped in poetry, but I suspect that to most Athenians it would sound as alien as Scots 'baillie' = 'senior town councillor' would sound to English ears. κάρτα would most probably strike an Athenian as familiarly non-standard, like the regional 'aye', with an additional poetic resonance.[8] Of its two[9] occurrences in comedy, Ar. *Av.* 342 ληρεῖς ἔχων κάρτα probably aims at the humour of incongruity (ληρεῖς ἔχων is colloquial; cf. p. 65), and in *Ach.* 544 καὶ κάρτα μεντἂν κτλ., 'You most certainly *would* . . .', καὶ κάρτα may be a fixed idiom (cf. Soph. *OC* 65, 301, Eur. *Hipp.* 90).[10] The solitary instance of κάρτα in Attic prose, Pl. *Tim.* 25 D πηλοῦ κάρτα βραχέος, occurs in the course of what purports to be a cosmogonic story of venerable antiquity, and by far the most plausible explanation of that κάρτα is that Plato

---

[7] Cf. *DGE* 687. B9 ἐπιθώϊος (Chios, s. vi/v), Pouilloux 150. 13 ἐνθωΐους (Thasos, s. iv).

[8] Its distribution in Euripides is curious: six times in *Hipp.*, three in *Med.*, and only three more in all the rest plus three in [Eur.] *Rhesus*.

[9] I wrongly said 'one' in Dover (1987) 23.

[10] And older men like Dicaeopolis may have been fond of it; uttered in a slow growl, it would be potent.

intended to impart to his story a little touch of early Ionic philosophical writing.[11]

The language of Attic documentary inscriptions has been treated above as if it exhibited a straightforward process of temporal change, but in fact it does not,[12] and the proof of that lies in a more detailed consideration of the history of the dative plural termination -ησι/-ᾱσι. Early in the fifth century we find it confused with the Ionic termination -ησι or -ης: *IG* i³ 6. A2]δραχμεῖς[, B10 ἐπ]οπτεῖσιν, 29 f. ἐν τεῖσι πόλεσιν, 34 f. ἐν τεῖσιν αὐτεῖσι. This shows that -ησι was no more part of the secretary's normal language than -ῃσι (*IG* i³ 7, which must, given its script, be close to *IG* i³ 6 in date,[13] has (12) Μοί]ραις). Whereas ταμίασι lasts a long time in formulaic prescripts, ἑλληνοταμίας, a word invented after the Persian War (Thuc. i. 96. 2), more often has -αις in the dative plural.[14] In 418/17 the composer of *IG* i³ 84 committed the solecism μυρίεσι δραχμέσιν (20), which is neither Ionic nor documentary Attic, after saying χιλίαισι δραχμέσι in 10 and τοῖς ταμίαισι in 17; we see here an incompetent attempt to perpetuate forms felt to be appropriate to the genre. The power and the limitations of precedent can be illustrated by the history of the three ways of saying in the documents 'in order to . . .': ἵνα, ὅπως ἄν, and ὡς ἄν. ἵνα occurs in three fifth-century inscriptions, *IG* i³ 71. 41, 46 (425/4), 79. 12 (422/ 1), and 203. 15 (date?), and ὡς ἄν in two,[15] ibid. 79. 9 and 156. 8 (*c*.430?). ὅπως ἄν outweighs them (14 examples) in the fifth century and eclipses them entirely in the fourth; it is only in the third that ἵνα reasserts itself.[16] There is at least one example of a temporary syntactical fashion—no other word but 'fashion' does justice to the data—in documentary language: in eight honorific decrees datable to the period 412–404 and two which may be earlier (*IG* i³ 162.

---

[11] Sakalis i. 101 f.

[12] On conservatism in *Kanzleisprache* and its reluctant but inevitable surrender to *Umgangssprache* see Rosenkranz 130–2, *ELDH* 386, Dover (1987) 35. In describing documentary language as 'langue d'une élite, donc langue de pouvoir' I think that López Eire 156 implicitly exaggerates the difference in vocabulary and grammar, but of course *Umgangssprache* has occasion to voice many lively utterances which *Kanzleisprache* does not.

[13] Lewis ad loc.

[14] Generally speaking, compound words need not follow their components in morphology or meaning. ὄρρος 'arse' (etymologically cognate) is vulgar in Attic, but ἄψορρος (e.g. Soph. *Ant.* 386) is not.

[15] In the index verborum of *IG* i² ΗΟΣ in 77. 6 (=*IG* i³ 131. 6) is mistakenly treated as ὡς. (ἵνα 'where' is common in documents.)

[16] Meisterhans 253, Henry 313 f.

3–6, 177. 4–8), ἐπαινεῖν governs the dative. This phenomenon does not occur earlier or later—there are four certain examples of the accusative during 430–415 and one probable and two certain (*IG* i³ 102. 6, 118. 37) from 410/09 and 408—nor is it ever found in Attic literature, whether poetry or prose.

There is one phenomenon of prose literature which was also comparatively short-lived. Attic documents from first to last use ττ and ρρ, not σσ and ρσ (ττ is a regional phenomenon, affecting Attica, Boeotia, and Euboea, though it appears also in Crete, and ρρ is a little more widespread), and this is also true of Anon. *Ath.*, all the orators from Andocides onwards, Plato, and Xenophon. In Antiphon and Thucydides, however, we find σσ and (Thuc.) ρσ, as always in tragedy. It should not be assumed that the formal language of oratory in the days when it was unwritten used σσ and ρσ.[17] The occurrence in the *Tetralogies* of non-Attic words which are attested in Ionic—ii. β. 7 ἀναγιγνώσκειν 'persuade', ii. β. 3 καταδοκεῖν 'suspect' (both common in Herodotus), ii. δ. 11 καταλαμβάνειν 'convict' (*DGE* 701. A7, Erythrae, s. v), ii. α. 3 οἴδαμεν = ἴσμεν (Hdt. ii. 17. 1 *al.*, Metrodorus DK 48 B 1)—suggests rather that some Athenian writers of the late fifth century took Ionic prose as a model.[18]

At the beginning of Chapter 4 the question was posed: what did the *first* Greek prose writer take as a model? The question was pursued in respect of the writer's relation to unwritten oratory and unwritten narrative; the question of phonology and morphology was allowed to lie, but must now be raised. It may be thought certain a priori that in those respects the language of oratory and stories was simply the language spoken in the community where the speeches were made and the stories told.[19] It might also be thought that the first prose writer had no motive to depart from that. This supposition, however, would be too facile, given that narrative transmitted in written texts, whether heroic or theological (cosmogony is one branch of theology), was the province of poets, and given also the freedom of the poets from regional constraints. Epic language was

[17] The inference is commonly drawn from Ael. Dion. σ 15 Erbse (e.g. by Rosenkranz 144) that Pericles inaugurated a change from σσ to ττ in oratory (despite the fact that all Antiphon's speeches are post-Periclean). Aelius in fact reports a tradition that Pericles avoided sigma because of the configuration of the mouth in uttering it.

[18] *ELDH* 404 f.

[19] Though this is not always so; among the Thulung of Nepal there is an elaborate and artificial language used for the telling of traditional stories in prose (Dover (1987) 12).

itself an artificial amalgam of alternative forms from different times
and places; Hesiod, a Boeotian, did not compose in Boeotian dialect, and Tyrtaeus, composing for Spartans, used the language of
Ionic elegiac poetry.[20] The lyrics of Sappho and Alcaeus superim-
posed upon a Lesbian base forms drawn from a 'poetic Koine'.[21]
We can see for ourselves how often the composers of funerary or
dedicatory epigrams used their own regional dialects as the basis of
their language but very readily drew upon epic and elegy in order
to impart a heroic tone, to adhere to a traditional formula—e.g.
γλαυκώπιδι κούρη in dedications at Athens (*CEG* i. 182, 282, 434)
side by side with Ἀθηναία (ibid. 189, 197, 202)—or to exploit metrically convenient alternatives: e.g. *CEG* i. 41. 2 θῆκε (Athens, s.
vi), ibid. 143. 3 ἐνὶ πόντῳ, 6 κασιγνήτοιο, beside 1 υἱοῦ, 3 πρόξενϝος,
5 ἐνθών (Corcyra, s. vii ex.).

The earliest prose literature is dominated by Ionians. There is no
doubt that there existed in Roman times written work attributed
to Thales (Galen, *Hipp. de Hum.* 1. 1), though scepticism about
its authenticity was in order (Simplicius, *Phys.* 23. 29, Plu. *Pyth.
Or.* 402 E, Diog. Laert. i. 23). With Anaximander and Anaximenes
we are on firmer ground; like Thales, they were natives of Miletus,[22] and Diogenes (ii. 3) says that Anaximenes wrote in 'straightforward and unadorned Ionic' (on Anaximander DK 12 B 1, see
below). Hecataeus too came from Miletus, the earliest geographer-
mythographer and a man of high standing at the time of the Ionian
Revolt (Hdt. v. 125 f.); Heraclitus came from Ephesus; Syros, the
native island of Pherecydes Syr., is one of the Ionian Cyclades;
and Herodotus' native city, Halicarnassus, though Dorian in origin
and proud of it, used in its fifth-century inscriptions a dialect in
which whatever Doric features it once had are swamped by Ionic.
Of other prose authors active in the first three quarters of the fifth
century, the majority were native speakers of East Ionic dialects:
Anaxagoras came from Clazomenae, Democritus from Abdera (a
colony of Teos), Charon from Lampsacus (a Phocaean–Milesian
foundation), Ion from Chios, and Melissus from Samos. All that

[20] Cf. Dover (1987) 101–3.
[21] Bowie 139; he fully demonstrates the inadequacy of Lobel's dogmatic view of
Sappho's language.
[22] We have no citations from Cadmus of Miletus (*FGrHist* 489), though Dion.
i. 359. 11–16 implies the availability of a work ascribed to him, and Clem. Alex.
Strom. vi. 26. 8 speaks of Bion of Proconnesus (*FGrHist* 332) as having summarized
Cadmus' work.

we have of these authors agrees with the Ionic inscriptions of their time in the universal mutation $\bar{a} > \eta$, e.g. Heracl. DK 22 B 40 πολυμαθίη, B 54 φανερῆς, Pherec. Syr. DK 7 B 1 Χθονίη, Hecat. *FGrHist* 1 F 305 ἱρή, μεταρσίη, and Heraclitus at least shares with Herodotus the characteristic mutation $k^w > \kappa$ of East Ionic, e.g. B 1 ὁκοίων, ὅκως, ὁκόσα, as in *SGDI* ⁿ62. 11 ὁκοῖα (Erythrae, s. iv), *SEG* xxxviii. 1036. 7 οκο = ὅπου (s. v m., from an area of Phocaean commercial activity in southern France). Psilosis, the loss of initial *h*, was shared by East Ionic with the Aeolic of Lesbos; fifth-century examples are: *DGE* 688. B5 πέντ᾽ ἡμέρη[ι]σιν (Chios, s. v), 701. A16 ἀπ᾽ ἑκάστης (Erythrae, s. v m.); 727. 5, 8 ἐπ᾽ ὧν (Miletus, s. v). This is the norm in our texts of Herodotus; other early Ionic prose texts provide little evidence except for Charon *FGrHist* 262 F 1 ἀπίξονται, though when Simplicius cites Anaxagoras DK 59 B 12 twice ἐπ᾽ ἑωυτοῦ appears as a variant on ἐφ᾽ ἑαυτοῦ the first time but not the second.

Whether the early Ionian prose writers each chose independently to use the dialect of his own speech-community, or chose to model his language on that of the very earliest,[23] the result would have been much the same, since the earliest were Ionic-speaking. However, the importance of the second alternative is strikingly shown by the fact that the extant citations from Pherecydes of Athens and Acusilaus of Argos are in Ionic. The fact that the works of the Hippocratic corpus, emanating from the centres of medical studies at Cos and Cnidos, use Ionic illustrates the cultural dominance of the eastern Aegean by Ionic.[24] In historiography this dominance extended to the central Mediterranean, where Antiochus of Syracuse (*FGrHist* 555), whose Sicilian history ended with the events of 424/3 (Diod. xii. 71. 2), wrote in Ionic.[25] By then a prose literature in Doric had been generated in Magna Graecia,[26] and it maintained its independence resolutely for a long time. Athens also, by virtue of its political and economic dominance in the Aegean and the universal appeal of the theatre, asserted itself; it was the powerhouse of oratory, the meeting-place of philosophers, and that is why Zeno

---

[23] The first was bound to be a powerful influence on the second, and the first two on the third (*ELDH* 380).

[24] For a survey of the distinctive features of Hippocratic language see *ELDH* 325–54.

[25] F 2 and F 5 are the only verbatim quotations from him.

[26] Cassio 145–9.

(from Elea) and Gorgias (an Ionic-speaker from Sicily) wrote in Attic.

Texts in dialects other than Attic were all subject in transmission to two conflicting processes. One was assimilation to Attic, often, no doubt, accidental, but sometimes (especially in short citations) through impatience of antiquarian niceties or deliberate assimilation (cf. the epitaph on the Corinthians killed at Salamis (*CEG* i. 131), which in the original has ποκ᾽ ἐναίομες but in Plutarch's quotation (*De Herod. Malign.* 870 E) ποτ᾽ ἐναίομεν). The other process is the 'restoration' of what Hellenistic scholars believed to be dialectal propriety and consistency. The texts of Pindar and Theocritus provide illuminating examples of both processes.[27] In Herodotus textual variants are abundant, e.g. in the declension of ναῦς and πόλις; in both, different branches of the manuscript tradition are internally consistent in different portions of the work.[28] Citations from Heraclitus show much variation, e.g. B 7 ὄντα~B 118 ἐόν (both in citations by Aristotle), B 115 ἑαυτόν~B 116 ἑωυτούς (both in Stobaeus), B 67 ὅκωσπερ . . . ὁπόταν (in Hippolytus). B 72 and B 73, both cited by Marcus Aurelius, are thoroughly Atticized. Citations of Hecataeus are hardly in better shape, e.g. F 163 πρὸς μεσημβρίαν ὁμουρέουσι and F 292, where οἰκέουσι and οἰκοῦσι are variants.

From the fifth century onwards the distinctive features of the Ionic dialects gave ground to Attic continuously,[29] so that it is no surprise to find e.g. ἡμέραις and ταῖς θωαῖς at Thasos *c.*350 (Pouilloux 141. 4, 7) contrasting with ἐν τῆις ἀποικίησιν (*sic*) there in 410 (ibid. 18. 7), but much variation, in all Ionic areas, is remarkably early, e.g. Iasos, s. v pr.: *SEG* xxxvi. 982. B8 κατάπερ~B10 καθόπερ, C5 καθάπερ, 983. 15 κατάπερ~17 καθόπερ; Erythrae, s. v pr.: *DGE* 701. A17 οἷσιν~B16 τούτοις. The most remarkable instance by far takes us right back into the sixth century at Chios: *SEG* xvi. 485. 3 f. δημαρχῶν~5 f. δημαρχέων.[30] Evidently the progress of innovation in Ionic dialects varied from place to place, time to time, and genre to genre. We have to reckon with changes of practice in the course

---

[27] Dover (1971) xxxiii f.

[28] Rosén (1962) 78–85, 87–9.

[29] Thumb–Scherer 248–50, *ELDH* 339–41, 431.

[30] Cf. Hartmann 105; it is disturbing to find that an ancient text on stone is not necessarily more consistent than a medieval text on paper. The bronze plate from Hipponion (*SEG* xxvi. 1139, *c.*400) presents us with (1, 6, 14) Μναμοσύνας, (12) Μνημοσύνης, (2) κρένα, (5) κράνας. The text is in verse, but scansion is not an issue.

of an author's lifetime[31] (how many years did Herodotus take to write books i–v?), idiosyncratic and varying preferences for certain rhythms and collocations of sounds, indifference to consistency,[32] the buffeting of fashion, aesthetic caprice. The idiolects of two authors may be so similar that we can regard them both as using the same recipe, but differing in the seasoning—as when, for example, F 4 of the *Argolika* of Agias and Dercylus (*FGrHist* 305) combines ἀπὸ τᾶς λοχείας φέρον[τι with the wildly un-Doric ἐπεί κέ τις.[33]

That last example is taken from the fourth century, but we cannot, given the precedent of the archaic poets, rule out comparable creativity in the first prose authors. Their texts, as transmitted, show certain features which cannot without more ado be ascribed to the Ionic vernaculars of their time. These features are:

1. Unaugmented past tenses in -σκ-, e.g. Acusilaus *FGrHist* 2 F 22 = DK 9 B 40a πολεμέεσκε, Hdt. i. 36. 1 διαφθείρεσκε. This is nowhere attested in Ionic documents, which is not surprising, since public documents rarely have occasion to use past indicative tenses.[34] -σκ- is common in epic,[35] and θύεσκε in Hipponax 104. 48 occurs in a very non-epic context charged with the pornographic gusto characteristic of that poet. In Archil. 96. 6 the immediate context of]σονδεσκεν και χαλ[is wholly obscure, but the wider context is undoubtedly seemly.[36] Whether -σκ- in early prose is taken from poetry or from the vernacular must remain an open question which may yet be decided in favour of the latter by the discovery of more lead-plate letters from Ionian sites in the Crimea.

2. α > ε before O-vowels, which has the effect of a partial transfer of thematic verb-stems in α to the category of stems in ε (e.g. Heracl. B 55 προτιμέω, Hdt. viii. 7. 1 ἐμηχανέοντο).[37] This conflicts

[31] After more than thirty years of work in Scotland and two in America I have observed many changes in my vocabulary; I am tending to use 'gift' = 'donate', 'outwith' = 'outside', as in Scots, and 'have to' and 'be about to' in their American senses; I am also vacillating over the placing of adverbs with auxiliary verbs.

[32] Aly (1927) 90 f., Untersteiner 17, *ELDH* 445. Much harm has been done to the study of Greek by the strange notion that consistency in choosing between linguistic alternatives is a virtue and that to impute caprice to a great writer is an insult to his memory; Rosén (1962) 236–9 cites amusing examples.

[33] Cassio 139 n. 5.

[34] Aly (1921) 270.

[35] Chantraine (1948) i. 321–5; and see Puhvel 13–20 on Anatolian -*sk*-.

[36] In Ar. *Eq.* 1242 the humour of βινεσκόμην lies in the Homeric tone given to a very obscene word.

[37] Smyth 568–70, Rosén (1962) 18. Rosén's explanation of the phenomenon in

with such evidence as there is in Ionic documents: *DGE* 710. B8 f.
αἰσυμνῶν (Teos, s. v m.), 726. 15 ἀμιλλῶνται (Miletus, s. v m.). It is,
however, a recurrent phenomenon elsewhere, including the south-
east and south Aegean (Rhodes—and its Sicilian colony Acragas—
with Crete and Cyrene),[38] where by Hellenistic times α-stems were
conjugated throughout like ε-stems, e.g. *SGDI* 3836. d10 τιμοῦντες
(Rhodes, s. iii), 4108. 4 ἐνίκει (Rhodes, s. i). It is not known in
epic,[39] e.g. *Il.* vii. 423 ἤντεον, xii. 59 μενοίνεον (ctr. xvi. 367 πέραον),
and that raises a crucial question:

> (*a*) Did the first prose writers adopt it
>   (i) because it was poetic,
>   or (ii) because it was vernacular?
> *or* (*b*) Was it imported in the transmission of their texts[40] for
>   reason (i)? (If (*b*) is true, (ii) can be ignored.)

The trouble is that it is by no means common in epic, and is
therefore recherché as an epic condiment. If such was wanted,
the obvious choice was diektasis[41]—ὁράᾳς, ὁρόωντες, etc.—which
would instantly proclaim 'epic' to an Ionian hearer, whereas αΟ >
εΟ was more likely to proclaim 'Rhodes'. Yet diektasis in Herodotus
is confined to what is patently deliberate Homeric reminiscence:
ἠγορόωντο as a variant on ἠγορῶντο in v. 11. 1 (cf. *Il.* iv. 1) and
κομόωσι as a variant on κομῶσι in ii. 36. 1 and iv. 191. 1 (cf. Homer's
κάρη κομόωντες, so well known a phrase in epic that it may have
influenced the treatment of κομᾶν in speech). For these reasons it
seems to me that αΟ > εΟ is very poor evidence for an epic ingredient in early prose.

    3. The writing of ε + ε as two vowels (and similar treatment of ε +
ει and ε + η). This is the norm in the surviving texts of Herodotus
(e.g. i. 1. 1 ἐσαπικνέεσθαι, iii. 104. 1 ἀφανέες), frequent in Democritus (e.g. DK 68 B 30 μυθέεται, B 38 ξυναδικέειν, B 181 ἁμαρτέειν),
occasional in Heraclitus (e.g. DK 22 B 113 φρονέειν (ctr. B 112
σωφρονεῖν), B 31 μετρέεται), once in Acusilaus (F 22 πολεμέεσκε),

accentual terms covers many instances, but not all, and I am sure he is wrong to
dismiss phonaesthetic preferences as a determinant of phonological change.

[38] Bechtel ii. 620 f., Thumb–Kieckers 191.
[39] Chantraine (1948) i. 361.
[40] So Bechtel iii. 10–16, Untersteiner 28, Thumb–Scherer 237 f., Hartmann 91–9,
ctr. Rosén (1962) 233.
[41] Chantraine (1948) i. 75–80.

once as a variant in Hecataeus (*FGrHist* 1 F 305 κινέεται),[42] and a
constantly recurring variant in Hippocrates.[43] There are, however,
many contrary instances (e.g. Hecataeus F 1 μυθεῖται and δοκεῖ, F 30
ἐκχωρεῖν). It is sporadically attested in Doric areas, most strikingly
in *SEG* xxxv. 479. 1. 2 ἐποίϝεε ἁργεῖος (Delphi, s. vi),[44] then *IG* xiv.
952. 11 πρεσβέες (Acragas, s. iii), ibid. 209. 15 ὑπογραφέες (Acrae, s.
iii),[45] and possibly γροφέ[ες in *DGE* 89. 4 (Argos, s. iii).[46] It gets no
support from early Ionic documents:[47] *DGE* 752 ἐϟρότε (Amorgos,
s. vi),[48] 723(2) ἐποίεν (Miletus, s. vi),[49] 744. 17 ἐπικαλ[έ]τω and 45
ἐπικαλὲν (Halicarnassus, s. v), *SEG* xvi. 495. C1 ἐκκαλέσθω (Chios,
s. v), xxvi. 845. 1 ἀδικέται (indicative) (Berezan', s. vi/v), Pouilloux
7. 3 ποιέτω (Thasos, s. v). It is certainly epic, sometimes metrically guaranteed,[50] e.g. *Il.* x. 116 ἐπέτρεψεν πονέεσθαι, xi. 526 Αἴας δὲ
κλονέει. Whichever prose author first wrote εε, or whichever transmitter of that author's text first introduced it, must have intended
pronunciation as two syllables. Why did he want to do that?[51] Considering that the inscriber of *CEG* i. 422 (Samos, s. vi pr.) wrote θηι
where the metre requires θεῇ—cf. *SEG* xlii. 785. 32 θῆς 'viewing',
33 θήσθω 'look at . . .' (Thasos, s. v pr./m.)—the writing of epic

---

[42] In F 30 ἀπολέεσθε is Cobet's emendation of the MSS' ἀπόλεσθε (Robortello's
ἀπόλησθε is better). Throughout this discussion I leave monosyllabic stems in ε out
of account.

[43] *ELDH* 347.

[44] The sculptor was Argive. I have reproduced the text of Faure, pls. III and IV,
which seem now to rule out earlier readings ἐποίεε ἁαρ- (Marcadé i. 115, cf. Jeffery
pl. 26 no. 4), ἐποίϝεh' Ἀρ- (Buck (1925) 139; cf. *CEG* i. 380. 7 ἐποίϝεhε : Ἀργεῖος), and
ἐποίϝε ἁαρ- supposing a stone-cutter's error, EE for FE (Buck (1913) 142, Solmsen
473 n. 1).

[45] The phenomenon is also—like Artemisia's mother—Cretan.

[46] The word is followed by the names of two men (like γροφέων ibid. 94. 10 f.),
hence not γροφε[ύς]; but perhaps γροφε[ῖς] (cf. Bechtel ii. 625, Thumb–Kieckers
132).

[47] Rosén's mention (26) of *IG* xii (5). 40. 15 as κὰ]γ[ί]νεεν (Boll's supplement)
(Naxos, s. vi/v) is not strong evidence; the traces on the stone as drawn in *IG*
resemble :ιννγεεν[, and the context is unintelligible (cf. Jeffery 289, 292 f.). In *SEG*
xxxi. 985. D14 (Teos, s. v pr.) μὴ 'ναλέξεεν is optative (=-ειεν), as often (e.g. ibid. C2)
in specifying the circumstances which would incur a penalty.

[48] Note that *SGDI* often prints ει when the stone has E (=ε+ε).

[49] If this means (as Bechtel iii. 99 thinks, surprisingly) that the composer said
ἐποιέεν, it also shows that he wrote εε as E.

[50] Chantraine (1948) i. 39 f., 322.

[51] Thumb–Scherer 225 treat the Herodotean εε as modelled on diektasis; but
it would be strange if a hypothetical extension of an epic phenomenon were so
much commoner than imitation of the phenomenon itself. Cf. Rosén (1962) 244.
Smyth consistently (e.g. 102) attributes εε to editorial intervention and grammatical
doctrine; cf. Eulenburg 149.

εε as ε *contra metrum* was far more likely than the writing of ε+ε as εε when there was no metrical constraint. We must again pose the question: if the introduction of epic colouring was important either to the author or to a transmitter, why pick on εε rather than diektasis, genitives in -οιο, or infinitives in -μεναι or -μεν? Rosén's hypothesis[52] that Rhodian εε infected the language of the Halicarnassian Herodotus by contiguity (in which case it must be supposed that the phenomenon was subsequently imported into the text of earlier prose authors by editorial intervention) can be seriously considered only if supplemented by the further hypothesis that there were two strata of language in Halicarnassus, ε+ε being written as two vowels and so pronounced by families proud of their Dorian ancestry[53] but written ε and pronounced as a single vowel in the language of administration.

As a footnote to the consideration of the phonology and morphology of early prose, it should be noted that the occurrence of βουλέωνται in *SGDI* 5633. 19 (Teos, s. iv), now supported by *SEG* xxxvii. 922. 13 ἦμ βουλε[(Erythrae, s. iv), reminds us of the chronic untidiness of real language.

Scepticism about the motives of an author or transmitter for importing certain specific features of poetry into a prose text in preference to more obvious features does not amount to scepticism about all desire to invest the text with the status and authority of poetry, which is by no means inexplicable. The test case is οὔνομα = ὄνομα (Hdt. *passim*, Hecat. F 282; not, however, the five citations of Heraclitus and Democritus containing ὄνομα).[54] οὔνομα is very frequent in epic because of the metrical utility of $- \smile \smile$ in so common a lexeme (whereas in ὀνομαστός and many parts of ὀνομάζειν short ο is required). If we knew that Herodotus actually wrote οὔνομα we would be a lot further on in understanding the relation between poetry and prose. The trouble is, we cannot know. He could have pronounced the vowel as long in reading his own work aloud, but could not have ensured that other readers did so except by violating the orthographic norm of his time and place, which made no distinction between /o/ and /o:/. Yet norms are not absolute rules, because in *DGE* 710. B26 f. we find βαρβάρους beside βολεύοι (24),

---

[52] Rosén (1962) 249; he does not deal with any objections.
[53] Cf. n. 45.
[54] Rosén (1962) 244 f., hostile to all ideas of ancient editorial *Homerisierung*, inappropriately associates οὔνομα/ὄνομα with ξεῖνος(< ξένϝος)/ξένος.

τὸ ξυνὸ (25), etc. (Teos, s. v m.), and in Attic sporadic instances of
ου=/o:/ begin in the sixth century.[55] The test case proves to be an
abortive test.

It may well be that to readers in the fourth century the Ionic prose
literature of the preceding century seemed to be heavily charged
with poetic resonances. Adoption of epic phrases in Herodotus[56]
would strengthen this impression, e.g. iii. 14. 10 (in dialogue) ἐπὶ
γήραος οὐδῷ=*Il.* xxiii. 60 (and cf. p. 108). With the eclipse of the
Ionic vernaculars—and no comparable decline in familiarity with
epic poetry—the true history of words which might or might not
have been current in speech two generations earlier could not be
known, and was not treated as an interesting subject. Thanks to
archaeology and epigraphy, we are better placed, and we have come
to terms with the fact that any language may be expected to change
continuously, but we are still handicapped by areas of irremedi-
able ignorance. In dealing with Classical Attic we can readily draw
distinctions between poetic and prosaic language, because from the
third quarter of the fifth century onwards we can see for ourselves
which is which, but with Ionic the matter is quite otherwise: no
prose contemporary with Homer, hardly a word of Ionic poetry
contemporary with Herodotus, and all known fragments of Ionic
documents earlier than the end of the fifth century, if put together
as a continuous text, would not equal more than fifteen pages of a
modern printed text of Herodotus. We can therefore ask, and should
ask, in respect of any lexeme confined to Homer and Herodotus, or
(say) to Archilochus and a Presocratic: was this lexeme taken from
poetry by the prose author, or was it taken by both independently
from an Ionic vernacular? The former alternative has in general
been favoured,[57] and taken to an extreme by Leumann,[58] but it is
time to try the latter alternative as a working hypothesis.

Before either hypothesis can be judged satisfactory certain con-
ditions must be fulfilled:

[55] Threatte i. 238–41; but he is mistaken about *IG* i³ 253/4 (=i² 186/7).
[56] Norden (1898) 40 f., Bechtel 19, Haberle 10, 13.
[57] e.g. Zarncke 21, 37–44; Haberle's admission (5 f.) that there may be something
to be said on the other side is a little grudging. He regards (e.g.) κάματος (11) as
'clearly poetic'.
[58] Leumann 305 f., treating (e.g.) ζωρός, λάβρος, μόρσιμος, σημάντωρ as epic vocabulary in Herodotus; he judges borrowing from Homer more likely '*a priori*' (314 f.;
the expression is his) than use of Ionic vernacular. Aly (1921) 273 admits that a lot
more inscriptions could make all the difference.

(i) There is no point in labelling any phenomenon 'non-Attic' unless we can say what an Athenian would have said instead.

(ii) A rate of change in Ionic comparable to what we observe in most other languages should be assumed. An Ephesian joker about 429 BC would not necessarily have used the same vocabulary as Hipponax in describing the same events. We are not in a position to say, in respect of any given lexeme, whether he would or not, but let us just not forget our ignorance.

(iii) Contrasting 'Ionic' with 'Attic' in no way entails denying the occurrence of 'Ionic' lexemes in other linguistic areas, including Aeolic and West Greek; the data refute such a denial. The contrast Ionic/Attic is relevant simply to the question: when a phenomenon is found in Ionic fifth-century prose but not in Attic prose of the fifth and fourth centuries, is poetry its source?

Ion of Chios *FGrHist* 392 F 6 is instructive (and close in date to the completion of Herodotus' work, because Ion is mentioned in Ar. *Pax* 835–7 as having recently died, at the beginning of 421). Excluding proper names and the verses and phrases cited from poets, the piece contains 104 mobile lexemes. Of these, seven are unknown in Attic: ἀμείβεσθαι = ἀποκρίνεσθαι, ἀσσότερα = ἐγγύτερον, ἀφαιρετεῖν (here denoting '(try to) fish out') = ἀφαιρεῖν, ἐπιράπιξις = ἐπίπληξις, νωπεῖσθαι = ἀθυμεῖν, πορφυροβάφος = (probably) *πορφυροβάπτης, ῥεκτήριος = δραστήριος (Thuc. ii. 63. 3). κάρφος is familiar in comedy, but extant Attic prose happens not to say anything about bits of straw. ἐπικροτεῖν, 'applaud', is in Men. fr. 771, but κροτεῖν is well attested in prose. ἀναγελᾶν (= ἀνακαγχάζειν) and συναντᾶν (= συγγίγνεσθαι, ἀπαντᾶν) are in Xenophon, like many other lexemes not found in other Attic prose authors,[59] but Ion's ἀγγελάσας (= ἀναγε-) has parallels in Hdt. i. 8. 3, vii. 181. 1 ἀμβώσας and (in the latter passage) ἀνθρώσκει (v.l.), none in Attic prose. ἀποφυσᾶν is in comedy (Ar. *Vesp.* 330), and no doubt it was the ordinary Attic for 'blow away', but the tmesis ἀπὸ τοίνυν φύσησον αὐτό has no parallel in Attic prose except with ἀντί/σύν (. . .), εὖ/κακῶς (. . .), ποιεῖν/πάσχειν, and Pl. *Phdr.* 237 A ξύμ μοι λάβεσθε as a deliberately grandiloquent poeticism in an invocation of the Muses.[60]

Ignoring ἐπικροτεῖν, κάρφος, and πορφυροβάφος as being of no interest for present purposes, four of the remaining phenomena owe nothing, on present evidence, to poetry: ἀφαιρετεῖν, ἐπιράπιξις,

[59] Gauthier 22–65.
[60] KG i. 537 f.

νωπεῖσθαι, ῥεκτήριος. There is no shortage of lexemes of that category in other fifth-century Ionic prose authors: διφάσιοι = δύο, τριφάσιοι = τρεῖς (cf. English 'two different . . .', where 'different' is often superfluous) Hdt., *DGE* 725. 2 (Miletus, s. vi ex.); λεώς = οἰκέτης Hecat. *FGrHist* 1 F 23, *DGE* 734. 6 (Zeleia, s. iv); μετεξέτεροι = ἔνιοι Hdt.; νόμαιος = νόμιμος Hdt., *DGE* 688. C8 (Chios, s. v).[61] Ionic documents contribute steadily to supplements to the lexicon, e.g. *SEG* xxxi. 985. D14 ἀναλέγειν = ἀναγιγνώσκειν (Teos, s. v pr.), xxii. 508. A5 *al.* ἐνηλάσιον = μίσθωσις[62] (Chios, s. iv m.), xvii. 451. 1 μοι[ρί]ζειν = διανέμειν (Thasos, s. iv ex.), xviii. 347. 9 νηϊδίη = ἄγνοια (Thasos, s. v pr.; Hdt. ἀϊδρείη), xxii. 508. A46 οἴη = κώμη (Chios, s. iv m.).

Of those lexemes which are shared by poetry and Ionic prose literature, a significant proportion appear also in documents, and there are some shared by poetry with documents but not yet attested in prose literature, notably:

ἀδηνής = ἄδολος
Cj. for ἀληνῆς Sem. 7. 53; ἀδηνέως *DGE* 688. B11 (Chios, s. v).

ἀτρεκής = ἀληθής
Epic; Hdt. *passim*, Democr. DK B 9, Diog. Apoll. DK B 5; cf. ML 29 ἀτρέκειαν (letter of Darius, s. vi ex.).

δαίνυσθαι = ἑστιᾶσθαι
Epic; Archil. 197, Hipponax 26. 3; Hdt.; Pouilloux 10. *c*3 (Thasos, s. iv pr.)

ἔρδειν = θύειν
Epic; Hdt.; *DGE* 726. 15 (Miletus, s. v).

εὐχωλή = εὐχή
Epic; Hdt. ii. 63. 1; *DGE* 748 (2) (Naucratis, s. vi).

---

[61] I have not included κιξάλλης, Democr. B 260, *DGE* 710. B19 (Teos, s. v pr.), because both Democritus and the Teian inscription treat κιξάλλης and λῃστής as distinct, and I do not know what the Athenians would have called a κιξάλλης; cf. Lewis in Craik 151 ff. I have also omitted one or two lexemes which occur only once each, or very rarely, in Attic prose: ἁλίζειν = συλλέγειν, epic, Hdt., *SEG* xxxviii. 851. 9 (Thasos, 407), and Xen. *Anab.* ii. 4. 3, vii. 2. 10; μετέπειτα = ὕστερον, epic, Hdt., *DGE* 710. B17 (Teos, s. v pr.), and Pl. *Epist.* 353 C; φάσθαι = φάναι, epic, Ionic prose, a letter as yet unpublished (Olbia, s. vi/v), and—not easily explained—Xen. *HG* i. 6. 3 οὐ φαμένου δέ (φάμενοι in Pl. *Alc. II* 142 D may be drawn from the passage of Simonides under discussion).

[62] 'Rent' in Attic is plainly μίσθωσις (e.g. *IG* i³ 84. 15, 23, 402. 18, 19)—not μισθός or μίσθωμα—although μίσθωσις also serves as a verbal noun, 'leasing' (e.g. *IG* i³ 149. 5 f.).

καρτερός = κύριος
Archil. 227; *DGE* 744. 21, 29 (Halicarnassus, s. v m.).

κατακτείνειν = ἀποκτείνειν
Epic; Hdt., Heraclitus B 56; *DGE* 727. 6 (Miletus, s. v m.).

καταφθίμενος = τεθνεώς
Epic; (καταφθίνειν Hdt. ii. 123. 2); *DGE* 766. Α1 (Iulis, s. v).

μιν = αὐτόν
Epic; Archil.; Hdt., Heraclitus DK 22 B 94, Protagoras DK 80 B 9; *SEG* xxvi. 845. 3, 9 (Berezan', s. vi/v).

μυθεῖσθαι = λέγειν
Epic; Hecat. F 1, Democr. DK 68 B 30; *SEG* xxvi. 845. 5.

ξυνός = κοινός
Epic; Hdt.; Heraclitus B 2 *al.*, Democr. B 3 *al.*; *DGE* 710. A3, B25 (Teos, *c.*470).

οὐδαμά, μηδαμά = οὐδέποτε, μηδέποτε
Hipponax 36. 2, 117. 7; Hdt., Melissus B 1; *DGE* 744. 41 (Halicarnassus, s. v m.), (Teos, s. v m.).

παρέκ = πλήν
Epic; (παρέξ Archil.); Hdt.; *DGE* 732. B4 (Cyzicus, s. vi), *SEG* xxii. 508. B49 (Chios, s. iv m.).

σφι = αὐτοῖς
Epic; Hdt., Democr. B 127; *DGE* 800.C D8 (Eretria, s. vi).

τό, τά = ὅ, ἅ
Epic; Hdt., Democr. B 198; *DGE* 721. 24 (Thebae ad Mycalen, s. iv pr.).

These data suggest that we should not think of the five phenomena in Ion F 6 which are shared with Herodotus and with poetry—ἀμείβεσθαι = ἀποκρίνεσθαι (cf. ἀνταμείβεσθαι in Archil.), κάρτα, tmesis, apocope of ἀνα-, and ἀσσότερα (Hdt., Hom. ἆσσον, *Od.* xix. 506 ἀσσοτέρω)—as modelled on poetic usage. The same must be said of χρῆμα, 'thing', with 'all', 'none', or superlatives; first attested in Archilochus 122. 1 χρημάτων . . . οὐδέν, it is commonplace in Ionic prose (Hdt. i. 35. 4, vii. 145. 1, Acusilaus F 22 μάλιστα χρημάτων, Anaxagoras B 12 οὐδενὶ χρήματι, Protagoras B 1 πάντων χρημάτων).[63] The question of the sources of the vocabulary of fifth-century prose

[63] Andocides shows a temporary enthusiasm for this use of χρῆμα in the *De Reditu* (ii. 1, 4, 21).

literature matters, because if we get it wrong the penalty is not just historical error but aesthetic deprivation. To treat the language of Herodotus as indiscriminately poetic is to diminish the power of those passages[64] in which it is plausible to believe that poetic reminiscence was deliberate, e.g. i. 155. 3 τὰ μέν . . . ἔπρηξα καὶ κεφαλῇ ἀναμάξας φέρω~*Od.* xix. 92 μέγα ἔργον ὃ σῇ κεφαλῇ ἀναμάξεις, iii. 14. 10 ἐπὶ γήραος οὐδῷ=*Il.* xx. 60, iii. 154. 1 μόρσιμόν ἐστι . . . ἁλίσκεσθαι~*Il.* xix. 417 μόρσιμόν ἐστι . . . δαμῆναι, iv. 181. 4 ζέει ἀμβολάδην~*Il.* xxi. 362–4 ζεῖ . . . πάντοθεν ἀμβολάδην, ix. 3. 1 ἀλλά οἱ δεινός τις ἐνέστακτο ἵμερος~*Od.* ii. 271 εἰ δή τοι σοῦ πατρὸς ἐνέστακται μένος ἠΰ.

Where a phenomenon whose distribution in classical literary prose is not universal cannot be associated exclusively with a period of history or a region of the Greek world, it is usually possible to ascribe it to the language expected of a particular genre. There are, however, some phenomena of restricted distribution which do not clearly reflect differences of period, region, or genre, and simply illustrate the freedom of the individual author to choose the ingredients of his idiolect—and to vary his choices between texts (cf. n. 8). A clear example is provided by τοῦτο μέν . . . τοῦτο δέ in the sense 'in the first place . . . and secondly . . .' (or '. . . and, again, . . .'); we find it sometimes with more than one τοῦτο δέ, or with some word for 'then' instead of τοῦτο δέ, or τοῦτο δέ without τοῦτο μέν. The usage is abundant in Herodotus (59 instances)[65] and is found also in Hippocrates, e.g. *Flat.* 7. 1. But it is not confined to Ionic, for Antiphon has 22 instances, Andocides 4, and Anon. *Ath.* one (3. 11, a double τοῦτο δέ without τοῦτο μέν). Is it therefore simply 'early'? Apparently not, because Thucydides does not use it at all, and though present in Antiphon i and v it is absent from vi and from the *Tetralogies*. In the fourth century it seems never to have appealed to Lysias or Plato; but it was not dead, for Isaeus uses it three times (iii. 28, v. 41, xi. 30), Demosthenes at least four (ix. 11, 24, xx. 59 f., xxv. 38),[66] and Isocrates at least once (iv. 21 f.), all in passages where we can see no reason why the speaker should have desired an archaic or Ionic flavouring.

[64] Examples selected from Leumann 305 f.
[65] I do not know what miscalculation led Powell to sum his examples as '111'.
[66] Rehdantz 103. Surprisingly, Denniston says nothing of this usage.

6

SPECIAL LANGUAGES

A. POETIC LANGUAGE

THE earliest explicit contrast between poetic and prosaic language is made (about 365) by Isocrates (ix. 9 f.). The lexemes, he says, which poets are able to use are not only τὰ τεταγμένα 'those pre-scribed' (sc. by general usage) but also those which are ξένα 'alien', καινά 'novel' or 'coined', and μεταφοραί 'metaphors'. Writers of λόγοι (cf. p. 185), on the other hand, have no such freedom, but are confined to τὰ πολιτικὰ τῶν ὀνομάτων 'citizens' words', i.e. 'words in circulation among ordinary people'. A somewhat more detailed and systematic analysis[1] is to be found in Arist. *Po.* 1457^{b}1–58^{a}7 and 1458^{a}17–59^{a}16, which should be taken in conjunction with *Rhet.* 1404^{b}1–7^{a}18. Aristotle draws a fundamental distinction be-tween κύρια ὀνόματα 'valid', 'legitimate', 'prevalent', hence 'nor-mal', words, and ξενικὰ ὀνόματα 'alien', 'unfamiliar', 'abnormal' words. Abnormal words comprise γλῶτται, metaphors, and length-ened forms. So *Po.* 1458^{a}17 ff.; in the earlier passage (1457^{b}1 ff.) he has given a longer list, adding κόσμος (an obscure term, because he offers no examples or further explanation),[2] forms of distortion other than lengthening, and coinages. Subsequently (1459^{a}5) he adds compound substantives. He recognizes that a γλῶττα is re-gional, so that the same word may be alien to Athenian ears but normal in Cyprus; but he has nothing to say about syntax.

[1] Halliwell's assessment of it (1986, 346) as 'desultory' and 'jejune' is just; but much may be forgiven to pioneers.

[2] Given the use of κόσμος to mean 'the (apparently ordered and orderly) universe' (e.g. Xen. *Mem.* i. 1. 11), we might suspect that Aristotle means the design apparent in the interrelation of the parts of the whole (none of which need be γλῶτται etc.). This, however, would be applicable just as much to prose as to poetry, and an alternative possibility is 'heightening', 'magniloquence'—which *can* be achieved without unusual vocabulary (e.g. by superfluous epithets; cf. Arist. *Rhet.* 1406^{a}18–35). The trouble is, in *Rhet.* 1404^{b}5–8 Aristotle says that 'the words of which I have spoken in the *Poetics* make one's language κεκοσμημένη'. This rules out the possibility that κόσμος refers to the ordering of words (σύνθεσις in Dionysius, e.g. ii. 9. 6–9, 11. 5–12. 3; cf. Ardizzoni 67–80).

Normal words are not sub-classified. We are simply told that they achieve the highest degree of clarity in communication (*Po.* 1458ª18–20), but at the price of being ταπεινός, for which 'ordinary' (in a derogatory tone of voice), 'cheap', or 'lowly' are appropriate translations. Their use is identified with τὸ ἰδιωτικόν (1458ª21, 1459ª2), i.e. the language of the ἰδιώτης, the 'layman', who, unlike the poet, has no τέχνη. It is positively desirable, according to Aristotle, that the language of poetry should avoid τὸ ἰδιωτικόν by being 'unusual' (παρὰ τὸ εἰωθός, 1458ᵇ3), but all the resources of poetic language have to be used πρεπόντως (1459ª4). If the poet does not observe the '(right) measure' (1458ᵇ12) what he writes will be enigmatic or gibberish (1458ª24). More precise guidance on what constitutes excess or deficiency is not offered.

In *Rhet.* 1404ᵇ1 Aristotle turns to the language of speeches, and refers back (1404ᵇ7, cf. 28) to what he has said in the *Poetics*. In a speech, as in a poem, normal words make for clarity, and clarity is the supreme fulfilment of utterance (λέξεως ἀρετή). A speech, like a poem, should be something better than ταπεινός, and the means of making it so are the same in both cases, but the 'appropriate measure' is different, for much that would be acceptable as moderate use in poetry would be regarded as going far beyond that if used in a speech (1406ª15), turning the speech into poetry (1406ª5, 37 ποιητικά, 1406ª14 ποίησις, 1406ª31 ποίημα, 1406ª32, 1406ᵇ10 ποιητικῶς). Abnormal words, compound words, and coinages must be used very sparingly (1404ᵇ26–37); but metaphor can be exploited more fully, since it is the kind of language that we all use (οἰκεῖος 1404ᵇ32). The speaker must conceal the artistic effort that has gone into his composition, so that the speech may sound 'natural' (1404ᵇ19 πεφυκότως).[3]

Throughout history, in a wide variety of cultures, both literate and illiterate, it has been normal practice to differentiate strongly between the language of song (or poetry) and the language of speech (or written prose).[4] Even if we had nothing but prose from the ancient Greeks, we would be justified in assuming that the differences to which Aristotle refers in general terms would be immediately apparent in a sample of Greek poetry. However, since we have no

---

[3] The concept 'nature' is often disastrous in linguistics, especially when (as in the views of which Dionysius repents in ii. 23. 1–27. 6) it rests on metaphysical foundations. Cf. also Dover (1988) 132 f., and on 'concealment of style' Sartre 39.

[4] Dover (1987) 1–15.

prose literature contemporary with archaic poetry and no Ionic poetry contemporary with Herodotus and the earliest historians and philosophers (cf. p. 91), it is only in Attic literature after about 430 that we can actually observe and describe the difference between prose and poetry composed for the same public at the same period.[5] Quantifiable comparison requires that we limit ourselves to serious poetry, i.e. tragedy; whenever tragedy can be contrasted with prose, Old Comedy aligns itself sometimes with tragedy, sometimes with prose, according to the dramatic function of a passage; in the course of the fourth century the alignment of comedy with prose is progressive.

Let us take a random[6] sample from tragic dialogue, Eur. *Hel.* 1043 f.:

$$\phi\acute{\epsilon}\rho\epsilon,\ \tau\acute{\iota}\ \delta'\ \epsilon\grave{\iota}\ \kappa\rho\upsilon\phi\theta\epsilon\grave{\iota}\varsigma\ \delta\acute{o}\mu o\iota\varsigma$$
$$\kappa\tau\acute{a}\nu o\iota\mu'\ \mathring{a}\nu\alpha\kappa\tau\alpha\ \tau\mathring{\omega}\delta\epsilon\ \delta\iota\sigma\tau\acute{o}\mu\omega\ \xi\acute{\iota}\phi\epsilon\iota;$$

But now suppose I hid in the palace and killed the king with this two-edged sword?

This brief utterance exhibits several phenomena which are abundant in poetry but rare or unknown in Attic prose:[7]

(1) The lexemes δόμος, κτανεῖν, and ἄναξ.

(2) The absence of the definite article with ἄνακτα and τῷδε . . . ξίφει.

(3) The simple dative, with no preposition, in a locative sense.

(4) The expansion of 'sword' to 'two-edged sword', where (as in *Hel.* 983) the compound adjective approximates to ornamentation.[8]

It would be pointless, even misleading, to call any phenomenon 'poetic' simply on the grounds that it happens to occur in extant poetry but not in extant prose. We need to specify what lexeme

---

[5] We have enough fourth-century Attic tragedy (a category to which some of the hundreds of *adespota* must belong) to assure us of the continuity of tragic language and therefore of the propriety of contrasting that language as a whole with Plato, Demosthenes, and their contemporaries.

[6] Or almost random. *Sortes Euripideae* led me to *Hel.* 1040–67, and chance to the top half of the page, from which I selected 1043 f. for the present purpose.

[7] It should at the same time be noted that φέρε, τί δ' εἰ κτλ. has a colloquial character (Stevens 30, 42).

[8] It is not 'meaningless', for it imparts an awareness of the fierce efficiency of the sword used against a man attacked from ambush; in English translation on stage this would best be conveyed not by an adjective but by tone, pace, and facial expression in uttering 'sword'. Similarly in *Hel.* 983 the adjective helps to convey the pathos of pain and death. On the analysis of δίστομος see Coughanowr 235.

or periphrasis or syntactical construction an Athenian would have used instead in his ordinary discourse. Of the three poetic lexemes identified in *Hel*. 1043 f., we can say that δόμος (much more often δόμοι) would be οἰκία 'house', or βασίλεια 'palace', in prose, and 'in the house' would normally be ἔνδον 'inside' (e.g. Pl. *Prt*. 310 E, *Rep*. 451 D); ἄναξ would be βασιλεύς 'king'; the aorist κτανεῖν 'kill' would be (-)κτεῖναι. If we put together a prose corpusculum consisting of Anon. *Ath*., Antiphon, Andocides i–iii, Thucydides, Lysias, early Isocrates, and early Plato (cf. p. 63), it is easy to compile a list of lexemes which are common in Sophocles and Euripides—that is to say, they occur at least fifty times (and often much more)— but are entirely absent from all those prose texts. Examples are αὐδᾶν 'speak', 'say' (=λέγειν), δῶμα 'house' (=οἰκία), κάρα 'head' (= κεφαλή), κασίγνητος 'brother' (=ἀδελφός), κλύειν 'hear' (=ἀκούειν),[9] λεύσσειν 'see' (=ὁρᾶν), μολεῖν (aor.) 'come', 'go' (=ἐλθεῖν), ναίειν 'dwell' (=οἰκεῖν), στείχειν 'go', 'come' (=βαδίζειν, ἰέναι), χθών 'land' (=γῆ). The differences in respect of ἀποκτείνειν/κτείνειν and certain other compound verbs, displayed in Table 6.1, are also of interest.

TABLE 6.1. *'Die' and 'kill' in poetry and prose*

	Soph. & Eur.	Prose corpusculum
ἀποθνῄσκειν 'die'	1 (Eur. fr. 578. 6)	*c*. 190
θνῄσκειν (excluding the perfective aspect)	*c*.620	55
ἀποκτείνειν 'kill'	47	*c*.300
κτείνειν	*c*.440	35
ἀπολλύναι 'destroy'	*c*.240	*c*.260
ὀλλύναι	*c*.270	none
διαφθείρειν 'destroy', 'ruin'	39	*c*.240
φθείρειν[a]	28	40

[a] Here it may be necessary to draw a semantic distinction, if we consider the different categories of object taken by διαφθείρειν and φθείρειν in Thucydides.

The frequency of the definite article is the most prominent and consistent difference between prose (and not only Attic prose) and serious poetry. This may be quantified in Table 6.2, which shows

[9] On Ar. *Ra*. 1173 (=Aesch. *Cho*. 5) κλύειν ἀκοῦσαι see Dover ad loc.

how many of the first 500 declinable tokens in each sample are the definite article (crasis of the definite article with an initial vowel has been dismantled throughout).

TABLE 6.2. *The definite article in seven texts*

Soph. *Phil*. 1 ff.	43	Thuc. i. 1. 1 ff.	119
Eur. *Or.* 1 ff.	35	Ant. v. 1 ff.	124
Hp. *VM* 1 ff.	90	Anon. *Ath*. 1. 1 ff.	152
Hdt. i pr. ff.	104		

Plato's prose paraphrase of *Il.* i. 15–24 in *Rep.* 393 D–394 A, overflowing with definite articles, is a famous illustration of the difference between archaic narrative poetry and fourth-century prose,[10] but it does not tell us at what period in the history of the language progressive debilitation of the demonstrative ὁ in the spoken language turned it into something which we would translate by 'the' or by nothing.[11] In particular, it does not tell us whether the comparatively low incidence of the definite article in Heraclitus— echoed in the Hippocratic *De Victu* i. 5–24—reflects an early stage in that process, an attempt to invest prose with the authority of poetry, or a tendency to think in terms which we would express by use of an indefinite article or of none.[12] Nor again can any firm historical conclusion be drawn from the absence of the definite article in many instances of proper names, titles, and institutions. It is therefore unwise to regard the opening words of ML 2 (Dreros, s. vii) ἇδ' ἔϝαδε πόλι 'the city's decision was as follows' as evidence that the definite article had not yet taken shape in the dialects of Crete, for at Argos *DGE* 78. 6 ἁ βōλά 'the Council' is half a century earlier (s. vi/v) than 83B. 21 βōλά (s. v m.). The fact is that the determinants of the presence or absence of the definite article in Greek are heterogeneous, sometimes in conflict, and the outcome of the conflict in particular instances is often unpredictable.[13]

---

[10] Delbrück i. 508.

[11] This debilitation of demonstratives is a general feature of languages which have a definite article; cf. Wackernagel ii. 127 f.

[12] See Rosén (1988) for discussion of citations from Heraclitus in which the definite article might have been expected but is absent; the explanations of its absence are, I think, more varied than he allows.

[13] See, most recently, Sansone (1993).

The locative dative,[14] terminal accusative[15] and spatial-ablatival genitive[16] differ from the low incidence of the definite article in so far as whereas the latter is pervasive and tells us within a few lines 'this is poetic'.(τῷδε . . . ξίφει in *Hel.* 1044 would be ungrammatical in prose), worthwhile quantifications of the former would be hard to extract even from much larger samples than I have used. We have to approach the phenomenon, so to speak, from the other direction, observing (and, if possible, explaining) sporadic instances of the bare substantive in prose where preposition plus substantive would have been expected.[17]

Much more easily quantified is the fourth phenomenon observed in *Hel.* 1043 f., the use of attributive adjectives, and in particular compound adjectives. Table 6.3 shows

(I) How many of the first 500 noun-tokens in each sample are accompanied by
   (A) one attributive adjective
   (B) two or more uncoordinated attributive adjectives,
   (C) two or more co-ordinated attributive adjectives.
(II) How many of the first 250 adjective-tokens in each sample are
   (A) adjective-lexemes,
   (B) compound adjective-lexemes beginning with a preposition, negative ἀ-, παν-, or πολυ-,
   (C) other compound adjective-lexemes.

'Noun', 'adjective', and 'attributive' all raise problems of definition. I count as a noun-token every =S which comprises a single declinable mobile, *excluding* all pronouns whatsoever, πολύς, πλείων, πλεῖστος, πᾶς and ἅπας, simple vocatives (e.g. ὦ παῖ), and proper names—then readmitting those vocatives and proper names which are accompanied by attributive adjectives. By 'adjective' I mean a

[14] KG i. 441–4, *GG* ii. 154–6, Bruhn 12 f., Bers 86–99; on Soph. *Oed. Col.* 411, however, see Lloyd-Jones and Wilson 230 f.

[15] KG i. 311 f., *GG* ii. 67 f., Bruhn 35, Bers 62–85.

[16] KG i. 394 f., *GG* ii. 91–5, Bruhn 27, Bers 99–101.

[17] Björck 98, 305 attributes the poets' lack of explicitness to their desire to reduce the elements which are *bedeutungsschwach* or *affektschwach* (should we discern in his terminology an unfortunate consequence of Aristotle's superficial distinction (*Po.* 1457ᵃ6–8, 32–4) between σημαίνων and ἄσημος?). Pl. *Alc. II* 147 B comments that poetry is essentially αἰνιγματώδης (cf. *Rep.* 332 B ᾐνίξατο . . . ποιητικῶς), 'allusive', and the omission of prepositions sometimes contributes to that effect; cf. Björck 304 f., Bers 190. Bers 62–101 discusses many individual passages and shows how often there is room for disagreement on the interpretation of a case.

TABLE 6.3. *Attributive adjectives in six texts*

	I			II		
	A	B	C	A	B	C
Soph. *Phil*. 1 ff.	118	5	3	162	40	28
Eur. *Or*. 1 ff.	91	6	2	156	38	27
Hdt. i pr. 1 ff.	31	3	5	121	32	14
Thuc. i. 1. 1 ff.	45		1	135	52	12
Pl. *Rep*. 357 A 1 ff.	31	1	3	95	14	12
Isoc. vii. 1 ff.	16		3	108	25	9

declinable mobile which is inflected for gender, *excluding* πολύς etc. (as above), all pronominal usages (e.g. οἱ ἄλλοι), numerals (ordinal and cardinal), πρότερον and ὕστερον,[18] and those tokens which are formally adjectival but require translation as nouns, e.g. ἱερά, ναυτικόν, οἱ πολέμιοι, but *including* the occasional participles which require translation as adjectives, e.g. μαινόμενος 'crazy', διαφέρων 'exceptional', and regular adverbs in -ως/ῶς. Difficulties are created by declinable mobiles which are morphologically nouns but function syntactically as adjectives, e.g. ἀγροβότης in Soph. *Phil.* 214 ποιμὴν ἀγροβότας. In such cases the compiler of the data has to take a decision and not spend too much time in repentance. As for 'attributive', it quite often happens that translators disagree over the interpretation of an adjective-token as attributive or predicative. For all these reasons there is an element of approximation (at least ±5%, I would say)[19] in the figures of Table 6.3. Verse quotations in prose passages are, of course, ignored.

The difference between poetry and prose revealed in the table accords with Aristotle's strictures (*Rhet.* 1405^{b}35–6^{a}6) on what he regards as excessive use of adjectives in prose: it turns prose into poetry (1406^{a}5). He extends his criticism (1406^{a}10–17) to all use of epithets which are lengthy, inappropriate to the occasion (ἄκαιρος), or too closely packed (πυκνός), since they make the language of a speech 'alien' (ξενικός). The low total of compound adjectives in our sample from Isocrates is particularly inter⸺ �ng, given his complaint that only πολιτικὰ ὀνόματα are permitte⸺ o the prose-writer,

---

[18] I considered that the frequency of these words in th⸺ hucydides sample might have a distorting effect, especially as they are used adv⸺ lly.

[19] But at least the decisions have all been taken by tl⸺ me person, so that there is some degree of consistency of principle.

and only one of his compounds, θεοποίητος 'divinely created' (62), is unattested in other Attic prose authors. It occurs impressively, resoundingly, at the climax of a value-judgement:

If we compare our political structure not with that which I have described but with that which was instituted by the Thirty, there is no one who would not regard it as θεοποίητος.

This reminds us that we can hardly rest content with the verdict that such-and-such an author favours a 'more poetic style' than such-and-such another; we must also look for explanations of poetic colouring in particular instances, even without the expectation that we shall always find what we seek.

The best starting-point is Pl. *Phdr.* 257 A, where Socrates says, at the end of the Myth of the Soul:

αὕτη σοι, ὦ φίλε Ἔρως, εἰς ἡμετέραν δύναμιν ὅτι καλλίστη καὶ ἀρίστη δέδοταί τε καὶ ἐκτέτεισται παλινῳδία, τά τε ἄλλα καὶ τοῖς ὀνόμασιν ἠναγκασμένη ποιητικοῖς τισιν διὰ Φαῖδρον εἰρῆσθαι.

So, dear Eros, I have given you, in atonement, the best and fairest recantation of which I am capable; in particular, I have been obliged, for Phaedrus' sake, to express it in some degree[20] in poetic language.

As Plato says this of something which he himself has composed, identification of the differences between the style of the Myth (beginning at 245 C 5 ψυχὴ πᾶσα ἀθάνατος) and his styles elsewhere should tell us what he regarded as poetic.

If we exclude indeclinable adverbs (e.g. εὖ, ἀεί, μάλα) and all the categories of lexeme listed on p. 47, the total number of mobile lexemes in the Myth is 702. We need to ask how many of them are attested in serious poetry before Plato but never, except in the Myth, in any Attic prose down to the end of the fourth century. We must then see how the figure compares with the figures from prose samples of equal size, and for this purpose I have chosen Pl. *Rep.* 357 A–372 D 5, Xen. *Mem.* i. 1. 1–4. 4, and Isoc. vii (this last, with 683 lexemes, falls just short of the desired 702, but not by a margin large enough to mattter). The lexemes which fall in the strictly defined category 'attested in serious poetry . . .' (and, of course, this is only a first step) are:

[20] On 'diffident' τις see p. 126 and KG i. 663 f., *GG* ii. 215, Ellendt s.v. τὶς V.3, Dover (1993) 269, 276.

Phdr. Myth

251 C ἀνακηκίειν 'bubble up' (as liquid does when boiled); (ἀνα)κηκί-
εειν epic, κηκίειν tragedy.

248 C ἀπήμων 'unharmed'; epic, lyric, tragedy; ἀβλαβής in prose.

247 B βρίθειν 'weigh down'; epic, lyric, tragedy; βαρύνειν in prose,
but βρίθειν is in the Pseudo-Aristotelian *Problemata* 915ᵇ3.

252 C δαίς 'banquet'; epic, tragedy; δεῖπνον, occasionally θοίνη, in
prose.

252 E δῖος 'noble', 'godlike'; epic, lyric, tragedy; θεῖος in prose.

264 D ἐνδάκνειν 'get . . . between the teeth'; tragedy.

244 E ἐξάντης 'healthy', 'cured'; tragedy (*TrGF* Adesp. 151); ὑγιής
in prose.

Ibid. κακηγόρος 'speaking ill'; Pindar.

253 E μελάγχρως 'dark-skinned' (tragedy).

256 E ὁμόπτερος 'alike in plumage' (tragedy).

251 D συναναίνειν 'dry up at the same time' (tragedy).

248 A ὑποβρύχιος 'submerged'; *H.Hom.* 33. 12.

247 B, 256 D ὑπουράνιος 'supporting the sky', 'under the sky'; epic.

253 D ὑψαύχην 'holding the neck high' (tragedy).

Rep. 357 A–372 D

364 B ἀγύρτης 'mendicant priest'; tragedy.

366 A λίσσεσθαι 'entreat'; epic, lyric, tragedy; ἱκετεύειν or ἀντιβολεῖν
in prose.

364 E ὅμαδος: in epic, sometimes 'throng', sometimes 'clamour'.

Xen. *Mem.* i. 1. 1–4. 4

1. 9 δαιμονᾶν 'be possessed by a (harmful) supernatural being';
tragedy.

3. 9 λεωργός 'wicked', 'illegal'; Archilochus, tragedy; ἄδικος or παρά-
νομος in prose.

2. 23 συμφυτεύειν '(im)plant at the same time'; lyric, tragedy.

3. 7 ὑποθημοσύνη 'prompting', 'instruction'; epic; παραίνεσις in
prose.

3. 12 φίλημα 'kiss'; tragedy.

Isoc. vii contains no lexemes in this category.

Plainly, not all these are significant; συναναίνειν and συμφυτεύειν
merely illustrate the freedom with which συν- could be prefixed
to any verb, and ἀγύρται happen not to be mentioned elsewhere in
Attic prose. Since κακηγορία was an actionable offence under Attic

law and κακηγορεῖν is common, it is improbable that κακηγόρος (it is in comedy) would strike a reader of Plato as a 'poetic word'. It will be observed that (in addition to κακηγόρος) three more of the poetic lexemes cited from the Myth are compound adjectives (type II.C in Table 6.3): μελάγχρως, ὁμόπτερος, ὑψαύχην; and it contains a further 25 such compounds (omitting those in which -ικός (see pp. 118 f.) is added to a stem already compound). These are:

(a) unique to the Myth: ἀεικίνητος, γλαυκόμματος, ἱππόμορφος, κρατεραύχην, νεοτελής, πτερώνυμος, σιμοπρόσωπος.

(b) elsewhere in Plato: εὐήνιος, εὐπειθής, θεοειδής, ὁλόκληρος, χιλι-ετής.

(c) first in Aristotle or Theophrastus among Attic prose authors: ἀρτιτελής, βραχυτράχηλος, μελανόμματος, ὁμόζυξ. Cf. p. 113.

(d) in other Attic prose authors: δύσκολος, εὐδαίμων, εὐσχήμων, ἰσόθεος, ἰσόρροπος, φιλόκαλος, φιλόπονος, φιλόσοφος, φιλότιμος.

The total of 29 out of 176 adjective-lexemes in the Myth, i.e. 16½%, puts the Myth on the level of the Euripides sample in Table 6.3. In 253 DE we have a block of seven compounds in six lines of text, a phenomenon not found elsewhere in prose. πτερώνυμος is peculiarly daring; as a one-word citation from a lost author it would baffle us, but the preceding lines, in which it is declared (in verse) that the gods call Eros Πτέρως, shows why τοῦ πτερωνύμου means τοῦ Ἔρωτος.

The compound adjectives in the other three texts chosen for comparison with the Myth are fewer: *Rep.* 6/118 = 5%; *Mem.* 9/139 = 6%; *Isoc.* 3/115 = 3%. Some of them are attested elsewhere in Attic prose (ἀξιοκοινώνητος, μισόδημος) and even commonplace (ἀγροῖκος, αὐτάρκης, θεοφιλής, λυσιτελής, μεγαλοπρεπής, φιλάνθρωπος, φιλότιμος); the exceptions are Isocrates' θεοποίητος (see p. 103) and in Xenophon ἀξιοθαύμαστος, ἐρασιχρήματος, θερμουργός, and ῥιψοκίνδυνος.

These data suffice to show why Plato should say ὀνόμασιν . . . ποιητικοῖς τισιν . . . εἰρῆσθαι; and there are other ingredients which contribute to its poetic character, notably its predominant rhythms (cf. p. 169), little nudges such as 250 C ἀπαθὴς κακῶν[21] 'untouched by ills' and 254 C θάμβος 'amazement', and its choices of poetic alternatives, e.g. λήγειν 'cease' five times (and only seventeen times in all the rest of Plato), and οὔποτε/μήποτε three times, with no οὐδέποτε/

---

[21] Cf. KG i. 401 f., Bruhn 28; the phrase ἀπαθὴς κακῶν occurs several times in Herodotus.

μηδέποτε, a reversal of the ratio in Plato as a whole.[22] The problem is to explain the occurrence of apparently poetic ingredients in the samples from the *Republic* and the *Memorabilia*.

The orators on occasion quote extensively from poetry, with ponderously didactic purpose, and Plato not only quotes freely but sometimes composes a couple of verses himself (*Smp.* 197 C, *Phdr.* 252 B). No problem there about what is poetic and what is not; but as well as partial quotation which is easily recognizable as such, there is partial quotation which is not so recognizable, and varying degrees of allusion.

In Hdt. vii. 159, when Gelon of Syracuse, asked for help against the Persians, has demanded supreme command of all the Greek forces, the Spartan envoy Suagros begins his reply with an exclamation:

ἦ κε μέγ᾽ οἰμώξειε ὁ Πελοπίδης Ἀγαμέμνων πυθόμενος Σπαρτιήτας τὴν ἡγεμονίην ἀπαραιρῆσθαι ὑπὸ Γέλωνος καὶ Συρακοσίων.

Oh! How Agamemnon, grandson of Pelops, would groan to hear that the Spartiates have been robbed of their hegemony by Gelon and the Syracusans!

This is an adaptation of *Il.* vii. 125:

ἦ κε μέγ᾽ οἰμώξειε γέρων ἱππηλάτα Πηλεύς . . .

Oh! How old Peleus, the great horseman, would groan . . .!

But the rhythm of the dactylic hexameter is adopted only for the first three feet. In Pl. *Rep.* 363 D, where Adeimantus is speaking of the poets' assurance that virtue is rewarded by the gods, he says

παῖδας γὰρ παίδων φασὶ καὶ γένος κατόπισθεν λείπεσθαι τοῦ ὁσίου καὶ εὐόρκου.

For they say that the children's children of the man who is pious and abides by his oath survive, and the family after them.

παῖδας γὰρ παίδων sounds like the first half of a pentameter in didactic elegiacs, and the same is true of 366 A, on the divine punishment of sin:

---

[22] Cf. Dover (1987) 22. It may be also that 253 D λευκὸς ἰδεῖν is modelled on the epic ἰδέσθαι following an adjective and (e.g.) Tyrt. 10. 29 θηητὸς ἰδεῖν (cf. KG ii. 15, *GG* ii. 384 f.), because in other prose instances ἰδεῖν is meaningful (e.g. Pl. *Rep.* 474 E ἀνδρικοὺς ἰδεῖν, 615 E ἄγριοι ἰδεῖν, Xen. *Eq.* 10. 17 ἅμα ἡδύν τε καὶ γοργὸν ἰδεῖν), whereas with 'white' it is pleonastic.

ἀλλὰ γὰρ ἐν Ἅιδου δίκην δώσομεν ὧν ἂν ἐνθάδε ἀδικήσωμεν, ἢ αὐτοὶ ἢ παῖδες παίδων.

But (it is said) we shall pay a penalty in the underworld for the wrongs we have committed—either we ourselves, or our children's children.

These are echoes of Solon 12. 31 f.:

> ἀναίτιοι ἔργα τίνουσιν
> ἢ παῖδες τούτων ἢ γένος ἐξοπίσω

The penalty for their deeds is paid by the blameless, either their children or their family after them,

and of Tyrtaeus 12. 29 f.:

> καὶ τύμβος καὶ παῖδες ἐν ἀνθρώποις ἀρίσημοι
> καὶ παίδων παῖδες καὶ γένος ἐξοπίσω.

His tomb and his children are famous, and his children's children and his descendants afterwards.

Yet in 363 D the rhythm is broken with φασί, and the hemiepes καὶ γένος ἐξοπίσω avoided; Plato could have created more obvious rhythm by inserting the article, as might have been expected in prose, and writing *καὶ τὸ γένος κατόπισθεν, but gave poetic language priority over poetic rhythm. So too Alcibiades in *Smp.* 214 B, inspired by drunken bonhomie, hails Eryximachus with a quotation of *Il.* xi. 154:

> ἰητρὸς γὰρ ἀνὴρ πολλῶν ἀντάξιος ἄλλων

For a doctor is worth a host of other men,

but when Plato wishes to praise informers in similar terms (*Lg.* 730 D) he breaks the rhythm by substituting ἑτέρων for ἄλλων:

ὁ μὲν γὰρ ἑνός, ὁ δὲ πολλῶν ἀντάξιος ἑτέρων, μηνύων τὴν τῶν ἄλλων τοῖς ἄρχουσιν ἀδικίαν[23]

That man is worth (just) one, but this one is worth a host of others, because he gives information to the magistrates about the wrongdoing of the rest.

In the case of *Rep.* 366 A:

ἄδικοι δὲ κερδανοῦμέν τε καὶ λισσόμενοι ὑπερβαίνοντες καὶ ἁμαρτάνοντες, πείθοντες αὐτοὺς ἀζήμιοι ἀπαλλάξομεν.

---

[23] I doubt whether the choice of ἑτέρων was determined by the need to use τῶν ἄλλων in the following phrase, because τῶν πολιτῶν 'his fellow-citizens' would have been a possible alternative to τῶν ἄλλων.

As wrongdoers we shall gain, and by entreating ⟨the gods⟩ when we transgress and err we shall persuade ⟨them⟩ and so escape scot-free from punishment,

λισσόμενοι and ὑπερβαίνοντες καὶ ἁμαρτάνοντες almost justify inverted commas, because the passage comes close on a quotation (364 DE) of *Il.* ix. 499–501, ending:

καὶ τοὺς μέν . . .
. . . παρατρωπῶσ᾽ ἄνθρωποι
λισσόμενοι, ὅτε κέν τις ὑπερβήῃ καὶ ἁμάρτῃ.

And . . . people avert their (sc. the gods') anger by entreaty, when someone has transgressed and erred.

Sometimes the choice of a poetic lexeme may be determined by the language of the immediate context. So in *Phdr.* 252 E, where it is said that a man whose soul, before its union with the body, was a follower in the train of Zeus will look for an object of love whose soul is δῖος, the adjective is dictated by the association of Δι- with δῖος. The use of δαιμονᾶν in Xen. *Mem.* i. 1. 9 is not dissimilar:

Socrates δαιμονᾶν ἔφη those who think that there is nothing δαιμόνιον [in the determination of one's future] . . . and he said [the same] of those who consult the gods on (sc. trivial and obvious) matters which the gods remitted to human understanding and decision.

Whether the sarcasm is Socrates' or Xenophon's own, the point is the same: not to understand τὰ δαιμόνια is itself δαιμονᾶν (without the echo which Xenophon's point requires, we might have expected μαίνεσθαι (cf. i. 1. 13), παραφρονεῖν, or παρανοεῖν).

In two cases contained in our samples we can see how the choice of poetic vocabulary is determined not by the wording of the context but by its substance. So in *Mem.* i. 3. 7:

He said with biting humour that Circe made (sc. men into) pigs by feasting them on abundant fare of that kind, but that Odysseus, through the ὑποθημοσύνη of Hermes, and because he was himself a continent man . . ., for those reasons was not turned into a pig.

ὑποθημοσύνη, 'prompting', is a thoroughly epic word (*Od.* xvi. 233), but happens not to occur in Homer's account of Hermes' advice to Odysseus; Xenophon thought it appropriate in alluding to a Homeric incident. Plato in *Rep.* 364 E takes the principle a stage further when he makes Adeimantus speak of a 'ὅμαδος of books by

Musaeus and Orpheus' on the afterlife. Again, an epic word, here delectably appropriate, because the poetry attributed to Musaeus and Orpheus was in epic metre and language, and ὅμαδος suggests a turmoil of books all clamouring for attention and bemusing the Athenian anxious to do the right thing for the future of his soul.

A touch of poetry may also invest one's words with an aura of religious solemnity and the authority of tradition.[24] This can be illustrated from the Plataeans' appeal to the Spartans in Thuc. iii. 54–9, a speech designed to implant the greatest πάθος. In 58. 5 the speaker says:

ἱερά τε θεῶν οἷς εὐξάμενοι Μῆδων ἐκράτησαν ἐρημοῦτε καὶ θυσίας τὰς πατρίους τῶν ἐσσαμένων καὶ κτισάντων ἀφαιρήσεσθε.

You are making a desert of the sanctuaries of the gods to whom the Greeks prayed before they defeated the Persians; and you will be taking away the ancestral sacrifices from those who founded and established them,

and in 59. 2:

ἱκέται γιγνόμεθα ὑμῶν τῶν πατρῴων τάφων καὶ ἐπικαλούμεθα τοὺς κεκμηκότας μὴ γενέσθαι ὑπὸ Θηβαίοις.

We are suppliants at the tombs of your fathers, and we call upon the dead not to let us come under the power of Thebes.

ἔσσασθαι (=Attic ἱδρύσασθαι) occurs in Pindar three times, but also in documents of several areas other than Attica. Given the absence of any sign elsewhere that Thucydides seasoned his speeches with the dialects of his different speakers, it is improbable that he made his Plataean say ἐσσαμένων because he believed it to be a Plataean word; it should be assumed to be affective, emphasizing the continuity of the sanctuaries with their heroic past. κάμνειν is not uncommon in Thucydides in the sense 'tire', and its perfective κεκμηκέναι (e.g. vi. 34. 5) is 'be exhausted'; in poetry οἱ κάμνοντες or οἱ κεκμηκότες are 'the dead', a usage unknown to the orators (even at their most sentimental) but revived in Pl. *Lg.* 718 A, 927 B, Arist. *EN* 1101^{a}35, with reference to the souls of the dead as sentient beings.[25]

However, we cannot expect to explain everything. For instance, Hdt. vi. 11. 1, on the gathering of the Ionians before the battle of Lade:

---

[24] Verdenius 25–37.
[25] There is a variant κεκμηῶτας in the text of Thucydides, an instance of the accidental intrusion of epic forms in the transmission of prose texts.

μετὰ δὲ τῶν Ἰώνων συλλεχθέντων ἐς τὴν Λάδην ἐγίνοντο ἀγοραί, καὶ δή κού
σφι καὶ ἄλλοι ἠγορόωντο, ἐν δὲ δὴ καὶ ὁ Φωκαιεὺς στρατηγὸς Διονύσιος λέγων
τάδε.

After that, the Ionians assembled at Lade, and discussions were held.
Among the many who spoke, Dionysius, the Phocaean commander, said . . .

appears to be modelled on *Il*. iv. 1:

οἱ δὲ θεοὶ πὰρ Ζηνὶ καθήμενοι ἠγορόωντο,

since ἀγορᾶσθαι occurs here only in Herodotus, and ἀγορά in the
sense 'assembly for public debate' is epic; everywhere else in Herodotus it is 'city centre' or 'market'. Why did Herodotus introduce
a reminiscence of *this* verse in *that* context? (Contrast viii. 49. 1 ὡς
δὲ ἐς τὴν Σαλαμῖνα συνῆλθον οἱ στρατηγοί . . ., ἐβουλεύοντο.)[26]

Similar questions press upon us throughout our reading of Xenophon. He was certainly willing to admit regional dialect as a contribution to vivid characterization, for two of his Spartan speakers
use the Doric τελέθειν instead of εἶναι/γίγνεσθαι (*An*. iii. 2. 3, *HG* vi.
6. 36).[27] There are a great many items in his vocabulary which are
alien to the rest of fourth-century Attic prose, and the assignment
of each item to its source in a region or a literary genre is rendered
impracticable by the paucity of our information on dialects. It is
unrealistic to imagine that in consequence of his travels Xenophon
was mixed-up and could not remember what was decent Attic and
what was not; acquaintance with many varieties of a language is
as likely to sharpen the ear for differences as to blunt it, especially
in so articulate a writer. The literature available (of which we have
only a fraction) is likely to have provided Xenophon with a much
more attractive array of models than regional dialects. We must
also take proper account of his own creativity, and when it comes
to 'attractiveness', the features of a lexeme which cause a particular
writer at a particular moment to *relish* it,[28] it is imprudent to attempt explanation. Moreover, we must allow, in Xenophon or any
other writer, for creative zest in the construction of new lexemes.

[26] And it is closely followed (11. 2) by the epic phrase ἐπὶ ξυροῦ ἀκμῆς (*Il*. x. 173).
[27] Cf. Gauthier 27, Dover (1987) 19. Gauthier classifies much of Xenophon's
vocabulary as Doric (22–47), Doric+Ionic (48–58), and Ionic (59–5). On φάσθαι
(Gauthier 65) cf. Ch. 5 n. 61.
[28] Cf. Winterson 172, 'Eating words and listening to them rumbling in the gut
is how a writer learns the acid and alkali of language.' Most of those who write
anything recognize the truth of that, and the fact that we cannot listen to a dead
writer's gut does not mean that it did not rumble.

As it happens, there are four interesting cases in our sample from *Mem.* i.

Mem. i. 2. 5:

ἀλλ' οὐ μὴν θρυπτικός γε οὐδὲ ἀλαζονικὸς ἦν οὔτ' ἀμπεχόνῃ οὔθ' ὑποδέσει οὔτε τῇ ἄλλῃ διαίτῃ· οὐ μὴν οὐδ' ἐρασιχρημάτους γε τοὺς συνόντας ἐποίει.

He was not fastidious or pretentious in his clothing or footwear or lifestyle in general; nor indeed did he make those who associated with him ἐρασιχρήματοι.

Mem. i. 3. 9:

"οὐ σὺ Κριτόβουλον ἐνόμιζες εἶναι τῶν σωφρονικῶν ἀνθρώπων μᾶλλον ἢ τῶν θρασέων καὶ τῶν προνοητικῶν μᾶλλον ἢ τῶν ἀνοήτων τε καὶ ῥιψοκινδύνων;" "πάνυ μὲν οὖν" ἔφη ὁ Ξενοφῶν. "νῦν τοίνυν νόμιζε αὐτὸν θερμουργότατον εἶναι καὶ λεωργότατον. οὗτος κἂν εἰς μαχαίρας κυβιστήσειε κἂν εἰς πῦρ ἅλοιτο."

'Didn't you think that Critobulus was one of the sensible people, not rash? One of those who think ahead, not those who can't think and are reckless of danger (ῥιψοκίνδυνος)?' 'Yes, indeed,' said Xenophon. 'Well, now you must think of him as completely hot-headed (θερμουργότατος), a man who'll do *anything* (λεωργότατος). That man would somersault on swords and jump into fire!'

The poetic flavour of ἐρασιχρήματος is unmistakable, because although 'Erasistratos' is a familiar Athenian proper name, the only two recorded lexemes beginning with ἐρασι- are Ibycus *PMG* 303 (Κασσάνδραν) ἐρασιπλόκαμον—so too Pi. *Py.* 4. 135 (Τυροῦς) ἐρασιπλοκάμου—and Pi. *Ol.* 14. 16 (Θαλία τε) ἐρασίμολπε. Neither φιλοχρήματος nor φιλάργυρος would have done, for a φιλοχρήματος may be a skinflint and a φιλάργυρος a robber (*Mem.* iii. 1. 10) or swindler (iii. 13. 4); cf. φιλ- in *Oec.* 20. 27–9. Xenophon wanted to describe people whose outward manifestation of wealth makes the beholder say, 'How gorgeous!',[29] and ἐρασιχρήματος was a very discriminating invention. θερμουργός occurs in a concentration of three unusual terms. In Ar. *Pl.* 415 Poverty, incensed with Chremylus and Blepsidemus for their plan to restore Wealth his eyesight, cries ὦ θερμὸν ἔργον κἀνόσιον καὶ παράνομον . . . τολμῶντε δρᾶν, 'O you who are venturing on a rash, unholy, illegal deed!' Ar. *Vesp.* 918 puns on the literal and metaphorical senses of θερμός; the latter appears in tragedy, but in Attic prose only in the *Tetralogies* (Ant. ii. α. 7, δ. 5). θερμουργός is modelled on πανοῦργος and κακοῦργος, though less deroga-

[29] Cf. Williger 6 n. 2 on ἐρασιπλόκαμος, against Debrunner 47.

tory than the former and much less so than the latter. What exactly the resonance of the poetic λεωργός was to Xenophon is uncertain.

From the very beginnings of Greek literature the composition of new lexemes and the combination of prosaic and poetic ingredients in the same context amounted to a distinctive art-form. Composition in particular was employed for a very wide range of purposes: it could be sonorous and impressive, as in the epithets of heroes and deities, or designed to express anger and hostility, as in *Il*. iii. 39, where Hector inveighs against Paris,

$$Δύσπαρι, εἶδος ἄριστε, γυναιμανὲς ἠπεροπευτά κτλ.$$

or for jocular and shaming ridicule, as when Solon 2. 4 envisages that his fellow-citizens will be mocked as Σαλαμιναφέται because they have 'let Salamis go'.[30] The vein of ridicule, with greatly varying degrees of hostility, is richly exploited in Old Comedy, e.g. in *Pax* 788–90~810–13, a total of nine novel compounds out of sixteen mobile tokens. When in *Nu*. 101 Strepsiades hesitatingly unrolls μεριμνοφροντισταί 'thinkers-about-problems' as a description of Socrates and his school, we are meant to laugh not so much *at* Socrates as *with* the author, admiringly. Cleverness seems to have played a part in the generation of multiple compounds[31] which we find in Comedy, e.g. *Nu*. 332 σφραγιδονυχαργοκομῆται, in which 'seal', 'fingernail', 'idle', and 'long-haired' are combined, and in monodic poetry such as the *Persians* of Timotheus, a style parodied in Ar. *Ra*. 1336*a* μελανονεκνείμων 'clad in the dark raiment of death'. This fashion does not seem to have caught on in prose, but there is one example in Gorgias (B 15): πτωχομουσοκόλακες 'parasites who beg in return for their poetry' (?).

B. TECHNICAL LANGUAGE AND LEXICAL INNOVATION

No less than ten of the compound adjectives in the *Phaedrus* Myth are concentrated in a description (253 DE) of the bodily characteristics of the two horses, one obedient and the other hybristic, which draw the chariot of the soul. We might expect to find some, at least, of these lexemes in Xenophon's chapter (*Eq*. 1) on the qualities to be looked for in the purchase of a horse, and there are in fact

[30] Wilamowitz 307 n. rightly observes the antiquity of this kind of compound, e.g. προδωσέταιρος in the skolion *PMG* 907. 1, but is hardly justified in designating it 'Attic'.
[31] Debrunner 80 rightly emphasizes the role of comedy.

two instructive points of contact between the two lists. The good horse drawing the chariot is ὑψαύχην 'holding its neck high', and in *Eq.* 10. 13 there is a reference to the ὑψηλαυχενία of a horse, a substantive which, in the absence of any other noun in -αυχενία on which it could have been modelled, presupposes *ὑψηλαύχην. In epic, lyric, and tragedy there are forty lexemes formed with ὑψ(ι), including ὑψαύχην (of a pine-tree) in Eur. *Ba.* 1061. ὑψηλο- appears in poetry first in [Aesch.] *Pr.* 4 f. πέτραις ὑψηλοκρήμνοις and Eur. *IA* 919 ὑψηλόφρων . . . θυμός. Except in *Phdr.* 253 D, prose has ὑψηλο-: Pl. *Rep.* 545 E ὑψηλολογουμένας, 550 B ὑψηλόφρων τε καὶ φιλότιμος ἀνήρ, *Phdr.* 270 A τό . . . ὑψηλόνουν τοῦτο. It seems that Plato has taken a term from the horse-fair and slightly adjusted it to give it a touch of poetry. A similar adaptation appears in the fact that the chari-oteer's two horses are respectively μελανόμματος 'black-eyed' and γλαυκόμματος 'grey-eyed', while Xen. *Eq.* 1. 9 describes a horse with sunken eyes as κοιλόφθαλμος. ὄμμα immensely prevails over ὀφθαλμός in tragedy (*c.*300:40), whereas the ratio in prose is *c.*60:100; the Hippocratic corpus contains compounds with -όφθαλμος (μελαν-, πλατυ-, πολυ-) but not with -όμματος; and all eleven examples of ὄμμα in Aristophanes are in lyrics or paratragedy.[32] Here again Plato in the Myth has transformed 'technical' compounds into 'poetic' compounds.

There are of course other compounds in *Eq.* appropriate to its subject, e.g. 1. 3 εὔπους 'well formed in the feet',[33] 1. 2 κακόπους 'badly formed . . .' (also of a horse in *Mem.* iii. 3. 4), and indeed inappropriate to any other subject, such as 1. 9 ἑτερόγναθος 'hard-mouthed on one side'. A comparable set of terms is used of hounds in [Xen.] *Cyn.* 3. 2 f., e.g. εὔπους, ἄπους = κακόπους, ἄρρις 'bad at pick-ing up the scent' (εὔρις, of a hound, is used in a simile in Soph. *Aj.* 8 and Aesch. *Ag.* 1093). ἄπους in its 'literal' sense (i.e. the sense we expect from analysis of its components) 'footless' is unremarkable; fishes, after all, are footless, and cf. Pl. *Phdr.* 264 C μήτε ἀκέφαλον . . . μήτε ἄπουν. But ἄπους = κακόπους is unlikely to be required except in referring to horses, hounds, or beasts of burden, and may rea-sonably be regarded as a 'technical term'; indeed, Arist. *Hist. An.*

---

[32] Aristotle appears (see especially *Hist. An.* 494^{b}12–15, 533^{a}4–10) simply to ring the changes on ὄμμα and ὀφθαλμός for the sake of variation.

[33] It is an epithet of Persephone in Callim. fr. 302. 2. LSJ translates it 'fleet of foot', but Pfeiffer ad loc. points out that Persephone is τανύσφυρος in *H. Cer.* 77. In *Eq.* 1. 3 there is no doubt at all that the formation of the foot is the point.

487ᵇ24 κακόποδες, οἵ . . . ἄποδες καλοῦνται (cf. *Met.* 1022ᵇ35 f., *An.* 422ᵃ28 f.) suggests that; on other instances of καλεῖσθαι see below.

'Technical term' is not a wholly satisfactory category of language, because it leaves out of account, as currently used, the fact that everyone belongs to a minority in some respects, and a very great number of minorities (e.g. drug-pushers, piano-tuners) use lexemes and phrases which are unlikely to be understood correctly by people outside the minority in question. I propose, however, to extend 'technical language' and 'technical terms' to cover all special languages used by minorities. The earliest allusions to technical language in Greek[34] are Anon. *Ath.* 1. 19 ὀνόματα μαθεῖν τὰ ἐν τῇ ναυτικῇ and Ar. *Nu.* 636–56, where Strepsiades totally misunderstands terms used by Socrates to denote rhythms and metres; cf. Pl. *Rep.* 400 B, where Plato's Socrates says 'I think I've heard Damon—though it wasn't very clear to me—speaking of a "composite enoplian" and of "dactyl" and "hexameter" too . . .'. The technical language of medicine is recognized in Thucydides' allusion (ii. 49. 3) to 'all the evacuations of bile which have been named by doctors'.

In this field four categories of phenomena need to be distinguished:

1. Lexemes which have no reference at all outside a specialized field, e.g. 'palimpsest', 'neutrino'. Although explicable by paraphrases of varying length, they have no synonyms in the language of the majority.

2. Lexemes which do have synonyms, e.g. 'tibia' = 'shin-bone', 'uterus' = 'womb'. From this category, in the course of time, many lexemes move into majority usage, e.g. 'diarrhoea'.

3. Lexemes which have different denotations in majority usage and in one or more specialized areas, e.g. 'induce' in ordinary language (= 'persuade', 'bribe', 'lure', ~'inducement') or in obstetrics (~'induction'), and indeed 'induction' in logic (~'inductive') or in churches and universities (~'induct').

4. Lexemes which become recognizable as technical because of the consistency with which they are used. The medical profession usually speaks of 'severe' pain rather than of 'ghastly' or '****** awful' pain. An example which straddles categories (3) and (4) is the

---

[34] Ar. fr. 205 (from *Banqueters*) is earlier (428/7), but its target seems to be more the general 'abnormality' of the language of political speakers and rhetoricians than particular features of that language.

distinction between 'descending' and 'going down', which is a great deal more important to an airline pilot than it is to a lift-operator.

In all categories it is essential that before we label any phenomenon 'technical' we ask ourselves 'how else could it be expressed?'. Neglect of this principle can lead to such absurdities as listing (e.g.) 'thumb' and 'liver' among 'anatomical terms', as if they showed the writer to have had some medical training.[35] It is a useful indication of technical status when the writer uses some part of καλεῖν, e.g. Diogenes of Apollonia DK 64 B 6 (p. 63. 8–11) 'the two largest veins . . . and one of them is called σπληνῖτις and the other ἡπατῖτις' and p. 65. 11, of certain other veins, 'and these are called σπερματίτιδες'. The first two of these three adjectives in -ῖτις occur also in the Hippocratic corpus.[36] Xen. *Mem.* i. 1. 11 'what is called κόσμος [(the universal) order] by the σοφισταί' is a little surprising, given the same use of κόσμος without apology by Isoc. iv. 179, xi. 12. A clearer case is Xen. *Eq.* 1. 3, 'High hooves have what is called the χελιδών [normally 'swallow'] far off the ground'; χελιδών is then used again without explanation in 4. 5 and 6. 2.

Medical language is perhaps the most easily parodied of all technical languages (Men. *Aspis* 444–64 is the best Greek example);[37] Thucydides' chapter (ii. 49) on the pathology of the Plague at Athens offers us something very different from parody, because it appears to incorporate a technical medical description in a historical narrative. In devoting so much space to that description (though not as much as to the social and moral consequences, 51. 4–53), Thucydides no doubt took as one of his models medical works of the type exemplified by the *Epidemics* and the *De Morbis*; he could hardly have done otherwise, since non-medical literature down to his time (and indeed afterwards), while regaling us with many stories of moral evil, tended to avoid what was aesthetically distasteful.[38] He created drama out of pathology, and in doing so inevitably used a vocabulary which we may regard as 'technical' in certain respects, though its coincidence with the vocabulary of Hip-

---

[35] It must be remembered that some anatomical terms will have been familiar from sacrifice and its related butchery; Eur. *El.* 841 f. νωτιαῖα . . . ἄρθρα 'joints of the spine' does not imply familiarity with (e.g.) Diog. Apoll. DK 64 B 6 (p. 63. 8 f.) ἄκανθα νωτιαία.

[36] Cf. Redard 102–4.

[37] Cf. W. G. Arnott in De Martino and Sommerstein 149–50, 163–4.

[38] Xen. *Mem.* i. 2. 54 is the only reference to sputum in non-medical literature, and there it is called σίαλον 'saliva' (cf. Pherecr. 73. 3, Arist. *Rhet.* 1407ᵃ9).

pocratic works is very limited,[39] being confined to 49. 7 ἐπεσήμαινε 'appeared (as a symptom)'; 49. 2 αἱματώδης 'bloody-looking' and 49. 6 ἕλκωσις 'formation of lesions' also happen not to appear in pre-Aristotelian Greek except in the Plague chapter and medical works.[40] In other respects Thucydides' vocabulary is distinctively non-medical; 49. 3, 6 ταλαιπωρία is 'suffering', not (as in medical works) 'physical exertion', and ibid. ἀσθένεια is 'weakness', not 'illness'. Moreover, φλεγμονή is the characteristic medical word for 'inflammation', but Thucydides uses (49. 2) φλόγωσις, in accordance with his love of words in -σις (cf. p. 49). It would be unjustifiable to treat 49. 3 βήξ 'cough' and 49. 5 φλύκταινα 'blister' as technical terms, because it is clear from comedy that they were the ordinary Attic terms for coughs and blisters. A more interesting point of resemblance to medical literature is the consistency (49. 2, 3, 4, 6) with which Thucydides uses ἰσχυρός. The lexeme is not in itself a medical technicality, as we see from (e.g.) Hdt. iii. 129. 1 f. 'sprained his ankle ἰσχυροτέρως', iv. 29 'ἰσχυρός cold spells', Pl. *Rep.* 388 E 'ἰσχυρός laughter', but the consistency is a gesture of acknowledgement towards existing pathological descriptions as a model.

The language of medicine is more fully attested in Greek literature than any other technical language, but, as Xenophon on horses, Pseudo-Xenophon on dogs, and Anon. *Ath.* on ships have served to remind us, there must have been as many special languages as there were specialized fields of practical and theoretical activity (not forgetting philosophy).[41] One of the most instructive texts in this respect is not a literary work at all, but a set of documentary inscriptions: *IG* i³ 474–9, the reports and accounts of the commission in charge of the building of the Erechtheion in the years 409–405. Here we find ourselves swimming in terms for parts of buildings, processes of fitting and carving, and related matters. It is interesting that many of these terms exemplify the types of word-formation which are just as characteristic of Attic tragedy

[39] Parry 156–71 is conclusive against the attempt of Page to show the technicality of Thucydides' description.

[40] Parry 166, 168 f. points out that both αἱματώδης and ἕλκωσις would be completely and immediately intelligible to a Greek ignorant of medicine, exemplifying as they do very familiar types of word-formation.

[41] In *Phd.* 79 A δύο εἴδη τῶν ὄντων 'two sorts of thing' Plato demotes εἶδος 'form' (as opposed to particulars) and εἶναι 'be' (as opposed to 'become') to everyday semantic level. I take it that in his 'technical' language the contrast between εἶναι and γίγνεσθαι is the contrast between the unchangeable and the changeable (cf. Code 54 f.).

from Aeschylus[42] onwards, e.g. 474. 10 ἄθετος 'not yet placed in position', 54 ἀκατάξεστος 'not filed smooth', 55 ἀρ(ρ)άβδωτος 'not fluted', 475. 261, 290 πρίστης 'sawyer', 292 τορνευτής 'turner', 476. 163 ὀπισθοφανής 'visible in the background'. Further examples are to be found in other documentary texts of the Classical period, e.g. *IG* ii² 244. 90 (337/6) ἄποτος 'watertight' ('not drinking' or 'undrinkable' in literature), *SEG* x. 394. 1 f. (s. v) ἐκ τοῦ ἀργυροκοπίου φυσητής 'bellows-man from the mint'. Similar formations occur in the language of administration, e.g. *IG* i³ 40. 10 ἀπρόσκλητος 'not in receipt of a summons', 84.16 f. ἀποδέκται, one of the boards of officials which handled payments and receipts.[43]

It is not that technological and administrative languages imitated poetry and literary prose, or that the learning process was the reverse, but simply that from the very beginning *all* genres of utterance in Greek exploited *in parallel* the creative potential of word-formation[44] and *also* interacted.

Although we may entertain a strong suspicion that a lexeme of unusual type attested just once in the Classical period was coined for the occasion by the author (cf. p. 111 on Xenophon's ἐρασιχρήματος), we possess so small a fraction of what once existed, and are so short of information on its chronology, that the mere fact that a lexeme is attested for the first time in such-and-such an author does not in itself tell us that the author coined it. Thucydides may have taken ἄγγελμα (vii. 74. 1) from Euripides (five instances, in four plays), or he and Euripides may have coined it independently, or it may have been widely current in both poetry and prose in the late fifth century and then edged out (though not for ever) by the long-standing ἀγγελία; we cannot know, and the discovery that a lexeme is 'first in Plato' or 'first in Xenophon' is of no stylistic interest.

Sometimes, though, we can discern evidence for fashions and tendencies in word-formation. Thuc. i. 70. 3 f. exhibits a curious concentration of nouns in -τής: τολμητής 'darer', κινδυνευτής 'risker', μελλητής 'hesitater', and ἀποδημητής 'goer abroad', four nouns of which only one (μελλητής Arist. *EN* 1124ᵇ24) recurs in the Classical period. Since the passage occurs in a contrast between the Athenian

[42] Cf. Kapsomenos 404–34 on -τος and 453–61 on -της, -τηρ, -τωρ. Hesiod's δώτης and ἀδώτης (*Op.* 355) take us back to an earlier time of word-formation.
[43] Cf. Dover (1987) 39 f.
[44] Hence e.g. παλιναίρετος in Pindar fr. 84 of buildings rebuilt after demolition, and of reconstituted iron in *IG* i³ 386. 131. On the variety of genres in which compound lexemes are created see Meyer *passim*, and Breitenbach on Euripidean lyric.

and the Spartan character (cf. p. 146), it could fairly be argued that 'they are (sc. by nature) riskers' is not quite synonymous with 'they take many risks', but that cannot be said of Antiphon v. 94 'Now you are acknowledgers (γνωρισταί) of the case, but then you will be assessors (δικασταί) of the witnesses; now, opiners (δοξασταί), but then, judges (κριταί) of the truth'; δικαστής and κριτής are, of course, very common lexemes, but γνωρισταί does not recur in the Classical period and δοξαστής only in Pl. *Tht.* 208 E (contrasted with ἐπιστήμων). A fondness for agent-nouns is similarly illustrated in Antiphon by ii. β. 2 ἐμοί . . . ἀνατροπεὺς τοῦ οἴκου ἐγένετο 'he was the overthrower of my house' and iii. β. 6 οὗτοι πράκτορες τῶν ἀκουσίων εἰσίν 'it is they who are the doers of involuntary acts' (there was a minor Athenian magistracy called πράκτορες, but πράκτωρ in the sense 'agent' or 'avenger' is tragic, and iii. β. 6 should probably be treated as poetic language).

There is one clue in documentary language to the growth of a phenomenon which became characteristic of the vocabulary of prose, perhaps the only type of lexeme which could be regarded as 'un-poetic'. *IG* i³ 138. 6, earlier than 434, refers to the ληξιαρχικὸν γραμματεῖον, the register of citizens eligible for appointment to office by lot, and in the Erechtheion accounts we find *IG* i³ 476. 123 τεκτονικόν, 180 f. ἀγαλματοποϊκόν, and 192 λιθουργικόν, designating the moneys available for the carpenters, sculptors, and stone-masons respectively; the usage continues in the fourth century, e.g. *IG* ii² 244. 31 τειχοποϊκά 'funds for wall-building'. In tragedy, however, -ικός is strikingly rare: only twelve such lexemes in the whole of Aeschylus, only one in the first 200 adjective-lexemes of Soph. *Phil.*, and none in the first 200 of Eur. *Orestes*. It does not occur in Heraclitus. The extant citations from Alcmaeon, Anaxagoras, Anaxarchus, the *Anonymus Iamblichi*, Diogenes of Apollonia, Ion of Chios, Critias, Melissus, Prodicus, Protagoras, Thrasymachus, and Zenon, with a total of 216 adjective-lexemes, provide only στρατιωτικός (Critias DK 88 B 34), εὐποιητικός (*Anon. Iambl.* p. 401. 29),[45] and three ethnics in Critias. Ethnics in -ικός appear early in the historians (Hecat. *FGrHist* 1 F 332 ὁ Ψυλλικὸς κόλπος) and are abundant in Herodotus (Ἑλληνικός, Δωρικός, Πελασγικός, etc.), but the first 200 adjective-lexemes in Herodotus (i. 1–84. 2) include only

---

[45] Cf. Ernst Fraenkel 209 f. and Chantraine (1933) 386; Debrunner 197 and Ammann 266 wrongly attribute the spread of -ικός to the 'Ionic sophists'.

two non-ethnics[46] in -ικός, and in the whole of Thucydides there
are only 34 (less than one-tenth of the total number in Plato). Attic
comedy, unlike serious poetry, readily accepted and exploited -ικός,
and one word in early comedy, ὡρικός 'attractive', 'sexy' (Crates
fr. 43, referring to a girl's breasts), being attested only in comedy
(Ar. *Ach.* 272, *Pl.* 963), was probably vulgar. Λακωνικοί as a noun,
'Spartans', is peculiar to comedy.[47]

It is plain from Ar. *Eq.* 1375–80, where 'young men in the scent-
market' are parodied, that the invention of new words in -ικός was
fashionable in the discussion of political and forensic oratory:

σοφός γ' ὁ Φαίαξ, δεξιῶς δ' οὐκ ἀπέθανεν.
συνερτικὸς γάρ ἐστι καὶ περαντικός
καὶ γνωμοτυπικὸς καὶ σαφὴς καὶ κρουστικός,
καταληπτικός τ' ἄριστα τοῦ θορυβητικοῦ.

In Sommerstein's translation:

Clever man, that Phaeax; ingenious, the way he escaped death! He's cohe-
sive and penetrative, productive of original phrases, clear and incisive, and
most excellently repressive of the vociferative.

The same fashion seems to be parodied in *Nu.* 1172 f. ἐξαρνητικὸς
κἀντιλογικός, and it is interesting to see that in serious literature -ικός
does have a tendency to occur in concentrations:[48] in Philolaus DK
44 B 11 three in one sentence (p. 411. 14 f.) and two, plus μουσική
as a noun, in another (p. 412. 6 f.); eight in one sentence in Xen.
Mem. i. 1. 7, and fifteen in Pl. *Phdr.* 248 c 8–E 3. The phenomenon
is perhaps generated by the classificatory character of the suffix;[49]
it is applied e.g. to subdivisions such as ἱππικόν 'cavalry', ξενικόν
'allied contingent', ναυτικόν 'fleet', and the principle of subdivision
is spectacularly employed in Plato's *Sophist*, where many new lexemes in -ική sc. τέχνη appear. Exposition of that kind is naturally
not a subject of poetry.

C. METAPHOR

Thucydides vi. 18. 4 represents Alcibiades as urging the assembly
to confirm the expedition against Syracuse ἵνα Πελοποννησίων τε

[46] Under the label 'ethnic' I include -ικός with reference to places, festivals, etc.
[47] LSJ s.v. Λακωνικός takes insufficient account of this usage.
[48] There is a similar concentration in Gorgias DK 82 B 3 (p. 280. 32–4, p. 282.
29 f.), but Sextus' fidelity to Gorgias' own terminology is questionable; the -ικός
lexemes are not in [Arist.] *MXG*.
[49] Ammann 259, 262 f.; cf. Ernst Fraenkel 212 f.

στορέσωμεν τὸ φρόνημα κτλ. 'so that we may lay flat the pride of the
Peloponnesians'. A scholion comments:

τῶν παρὰ Θουκυδίδῃ τροπικῶν ὀνομάτων τὸ σκληρότατον τοῦτό ἐστιν, ἀλλὰ κατ'
Ἀλκιβιάδην.

τροπικός here means 'metaphorical' (or 'figurative', which I use of
the genus of which metaphor is a species); Hermogenes 199. 4–
23 equates τροπή and μεταφορά (rejecting a narrower definition of
metaphor; see below),[50] and (248. 21–3) he applies σκληρός 'hard'
or 'harsh' to certain metaphors in Demosthenes.

Since στορ-/στρω- most often denotes creating a layer wider than
it is deep, covering something with such a layer, or flattening the
irregularities of a surface, encountering 'pride' as its object gives
the hearer a jolt. Such abnormal collocation, in which a verb has
an unusual subject, object, or adverb, or a noun an unusual epithet,
is what we and the ancients most commonly call a metaphor, and
it would seem to lend itself readily to statistical treatment: if we
find in a corpus of texts 903 examples of a given verb with one
kind of subject and only one in which it has a different kind of
subject, we may prima facie treat the odd one as metaphorical (de-
ferring scrutiny of the treacherous term 'kind'). For instance, on
the opening page of Stephen Crane, *The Red Badge of Courage* (a
self-indulgent work in respect of metaphor), we read:

The smoke from the fire at times neglected the clay chimney and wreathed
into the room, and this flimsy chimney of clay and sticks made endless
threats to set ablaze the whole establishment.

The reader is unlikely to have encountered neglectful smoke, and
although a chimney may 'threaten' to fall we don't speak of it as
'making threats'. Crane's two metaphors exemplify the definition
of metaphor which Hermogenes 199. 8 f. attributes to οἱ γραμ-
ματικοί, using of inanimates language appropriate to animates and
vice versa. Hermogenes himself (333. 16–335. 7) makes that distinction in a slightly different form, finding γλυκύτης in the implicit
attribution of an exercise of will or choice (προαιρετικόν τι) to what

---

[50] In Dion. i. 358. 14 f., 359. 23 f. τροπικὴ λέξις (or φράσις) is contrasted with κυρία,
and that agrees with Hermogenes' definition of τροπή as the use of ἀλλότρια ὀνόματα,
though elsewhere Dionysius implies by listing (i. 361. 5 f., ii. 137. 7 f.) that archaisms
and dialectal or poetic words are not τροπικὰ ὀνόματα. In [Longinus] 32. 2 f. μεταφορά
is plainly classed among τροπικαί (sc. λέξεις? cf. 32. 6), and his examples of τροπικαὶ
λέξεις are all metaphors. On the problems of τρόπος and σχῆμα see Russell (1964)
126–8.

in reality lacks that faculty (ἀπροαίρετα), and indeed the attribution to animals of emotions and purposes which he believes to be purely human (335. 8–22).

Personification, as defined by Hermogenes, plays a larger part in modern discussion of Greek metaphor than is warranted by difference between Greek and other languages, considering the readiness with which we say (e.g.) 'the situation compels/demands/ requires . . .', 'the schedule forbids/says/spells out . . .' (to say nothing of 'personification . . . plays a larger part' and 'is warranted by difference').[51] There is, however, one very significant difference in outlook between the Greeks of the archaic and classical periods and people like Hermogenes and ourselves:[52] a long-standing tendency to speak in personal terms of phenomena later classified as natural phenomena or abstractions.[53] The list of the offspring of Night and of Strife in Hes. *Th.* 211–32 amounts to a taxonomy of a very large area of human experience, and in *Il.* ix. 502–12 the physical appearance of Prayers is described vividly, while their operation and effect is that of prayers in interpersonal relations. To this tradition belong the sermons uttered by the Laws in Pl. *Crito* 50 A–54 D and the enticements and exhortations offered to Herakles by Virtue and Vice, which Xen. *Mem.* ii. 1. 21–34 took from Prodicus; and in the ephebic oath at Athens (Tod no. 204. 29 ff.) the invocation of 'boundary-stones, wheat, barley, vines, olive-trees, and fig-trees' as witnesses illustrates the readiness with which inanimates could be personified in a culture far removed from Hesiod's. Such passages should be regarded not simply as the novel and adventurous adoption of poetic conceits, but rather as the exploitation of a larger inheritance. So Heraclitus B 53 calls War 'father of all and king of all', and in Democritus B 76 misfortune (συμφορή) is the teacher (διδάσκαλος) of the foolish. So too in Thuc. iii. 82. 4 war is βίαιος διδάσκαλος 'a teacher by violence',[54] and the Syracusan speaker in vi. 41. 4 calls arms and equipment the things

---

[51] Radford 5 compares authors in respect of the number of non-personal subjects per Teubner page, the figures ranging from 1.43 (Sophocles) to 0.11 (Lysias), with Antiphon i–iv (1.19) and Thucydides' speeches (0.92) at the head of the list for prose.

[52] The scholia in the medieval MSS of Thucydides were probably for the most part composed in very late antiquity (Wilhelm Schmid I. v. 216).

[53] On this matter Lloyd (1966) is very important; see especially 192–202, 237, 299 f.; cf. Louis 165, and for personification in comedy Newiger *passim*.

[54] I prefer this oxymoron, given the common contrast between violence and rational persuasion, despite Gomme's argument (*HCT* ii. 373) for 'teacher *of* violence'.

in which ὁ πόλεμος⁵⁵ ἀγάλλεται 'which War exults in possessing' (elsewhere in prose ἀγάλλειν has personal subjects and objects and ἀγάλλεσθαι personal subjects; cf. however *Od.* v. 176, where ships enjoy (ἀγαλλόμεναι) a favourablẹ wind).⁵⁶

Identifying metaphors in the language of one's own time, nation, class, and culture is not difficult, thanks to the vast linguistic store which we carry within us. Identifying them in a past language is a very different matter, because the available evidence is exiguous in the extreme compared with what we need for statistical justification of our identification. To take Thuc. vi. 18. 4 as a case in point: as against more than 50 instances of στορ-/στρω- with an object which is a spatio-temporal continuum, there are just three other passages in which it takes other kinds of object, and one in which it is a plausible emendation. In descending order of physicality, they are: Eur. *HF* 365 f. Κενταύρων ποτὲ γένναν ἔστρωσεν (Reiske, 'laid low': ἔτρωσεν codd.)⁵⁷ τόξοις φονίοις; a Marathon epigram (Page, *Further Greek Epigrams*, pp. 230 f., from Lycurgus *Leocr.* 109) χρυσοφόρων Μήδων ἐστόρεσαν ('laid low') δύναμιν; Eur. *Hcld.* 702 λῆμα μὲν οὔπω στόρνυσι ('diminishes') χρόνος τὸ σόν; [Aesch.] *Pr.* 190 τὴν δ' ἀτέραμνον στορέσας ('abating') ὀργήν. All three tragic passages are in choral lyric.

And yet these data could be described without resource to the category 'metaphor'. We might say (with justification) that in poetry many lexemes (of which στορ-/στρω- is one example) are 'more polysemous' than in prose, or have a greater 'semantic stretch' or range, or that their 'multireferentiality' is greater.⁵⁸ One implication of that

---

⁵⁵ Modern editors, unlike ancient writers, are beset by the need to decide whether or not to print an initial capital.

⁵⁶ Plu. *Dem.* 2. 4 evidently recalls Thuc. vi. 41. 4: 'metaphor and rhythm καὶ τῶν ἄλλων οἷς ὁ λόγος ἀγάλλεται'.

⁵⁷ I have assumed synonymy of στορέσαι and στρῶσαι; cf. Eur. *Cy.* 387 ἔστρωσεν (Pierson: ἔστησεν cod.) εὐνήν~Ar. *Pax* 844 στόρνυ . . . λέχος; and I have heeded Silk's warning (30, 48) against the assumption that what can be said about the metaphorical use of a given lexeme can be said equally of its cognates (in the present case καταστρῶσαι and καταστορέσαι).

⁵⁸ 'Polysemy': Lyons (1977) 550–5, 566; 'semantic stretch': Lloyd (1987) 174 f. A similar question can be asked about technical language, in which a lexeme common in non-technical usage can be given a specialized denotation unintelligible to those outside the technical field, e.g. 'proud', used of a screw-head which is not flush with, or sunk into, the surface into which the screw is put. ἀτέραμνος is used six times of 'hard' water in Hp. *Aer.* (plus ἀτεραμνίη, p. 59. 2 Heiberg) and once of costive bowels (p. 58. 12), and in Aristotle and later Greek in various physical connections. It denotes hardness of heart in *Od.* xxiii. 167 and [Aesch.] *Pr.* 160. Which instances are metaphorical? (ἀτεράμων is plainly cognate.)

is that collocations which are well attested in poetry might strike
the hearer, if they occur in prose, more as an injection of poetic
colour than as an enterprising autonomous development of prose.
Moreover, since we know from acquaintance with our own language
that a collocation normal in one region can be abnormal (and ludi-
crous) in another,[59] the old problem of determining the sources of
Presocratic vocabulary—poetry or regional vernacular?—acquires
a new dimension: what was the semantic coverage of lexeme A in
region B at period C? For instance, Philolaus DK 44 B 11 says
(p. 412. 12) ψεῦδος δὲ οὐδαμῶς ἐς ἀριθμὸν ἐπιπνεῖ, lit. 'falsehood in
no way breathes into number' ('affects'? 'inspires'?). Highly metaphorical in Attic, but was it so in the Doric of Magna Graecia?
Similar doubts must arise over Democritus' use of κῆρες 'vicissi-
tudes' (DK 68 B 191, B 285) and ῥυσμοῦν (B 266), ῥυσμός (B 197;
cf. B 139 ἀμειψιρυσμεῖν). Such uncertainties do not invalidate *all* attempts to identify metaphors in early prose; they simply remind us
that every putative metaphor has to be scrutinized rather carefully,
and the consequences of scrutiny are not invariably negative. For
instance, Democritus B 11 distinguishes two kinds of γνώμη, one
γνησίη 'legitimate' and the other σκοτίη (lit.) 'hidden in darkness'.
γνήσιος is attested in several Greek dialects (including Attic) as a
designation of legitimate children; σκότιος in *Il.* vi. 24 refers to an
illegitimate child, and Euripides uses it (e.g. *Tro.* 44) of sexual relations out of wedlock. The probability that Democritus originated
the application of the antithesis to the formation of judgements is
reasonably high.

It would be wrong, however, to regard σκότιος itself as metaphorical simply because it means 'in darkness' as well as 'illegitimate'
and is formed from σκότος 'darkness'. 'Literal translation' is an indispensable term for a useful activity, but 'literal meaning', when
applied not to tokens in context but to lexemes abstracted from a
context, is best avoided, even though, unfortunately, we have no
concise term for 'denotation which, on the etymological evidence
at present available, would have been expected'. 'Real meaning'[60]
and 'true meaning' should never pass the lips of any serious student

---

[59] I have heard the Russian language described (by a young woman teacher, *c.*1980,
West Midlands, Baptist) as 'cheeky', because the accentual patterns of Russian nouns
often take the learner by surprise.

[60] Cf. Firth 8 f. Roschatt (e.g. 8–10, 29) overworks *eigentliche Bedeutung*, even saying that προπηλακίζειν 'really' means 'spatter with muck' (cf. Ronnet 173), although
it is attested only in the senses 'vilify', 'abuse', 'insult'.

of language, and even 'original meaning' requires the caveat that we cannot know the semantic range of a lexeme at a time earlier than that of its first attested occurrences. Etymological expectations and hypotheses about prehistoric semantics do not justify the identification of any usage as metaphorical. For instance, διασπείρειν occurs thirty-three times in Attic prose, but never with seeds as its object (how often does 'broadcast' in contemporary English denote, as it did in the eighteenth century, something one does with seeds?), and ὑποστέλλεσθαι seven times, but only once in connection with sails. It must be remembered that the second time a metaphor is used it is less metaphorical than it was the first time; as in a living creature, its birth is the first step to its death.

Or is it embalmed, ready for parade on appropriate occasions? That part of the semantic coverage of a given lexeme in poetry which exceeds the coverage common to poetry and prose could perhaps be called 'stock' or 'conventional' metaphor, a very different thing from the creation of a new and striking metaphor.[61] The case of ποιμήν is instructive. When it occurs without a dependent genitive the context nearly always shows that its referent is a man who drives and tends sheep; but with a genitive, the referent may be a commander, ruler, or organizer, as shown in Table 6.4.[62]

To insist on distinguishing here between 'normal' and 'abnormal' collocation on crude arithmetical grounds would be absurd, because 65 of the 68 instances of 'non-sheep, with dependent genitive' are tokens of the epic formula ποιμένα/-νι λαῶν (the remaining three are Aesch. *Su.* 767, Eur. *Su.* 674, *Pho.* 1140). It is inconceivable that the audience of a rhapsode gasped with admiration on hearing ποιμένα λαῶν for the two-hundredth time, and we may be tempted to classify it as a metaphor which is not just 'dead' but past the stage of putrefaction.[63] Yet Xenophon's Socrates thinks it worth expounding ('Just as the shepherd must ensure that the sheep are safe . . .'); the dictum that the great legislators of the past were 'herdsmen and shepherds of men' ([Pl.] *Minos* 321 C) comes at

[61] I agree with Stanford 84 that the term 'metaphor' is best restricted to 'conscious and deliberate' usage, i.e. artistic action; cf. Earp (1944) 94. Lloyd (1987) 172 mentions contemporary 'challenges' to the distinction between the metaphorical and the non-metaphorical—and I am mounting one or two (limited) challenges in this chapter—but the notion that all language is metaphorical displays ignorance of the experiential difference between trying to create a metaphor and not trying to.

[62] See Lloyd-Jones and Wilson 17 f. on Ajax' ποιμένες (Soph. *Aj.* 360).

[63] On the problem of 'dead' metaphor cf. Earp (1948) 93–6, 107 and Silk 27–56.

TABLE 6.4. *Use of* ποιμήν *in poetry and prose*

	Controlling sheep	Controlling other beings	
		With dependent genitive	Without dependent genitive
Poetry	32[a]	68	4[b]
Prose	31	1[c]	—

[a] Including 6 in Comedy.
[b] Aesch. *Ag.* 657, fr. 132c. 8, Soph. *Aj.* 360, Eur. *Su.* 191.
[c] Plus explicit quotation and exegesis of Homer in Xen. *Mem.* iii. 2. 1 and [Pl.] *Min.* 321 C 2.

the end of a long argument about law-making, which exploited the relationship between νόμος 'law' and νομεύς 'herdsman' and drew an analogy between the 'laws' made by the shepherd for his sheep and the laws made by legislators for 'the souls of men' (317 E–318 A); and *Plt.* 274 E 'the shepherd of the human flock in those days' refers back (εἴπομεν) to the simile (οἶον νομῆς θεῖοι) of 271 D, with an intermediate reminder in 274 B 'the god who owns (κεκτημένου) and herds (νέμοντος) us'. Here we may suspect that (as so often) there is a non-linguistic determinant of the data: in this case, the tradition of Homeric exegesis and the educational need to find wisdom in Homer's language.

The history of ποιμήν points to a further two important aspects of metaphor.

The first concerns the relation between metaphor and simile. Arist. *Rhet.* 1406[a]20–6 and 1410[b]17–20 regards them as essentially the same. Demetrius 80 recommends that when a metaphor seems 'risky' (κινδυνώδης) it can be made 'safer' (ἀσφαλέστερον)[64] by the insertion of ὥσπερ, and [Longinus] 32. 3 calls ὡσπερεί, οἱονεί, etc. μειλίγματα ('softening', 'toning down') of 'bold' metaphors. Stanford's assertion[65] that 'metaphor and simile are not generically related at all' is not easily reconciled with the ease with which 'like . . .' comes and goes, e.g. Thuc. iv. 73. 2 'they would get the credit of a victory ὥσπερ ἀκονιτί' ~ Dem. xix. 77 'so that he could subject everything to himself ἀκονιτί' ('without a fight' ~ κόνις 'dust'). There is, however, a hard grain of truth in Stanford's judgement: a simile

[64] He means 'less likely to produce an adverse reaction in a critical hearer'.
[65] Stanford 28; but cf. Silk 18 f. and Tarrant (1946) 29 on the merging of metaphor and simile.

informs us of an author's perception, but a metaphor makes us *work* to understand his meaning.

While ὥσπερ and οἷον signal 'simile', there are other usages which blur the boundary with metaphor. In Dem. i. 2

ὁ μὲν οὖν παρὼν καιρός . . . μόνον οὐχὶ λέγει φωνὴν ἀφιεὶς ὅτι κτλ.

This present crisis practically cries out and tells us . . .

'practically'/'virtually' is crucial as 'softening' the metaphor. τις, which often goes with οἷον or ὥσπερ/ὡς in similes (e.g. Aesch. *Ag.* 1194 τοξότης τις ὥς),[66] may also occur without them (e.g. Pl. *Hp. Ma.* 297 B ἐν πατρός τινος ἰδέᾳ εἶναι τοῦ καλοῦ τὸ ἀγαθόν) in contexts where an English-speaker would convey consciousness of metaphor by prosody and facial expression.[67] Also, in 'A καί B' one of the two terms may be a metaphor and the other an explanation of it, e.g. Democritus DK 68 B 280

ἔξεστιν οὐ πολλὰ τῶν σφετέρων ἀναλώσαντας παιδεῦσαί τε τοὺς παῖδας καὶ τεῖχός τε καὶ σωτηρίην περιβαλέσθαι τοῖς τε χρήμασι καὶ τοῖς σώμασιν αὐτῶν.

It is possible, without much expense of one's own, to educate one's children and put a wall around their persons and property and ⟨so ensure their⟩ security.

The metaphorical use of πηγή '(well-)spring' illustrates the difficulty of keeping metaphor and simile apart. Well established in poetry with non-physical referents (Pi. *P.* 4. 299,[68] Aesch. *Pe.* 743, *Se.* 584, Emped. DK 31 B 3. 2),[69] its metaphorical use in prose is handled circumspectly until we reach late Plato, where we encounter *Ti.* 85 D πηγὴ πάντων νοσημάτων, *Lg.* 808 D πηγὴ τοῦ φρονεῖν, 893 D τῶν θαυμαστῶν . . . πηγή, but with 'apologetic' τις in *Lg.* 690 D στάσεων πηγήν τινα and with both οἷον and τις in *Ti.* 79 D οἷον . . . πηγήν τινα . . . πυρός, *Lg.* 891 D οἷον πηγήν τινα ἀνοήτου δόξης. Compare *Phdr.* 245 C πηγὴ καὶ ἀρχὴ κινήσεως and Hp. *Flat.* 1. 4 ἀρχὴ καὶ πηγή . . . τῶν . . . κακῶν. In Xen. *Cyr.* vii. 2. 13 αἱ τέχναι . . . ἃς πηγάς φασι τῶν καλῶν εἶναι there is an ambivalence, ostensibly

---

[66] Cf. Italie 300.

[67] By no means all such cases involve metaphor (Silk 55), and the range of nuances conveyed by τις (cf. n. 20) frustrates precise classification. πως may also be used diffidently, e.g. Soph. *El.* 372 f.

[68] εὗρε παγὰν ἀμβροσίων ἐπέων is not just a one-token metaphor, but an image (cf. p. 127), evoking as it does the joy of coming upon water when one is seeking it.

[69] In Aesch. *Pe.* 238 ἀργύρου πηγή τις αὐτοῖς ἐστι, silver is not fluid, but note τις, which is likely here to mean 'virtually', 'somewhere', or 'I believe' rather than 'a certain'.

reporting common opinion but also hinting at some well-known (quasi-proverbial, and therefore legitimately poetic) dictum. Plato is famously the most metaphorical of all Greek prose authors,[70] and there is a hint in Aeschines ii. 21 that πηγή with a non-physical referent was stylistically pretentious by the standards of mid-fourth-century oratory: Demosthenes, he says, during the envoys' discussion of tactics before their meeting with Philip, πηγὰς δὴ λόγων ἀφθόνους ἐπηγγέλλετο 'professed ⟨to have⟩ inexhaustible springs of argument'. δή shows that Aeschines claims to be using Demosthenes' very words.[71] Whether that claim is true or false, passages in which orators criticize each other's style (e.g. Dem. xviii. 35, Aeschines iii. 166) are a valuable indication, like passages of comedy in which exaggeration is ridiculed or abnormal language deliberately misunderstood, of the linguistic constraints on political and forensic discourse.

The second important aspect of metaphor which emerges from the examination of ποιμήν is illustrated by the handling of ποιμήν and νομεύς in *Minos* and *Politicus*. Some metaphors are comprised in a single token, e.g. Eur. *Su.* 191 νεανίαν ἔχει σε ποιμέν' ἐσθλόν 'it (sc. Athens) has in you a good and vigorous ruler', continuing 'for lack of which many cities have perished, having no general (στρατηλάτης)'; cf. ibid. 879 f. 'a city getting a bad name through a bad helmsman' (κυβερνήτης, i.e. 'ruler'). Others are more extensive, e.g. Pi. *P.* 1. 86 ἀψευδεῖ πρὸς ἄκμονι χάλκευε γλῶσσαν 'forge your tongue on an anvil of truth' (*ἀψευδῆ χάλκευε γλῶσσαν would have been a one-token metaphor). And that image is expanded further in what follows:

> εἴ τι καὶ φλαῦρον παραιθύσσει, μέγα τοι φέρεται
> πὰρ σέθεν

(literally) If something even trivial flits aside (or 'flits past'), it is borne great from you,

i.e. 'even a spark (sc. from the forging) . . .'. When the Watchman in Aesch. *Ag.* 31–3 says that he will dance because his long watch for the beacon-fire has 'thrown a triple six', that is an extraordinary collocation, but the intervening line (32) τὰ δεσποτῶν γὰρ εὖ πεσόντα θήσομαι (literally) 'my master's has fallen well and I'll make its

---

[70] Lloyd (1987) 181, 185. Louis's rich catalogue of Plato's metaphors classifies them by what Silk (e.g. 9 f.) calls 'tenor', not by technique.
[71] Denniston 235.

move' has constructed the image of a board-game. In the Herald's description (ibid. 657) of the loss of ships ποιμένος κακοῦ στρόβῳ, literally 'by the whirling of a bad shepherd', the referent of 'bad shepherd' is the storm, but the construction of the image has begun two lines earlier, in the description of ships as κεροτυπούμεναι[72] 'violently butting each other'; a good shepherd keeps the peace and does not 'whirl' his flock round in a panic which generates aggression, but moves them purposefully to the right destination.

The construction of extended images[73] is virtually confined in prose to Plato, and there it is abundant. *Smp.* 209 E–210 A is a simple example. Diotima has expounded her doctrine of Eros to Socrates, and then she says

ταῦτα μὲν οὖν τὰ ἐρωτικὰ ἴσως . . . κἂν σὺ μυηθείης· τὰ δὲ τέλεα καὶ ἐποπτικά . . . οὐκ οἶδ᾽ εἰ οἷός τ᾽ ἂν εἴης.

In these (sc. mysteries) of Eros you too can perhaps be initiated; but I do not know whether you could be initiated in the complete revelation

(ἐπόπτης is one to whom the revelation of sacred objects is vouchsafed at the last stage of initiation). No explicit reference to initiation recurs in the rest of Diotima's speech,[74] but there are passages in which an image is sustained far longer. When the young Theaetetus in *Tht.* 148 E admits that he is in an intellectual quandary, Socrates says to him

ὠδίνεις γάρ . . . διὰ τὸ μὴ κενὸς ἀλλ᾽ ἐγκύμων εἶναι.

That is because you are suffering birth-pangs, for your womb is not empty;[75] you are pregnant.

ὠδίνειν is used of birth-pangs in comic dialogue (Ar. *Th.* 502, *Ec.* 129) and science (e.g. Arist. *HA* 584^{a}31, 586^{b}27), but also of other severe pains (first in *Od.* x. 415). Here in *Tht.* we are plainly meant to think of birth-pangs, as the continuation shows. The image of

[72] LSJ 'buffeted by the storm' misses the point.

[73] Hermogenes 199. 23–200. 13 evidently thinks that he has found an extended image, which he commends, in Dem. iii. 22. Unfortunately, he has misremembered a metaphor in Dem. iv. 49 as following on iii. 22, and it is virtually certain that he mistakenly believes προπέποται in iii. 22 to be making the same point as προπεπωκότες in xviii. 296. Extended images must, of course, be distinguished from a clot of metaphors such as Antiphanes 5. 12 Βρομιάδος δ᾽ ἰδρῶτα πηγῆς 'sweat of the Dionysiac spring' = 'wine', which is meant (as the reaction of the interlocutor shows) to be regarded as preposterous.

[74] Though it is sometimes imported by translators.

[75] Not 'barren', which would be στέριφος.

pregnancy and delivery by a midwife, once developed as an elaborate introduction (149 A–151 D) to an epistemological argument,
culminates in the birth and inspection of a hypothesis (160 E–161 A),
having surfaced halfway through (157 CD; cf. p. 125 on *Plt.* 274 B)
in a reference to the midwife's encouraging incantations.[76] At its
fullest development, an image of this kind can turn into a playlet.
In *Rep.* 432 B–E Socrates and his interlocutors have reached a point
at which they must identify and define moral integrity: 'Now, like
huntsmen, we must encircle the thicket and keep a sharp eye . . .
It's tangled and dark and hard to get through . . . Hey! I think I've
picked up a track . . . Our quarry's been thrashing around at our
feet all the time . . .'.

We should not expect to find imagery of that kind employed in
prose for any but didactic, argumentative, or expository purposes—
certainly not for narrative—and I would assign it to a stylistic level
(cf. pp. 3 f.) higher than the linguistic level.

Although modern students of Greek prose literature would probably agree that they are more often struck by metaphor in Demosthenes and Aeschines than in the other orators, and confident attempts have been made to assess its frequency in fourth-century
authors, precise quantification is hardly to be expected.[77] When a
lexeme is rare, it is safest to treat its semantic coverage simply as
that which is indicated by its tokens in context, and identification
of the originator of a new metaphor is as insecure as identification
of the creator of a new lexeme. Bold metaphors are memorable,
and attribution to their originators, such as we find in Arist. *Rhet.*
1411[a]1–[b]10, may sometimes have been correct, but the ancient critics are not necessarily reliable guides. Hermogenes 199. 4–13 gives
pride of place to Dem. iii. 22 προπέποται τῆς παραυτίκα χάριτος τὰ
τῆς πόλεως πράγματα 'Athenian concerns have been treated as gifts
in return for temporary popularity'. προπίνειν takes as its direct object (explicit or implicit) a drink, a drinking-vessel, or a gift which
accompanies the drinking of someone's health, in fourteen passages

---

[76] A metaphor which surfaces relies on the hearer's recollection of the previous
occasion on which it was used; thus in Stephen Crane 'staring at the red eyes across
the river' recalls, from thirteen pages earlier, the combined image 'One could see
across it the red, eyelike gleam of hostile camp-fires set in the low brows of distant
hills.'

[77] Ronnet 153 states confidently that there are 80 metaphors in Dem. xviii, plus 24
injures imagées. Wankel's index s.v. *Metaphern* lists 23; I question the metaphorical
status of at least half of them.

(first in Anacreon *PMG* 356(*a*). 2 f., and including Dem. xix. 128 and 139), but in seven, including Dem. iii. 22, xviii. 296, and *Ep.* 1. 10, it has a different kind of object and is translatable as 'give away (recklessly or too generously)', 'grant freely', or 'sacrifice'. The four non-Demosthenic instances of that denotation are Anacreon *PMG* 407, Aesch. fr. 131b, Anon. *PMG* 917(*b*). 2, and [Eur.] *Rhes.* 405, of which the first two are certainly much earlier than Demosthenes and the other two may well be.

Not only does a usage which appears prima facie to be a metaphor in a fourth-century prose author often turn out to be the adoption into prose of a semantic coverage long established in serious poetry; a contribution made by comedy to prose must also be acknowledged, and it is not always possible to decide whether to classify such a phenomenon as comic invention and fantasy or as well-established slang. Within comedy itself, slang is most likely to appear with anatomical and physiological reference (e.g. Ar. *Ra.* 545 ἐρέβινθος 'penis', elsewhere 'chick-pea'; cf. *Ach.* 801), and such usage is not to be expected in serious prose (cf. p. 61), but insult and invective are a different matter.[78] In Ar. *Nu.* 444–52 Strepsiades says 'I shan't care if they call me . . .'—and then follows a list of twenty-one opprobrious terms, of which some (e.g. μιαρός) are commonplace, one or two may be invented for the occasion by Aristophanes (e.g. γνωμῶν συγκολλητής; cf. pp. 112, 117), and some had previously been used in a complimentary sense (e.g. εὔγλωττος, εὑρησιεπής). At least one, κύρβις, is metaphorical in the sense that elsewhere it denotes an object on which laws were inscribed, but here a person who knows the law too well. At least one other, περίτριμμα δικῶν, recurs in Dem. xviii. 127, where Aeschines is vilified as περίτριμμ᾽ ἀγορᾶς. If περίτριμμα were known to us only as an item in a list of lexemes out of context, we might infer, on the analogy of περίβλημα and περιτείχισμα, that it denoted something worn away or rubbed all round, but we could hardly infer that we would encounter it in context only as an opprobrious term for a habitual litigant or politician. We have no evidence that it ever denoted anything else, a reminder that 'figurative' references may not always or necessarily be later in date than so-called 'literal meanings'.[79]

---

[78] Demosthenic invective has much in common with comedy (cf. Dover (1974) 30–3), e.g. xviii. 242 πίθηκος 'ape', 'monkey'.

[79] Cf. n. 60.

7

VARIETY

A. VOCABULARY

A PAPYRUS published in 1915 (*P.Oxy.* 1364) was recognized as containing part of Antiphon the Sophist's περὶ Ἀληθείας, thanks to Harpocration's attribution of the words τοὺς νόμους μεγάλους ἄγοι, which occur in col. i 18–20 of the papyrus, to that work. This was the first, and it remains the only, truly random sample of a fifth-century sophistic text to become available to us; what else we have of such works has survived because later authors chose to quote it for its content or form. Five years later *P.Oxy.* 1797 yielded a substantial piece of what is almost certainly the same work, though not written by the same copyist; and if it is not the same work, so much the better, because it would then be a second random sample of a sophistic treatise. In 1984 *P.Oxy.* 1797 was augmented by *P.Oxy.* 3647.

One passage of *P.Oxy.* 1797 (DK 87 B 44 col. i 1–ii 25) runs thus:

]τοῦ δικαίου [σπουδ]αίου δοκοῦν[τος τὸ] μαρτυρεῖν ἐν ἀλλήλοις τἀληθῆ [δίκαιο]ν νομίζεται [εἶναι] καὶ χρήσιμον [οὐδὲν] ἧττον εἰς [τὰ τῶν] ἀνθρώπων [ἐπιτ]ηδεύματα.

. . . right[1] being taken seriously, giving true evidence before one another is regarded as right and, equally, useful for human pursuits.

[τοῦτο] τοίνυν οὐ δί[καιος] ἔσται ὁ ποιῶν, [ἐπείπε]ρ τὸ μὴ ἀδικεῖν [μηδ]ένα μὴ ἀδι[κού]μενον αὐτὸν [δίκ]αιον.

Now, the man who does that will not be right, since right consists in not wronging anyone if one is not wronged oneself.

ἀνάγ[κη] γὰρ τὸν μαρτυ[ροῦ]ντα, κἂν ἀλη[θῆ μ]αρτυρῆι, ὅμως [ἄλλον] πως ἀδικεῖν [καὶ ἅμα] αὐτὸν ἂ[ν ἀδι]κεῖσθαι [ὕστερον, ὦ]ν ἕνε[κα εἶπεν, ἔ]ν ὧι διὰ τ[ὰ ὑπ᾿ αὐτ]οῦ μαρτ[υρηθέν]τα ἁλίσκ[ε]ται ὁ καταμαρτυρούμενος καὶ ἀπόλλυσιν ἢ χρήματα ἢ αὐτὸν [δ]ιὰ τοῦτον ὃν οὐδὲν [ἀ]δικεῖ·

for it is inevitable that he who gives evidence, even if his evidence is true,

---

[1] I have adopted 'right' and 'wrong' throughout for consistency; on the scope of ἀδικεῖν cf. Dover (1974) 181 f.

nevertheless wrongs another in some way and at the same time is likely himself to be wronged later because of what he said, in that because of the evidence he gave the man against whom he gave it is convicted and loses either money or his life, because of that man (sc. the witness) whom he (sc. the accused) does not wrong.

ἐν μὲν οὖν τούτωι τὸν κατα[μ]αρτυρούμενον [ἀ]δικεῖ, ὅτι οὐκ ἀδι[κο]ῦντα ἑαυτὸν ἀ[δι]κεῖ, αὐτὸς δὲ ἀδικεῖ[ται ὑ]πὸ τοῦ καταμαρ[τυρηθ]έντος, ὅτι μι[σεῖται] ὑπ' αὐτοῦ τὰ [ἀ]ληθῆ μαρτυρ[ή]σας·

Therein he (sc. the witness) wrongs the man against whom the evidence is given, because he wrongs one who does not wrong *him*, and is himself wronged by the man against whom evidence has been given, because he is hated by him, having borne witness to the truth;

καὶ οὐ μόν[ον] τῶι μίσει, ἀλλὰ [καὶ] ὅτι δεῖ αὐτὸν τὸ[ν] αἰῶνα πάντα φυλάττεσθαι τοῦτο[ν] οὗ κατεμαρτύρ[η]σεν,

and (sc. he is wronged) not only by that hatred, but also because he must be on his guard for the rest of his life against the man against whom he gave evidence,

ὡς ὑπάρχε[ι] γ' αὐτῶι ἐχθρὸς τοιο[ῦ]τος, οἷος καὶ λέγειν καὶ δρᾶν εἴ τι δύν[αι]το κακὸν αὐτόν.

since he has an enemy of such a kind as to do him whatever harm he can by word or deed.

καίτοι ταῦτα φαίνεται οὐ σμικρὰ τἀδικήματα, οὔτε ἃ αὐτὸς ἀδικεῖται οὔτε ἃ ἀδικεῖ·

Now it is clear that neither the wrongs done to him himself nor the wrongs he does are small wrongs;

οὐ γὰρ οἷόν τε ταῦτά τε δίκαια εἶναι καὶ τὸ μη[δ]ὲν ἀδικεῖν μη[δὲ] αὐτὸν ἀδικεῖσθαι, [ἀλ]λ' ἀνάγκη ἐστὶν [ἢ] τὰ ἕτερα αὐτῶν [δ]ίκαια εἶναι ἢ ἀμφότερα ἄδικα.

for it is impossible that both this procedure (sc. the giving of true evidence) should be right and (the principle of) neither wronging nor being oneself wronged should be right, but it must be the case either that one of the two is right or that both are wrong.

φαίνεται δὲ καὶ τὸ δικάζειν καὶ τὸ κρίνειν καὶ τὸ δια⟨ι⟩τᾶν ὅπως ἂν περαίνηται οὐ δίκαια ὄντα·

And it is clear that acting as juror or judge or arbitrating to decide an issue are not right;

τὸ γὰρ [ἄ]λλους ὠφελοῦν [ἄλλο]υς βλάπτει· ἐν δὲ [τού]τωι οἱ μὲν ὠφελούμενοι οὐκ ἀδικοῦ[νται, οἱ] δὲ βλαπτόμε[νοι ἀδικο]ῦνται[ι.

for that which benefits some harms others, and therein those who are benefited are not wronged but those who are harmed are wronged.

This text exhibits a stylistic feature which must appear singular to any reader accustomed to the Classical authors: the intensive use of a comparatively small vocabulary. The lexeme ἀδικεῖν occurs fifteen times, δίκαιος seven times, μαρτυρεῖν five, and καταμαρτυρεῖν four, all in a passage of 103 mobile tokens. The 'lexeme–token ratio' is 55:103, and one would have to search a long time to find a passage exhibiting a ratio as high as that. Comparison of authors in respect of their lexeme–token ratios lends itself admirably to precise quantification, but—like 'average sentence-length' (see p. 50)—it needs some refinement before it becomes interesting.

In the first place, it is not simply the recurrence of a lexeme within a passage (how is 'passage' to be defined?) that matters, but the size of the interval between occurrences. A fair range of experiments has indicated to me that it is not rewarding to record recurrence beyond the twentieth mobile. In the text quoted above, the second μαρτυρεῖν occurs as eighteenth mobile after the first, and that matters; but the second ἀνάγκη is seventy-fourth after the first, and that assuredly does not matter. Since recurrence is more obtrusive when the interval is short, the assignation of a 'score' for recurrence must use not the intervals themselves, but their reciprocals. Thus in the Antiphon passage the second occurrence of δίκαιος ([δίκαιο]ν) scores 1:6 (0.17, to two places of decimals) because it is the sixth mobile after δικαίου; the third (δί[καιος]) 1:8 (0.13), as it is the eighth mobile after [δίκαιο]ν; and so on. Total the reciprocals for a given text, multiply by 100, divide by the total number of mobile tokens in the text, and you have an 'index of recurrence' for that text.

Secondly, I have generally found that differences between texts in respect of recurrence are sharpened if the enquiry is limited to nouns (excluding proper nouns), adjectives (excluding pronominal adjectives, πολύς and πᾶς, and numerals), regular adverbs in -ως/ -ῶς, εὖ, and verbs;[2] that is to say, they are the only mobiles whose recurrence is counted, but, of course, in calculating the *interval* between one occurrence and the next *all* mobiles are counted.

Table 7.1 shows the index of recurrence for certain samples. Data

[2] I have not treated any part of the copula εἶναι as mobile unless it comes immediately after pause or is negatived; I have treated the present indicative of φάναι in the same way, and have ignored parenthetic ἔφη. A combination of prepositive and postpositive, e.g. πρὸς αὐτόν, is treated as mobile for the calculation of intervals.

TABLE 7.1. *Index of recurrence for four texts*

Sample	Total of mobile tokens	Total of reciprocals	Index of recurrence
Hdt. vii. 8–11. 4	976	7.45	0.76
Gorgias, *Helen*	750	33.20	4.42
Thuc. vi. 76–87.2	1008	3.18	0.32
Isoc. vii. 1–38	1020	1.28	0.13

of this kind might reasonably be expected to explain one aspect of the impressions that different authors make on us—including negative impressions, because many readers of Thucydides and Isocrates somehow become aware that they are *not* encountering the same lexemes at frequent intervals.

There are, however, certain common configurations in which tokens of the same lexeme appear in immediate or close proximity to one another, and it is always possible that a writer may combine a liking for such configurations with a desire to vary his vocabulary otherwise. That practice could be obscured by an undiscriminating calculation of the index of recurrence, and for that reason it is advisable to separate data on close proximity (intervals 1–5) from data on intervals ranging from 6 to 20.

Some recurrences in close proximity can reasonably be called 'formal'. That would apply to polyptota,[3] e.g. Hdt. i. 2. 1 ἴσα πρὸς ἴσα, to combinations of moods, tenses, and voices,[4] such as Hp. *VM* 2. 2 ἐξηπάτηται καὶ ἐξαπατᾶται, Pl. *Rep.* 358 E ἐπειδὰν ἀλλήλους ἀδικῶσί τε καὶ ἀδικῶνται, Dem. xxi. 191 τοιαῦτα παθὼν καὶ πάσχων, and to resumptive constructions of various types,[5] e.g. Anon. *Ath.* 1. 1 ταῦθ᾽ ἑλόμενοι εἵλοντο τοὺς πονηροὺς κτλ., 2. 3 ὁπόσαι δ᾽ . . . εἰσι . . . ἀρχόμεναι, αἱ μὲν μεγάλαι διὰ δέος ἄρχονται, Hdt. i. 8. 1 ἠράσθη τῆς ἑωυτοῦ γυναικός, ἐρασθεὶς δὲ ἐνόμιζε . . .· ὥστε δὲ ταῦτα νομίζων, Democritus DK 68 B 33 ἡ διδαχὴ μεταρυσμοῖ τὸν ἄνθρωπον, μεταρυσμοῦσα δὲ φυσιοποιεῖ, Pherec. Ath. *FGrHist* 3 F 105 διέβαινε τὸν ποταμόν, διαβὰς δὲ κτλ., Pl. *Rep.* 614 B ἀνεβίω, ἀναβιοὺς δὲ κτλ.,

[3] On polyptota see Gygli-Wyss *passim*, *Wf* 45 n. 41, 57–9, 82 f., 221, 234 and Rehdantz 27.
[4] Cf. *Wf* 264–7.
[5] *SPG* 129–33, 147 f., *Wf* 134–6, 143, 146 f., Lilja 42, *ELDH* 456. Lucian observed and parodied this feature of Herodotean prose (*Wf* 138, 140).

Hdt. i. 12. 2 ἔσχε καὶ τὴν γυναῖκα καὶ τὴν βασιληίην Γύγης . . . ἔσχε δὲ τὴν βασιληίην καὶ ἐκρατύνθη κτλ. It applies also to some (not all) examples of anaphora, e.g. Xen. *HG* vii. 1. 14 μέρος μέν . . . μέρος δὲ κτλ.

We must expect recurrence when an individual lexeme is discussed or defined,[6] e.g. Dem. xxi. 189 καὶ "ῥήτωρ ἐστὶν οὗτος" φήσει . . . ἐγὼ δ᾿ εἰ ὁ συμβουλεύων . . . ῥήτωρ ἐστίν, οὔτε φύγοιμ᾿ ἄν . . . εἰ μέντοι ῥήτωρ ἐστὶν κτλ., Pl. *Smp.* 219 c (Alcibiades telling his fellow-guests of his 'rejection' by Socrates) ᾤμην τι εἶναι, ὦ ἄνδρες δικασταί· δικασταὶ γάρ ἐστε τῆς Σωκράτους ὑπερηφανίας. Such phenomena are 'intellectual' rather than 'formal', and naturally prominent in philosophical argument (as in Pl. *Rep.* 357 A–368 c on right and wrong). No less so in scientific exposition, where clarity demands consistent terminology;[7] hence the index of recurrence in Diogenes of Apollonia DK 64 B 6, on the vascular system, is 2.5 (close recurrence, i.e. intervals 1–5, occurring six times in 214 mobile tokens).

Where the intellectual requirement of clarity is not in evidence, recurrence is an instrument of affect; thus the anaphora[8] in Antiphon v. 12:

ἀνώμοτος γὰρ αὐτὸς ἐμοῦ κατηγορεῖ, ἀνώμοτοι δὲ οἱ μάρτυρες καταμαρτυροῦσιν.

He himself accuses me *unsworn*, and the witnesses give evidence against me *unsworn*,

is not just a formal pattern, but strengthens the indignation which the speaker hopes to provoke in the jury. Passion is obvious in Dem. xviii. 24 ἀλλ᾿ οὐκ ἔστι ταῦτα, οὐκ ἔστι (cf. Ar. *Nu.* 1470 οὐκ ἔστ᾿, οὐκ)[9] and scorn, as in Thucydides' summary (viii. 27. 2 f.) of Phrynichus' advice to his colleagues at Miletus:

οὐκ ἔφη . . . οὐδέποτε τῷ αἰσχρῷ ὀνείδει εἴξας ἀλόγως διακινδυνεύσειν. οὐ γὰρ αἰσχρὸν εἶναι Ἀθηναίους μετὰ καιροῦ ὑποχωρῆσαι, ἀλλὰ καὶ μετὰ ὁτουοῦν

---

[6] *SPG* 144–7 = *GPS* 92–5, Lilja 40, 50, *Wf* 144 f., 149.

[7] Thesleff (1966) 93 n. 16, 99. Cf. Bannier (1912) on documentary style, esp. 516 f.; id. (1914) covers all genres of text.

[8] On anaphora in general see Rehdantz 4 f., *SPG* 133–7 = *GPS* 84–7, *Wf* 184 f., 192–213.

[9] Cf. *SPG* 141–4 = *GPS* 90–2, *Wf* 169–72, 176 f. Demosthenes' fondness for this repetition (*SPG* 142 f. = *GPS* 91 f.) is further evidence (cf. p. 65) for his liking for colloquial elements which are well attested in comedy and anecdote, e.g. Ar. *Thesm.* 514 (exultant) λέων λέων σοι γέγονεν, Plu. *Per.* 10. 6 (a putting-down joke) γραῦς εἶ, γραῦς εἶ.

τρόπου αἴσχιον ξυμβήσεσθαι ἢν ἡσσωθῶσιν· καὶ τὴν πόλιν οὐ μόνον τῷ αἰσχρῷ, ἀλλὰ καὶ τῷ μεγίστῳ κινδύνῳ περιπίπτειν, κτλ.

He said that he would never be induced by the reproach of '*disgrace*' to take a thoughtless risk. It was not *disgraceful* for Athenians to withdraw when the moment was right; the terms they would be making if they were defeated would be more *disgraceful*, whatever happened, and the city was incurring not just *disgrace*, but extreme danger . . .

One can hear the scornful emphasis on αἰσχρός, which is reminiscent of some passages of comic dialogue, e.g. Ar. *Lys.* 430–2 (Lysistrata's reaction to the Proboulos' command that the gates of the Propylaea be prised open with crowbars):

μηδὲν ἐκμοχλεύετε·
ἐξέρχομαι γὰρ αὐτομάτη. τί δεῖ μόχλων;
οὐ γὰρ μόχλων δεῖ μᾶλλον ἢ νοῦ καὶ φρενῶν.

Don't *crowbar* anything. I'm coming out of my own accord. What do you want *crowbars* for? It isn't *crowbars* that are needed, it's good sense.

It is possible, with a sufficiently sensitive stylistic thermometer, to detect the presence of a touch of affect wherever there is recurrence of a lexeme denoting size, strength, or menace,[10] e.g. Thuc. vii. 80. 3 διὰ πολεμίας καὶ ἀπὸ πολεμίων οὐ πολὺ ἀπεχόντων ἰοῦσιν, Pl. *Rep.* 361 A δοτέον οὖν τῷ τελέως ἀδίκῳ τὴν τελεωτάτην ἀδικίαν; cf. *Il.* i. 267 κάρτιστοι γὰρ ἔσαν, καὶ καρτίστοις ἐμάχοντο 'Mighty men they were, and mighty the foes they fought.'

These considerations are crucial to the interpretation of Table 7.2, which shows the extent of recurrence in fifteen samples. Gorgias must have sought close recurrence deliberately (for remoter recurrence, he resembles the Hippocratic sample), and that conclusion from his *Helen* is supported by the famous citation (*AS* B VII 42 = DK 82 B 6) from his Funeral Speech (e.g. ὑβρισταὶ εἰς τοὺς ὑβριστάς, κόσμιοι εἰς τοὺς κοσμίους, ἄφοβοι εἰς τοὺς ἀφόβους, δεινοὶ ἐν τοῖς δεινοῖς and ἀθάνατος οὐκ ἐν ἀθανάτοις σώμασι ζῇ οὐ ζώντων) and, in less concentrated form, from his *Palamedes* (*AS* 44 = DK B 11a), for which (1,341 mobile tokens) the first five columns of Table 7.2 would read 11–14–17–13–7 (scaled down, 8–10–13–10–5). In this respect, Gorgias' influence on Greek prose was somewhat limited, and whatever praise or blame is deserved for the 'invention' of close

---

[10] Cf. *Wf* 227 f.

TABLE 7.2. *Intervals of recurrence in fifteen texts*

Sample	Total mobile tokens	Intervals of recurrence							
		1	2	3	4	5	6–10	11–15	16–20
Anon. *Ath.* 1.1-2.12	1006	5	9	7	12	8	56	33	24
Hdt. i. proem.–14.									
2	1000	2		5	6	11	26	20	11
Hdt. vii. 8–11	976		3	2	4	3	21	24	7
Hp. *VM* 1–10. 3	1019	3	4	5	6	4	26	23	19
Gorgias, *Helen*	750	18	14	7	4	5	20	16	15
scaled up to /1000:		24	19	9	5	7	27	21	20
Antiphon v. 1–29	1015	1	4	4	10	9	28	21	8
Thuc. i. 1–11	1002				1	1	7	6	12
Thuc. vi. 76–87. 2	1008			2	1		10	6	5
Lys. xii. 1–39 (om. §25)	1028		1	1	3	4	17	18	11
Pl. *Smp.* 215 A 4–218 B 7, 219 B 3–221 D 1	1010	5	5		5	2	16	23	13
Pl. *Rep.* 357 A 1–363 B 4 (om. poetic quotations)	999	2	13	2	1	5	25	16	12
Isoc. iv. 1–37	1006		1			1	5	7	10
Isoc. vii. 1–38	1020				1	1	2	3	6
Dem. xxi. 175–200	1005		1	1	3	1	6	12	8
Dem. xviii. 1–26	1006	1	3	2		1	7	10	4

recurrence should be attached not to him but to moralizing aphorisms,[11] which abound in Hesiod's *Works and Days*, e.g. 352–5:

> μὴ κακὰ κερδαίνειν· κακὰ κέρδεα ἶσ' ἄτῃσιν.
> τὸν φιλέοντα φιλεῖν καὶ τῷ προσιόντι προσεῖναι,
> καὶ δόμεν ὅς κεν δῷ καὶ μὴ δόμεν ὅς κεν μὴ δῷ·
> δώτῃ μέν τις ἔδωκεν, ἀδώτῃ δ' οὔ τις ἔδωκεν.

Seek not ill gain. Ill gains are no better than losses. Be a friend to him who is your friend, and keep company with him who seeks yours. And give to him who gives, but do not give to him who does not give. To a giver one gives, but to a non-giver one does not give.

Anon. *Ath.* comes second to Gorgias—a distant second—in the closest recurrence, but outstrips Gorgias and everyone else in recurrence at intervals from 4 to 15. Thucydides shows a quite remarkable fall in recurrence across the whole range from 1 to 20 intervals; Isocrates takes this development further in the range 1–5, and one of his samples also shows a very low figure for 6–15, while there seems

[11] Cf. *Wf* 136, 166, 225 f., 231, *ELDH* 454, Deichgräber (1971) 73.

to be a clear chronological trend towards reduction of recurrence in oratory from Antiphon, via Lysias, to Demosthenes. The Plato samples are striking. We might have expected the *Republic* sample to show much more recurrence, because of its philosophical character, than the narrative of the *Symposium* sample, but that turns out not to be so. There is a reason for that, which we have glimpsed already in the passage of *Lysis* analysed on pp. 19 f. Much pre-Platonic prose was insensitive to avoidable recurrence, and the tradition inaugurated by Thucydides and taken to extremes by Isocrates was over-sensitive and therefore blatantly artificial. The peculiar— I would say, unique—'naturalness' of Plato's style is achieved in large measure by his willingness to float between consistency and inconsistency of vocabulary as good articulate conversation does. A striking example is afforded by *Rep.* 357 B–358 A: αὐτὸ αὐτοῦ ἕνεκα ἀσπαζόμενοι . . . αὐτό τε αὐτοῦ χάριν ἀγαπῶμεν . . . δι' ἀμφότερα ἀσπαζόμεθα . . . αὐτὰ μὲν ἑαυτῶν ἕνεκα οὐκ ἂν δεξαίμεθα ἔχειν . . . δι' αὐτό . . . ἀγαπητέον, where maximum variation is attained by the sequences ἕνεκα/χάριν/διά/ἕνεκα/διά, ἀσπάζεσθαι/ἀγαπᾶν/ἀσπάζεσθαι/ δέχεσθαι ἔχειν/ἀγαπᾶν.

Plato apart, when it comes to illustrating by examples the movement from early insensitivity to later over-sensitivity—*statistically* demonstrable, as we have seen—the inevitably subjective element in the assessment of sensitivity raises problems. Only extreme cases (and not all of them) are unproblematic,[12] e.g. Anon. *Ath*. 2. 11:

If a city is rich in shipbuilding timber, where will it dispose of it without consent of the ruler of the sea? Or again, if a city is rich in iron or bronze or flax, where will it dispose of it without consent of the ruler of the sea?

Cf. ibid. 2. 20 'in a democratic city more than in an oligarchy . . . (3 mobiles) . . . more . . . (3 mobiles) . . . in a democratic city ('more' repeated) than in an oligarchy', and 3. 11 'whenever they tried to choose the best men (. . . 1 mobile . . .) within a short time the people . . . (2 mobiles) . . . and again when . . . (1 mobile) . . . they chose the best men, within a short time . . . (3 mobiles) . . . and again when they chose . . . (2 mobiles) . . . within a short time . . .'. And in the papyrus text of Antiphon the Sophist, DK 87 B 44 A col. i. 30–iii. 18:

Laws have been imposed on our eyes, prescribing what they must see and

---

[12] *ELDH* 458.

what they must not; and on our ears, what they must hear and what they must not; and on our tongue, what it must say and what it must not; and on our hands, what they must do and what they must not; and on our feet, where they must go and where they must not; and on our mind, what it must desire and what not.[13]

There, of course, there is a point, made in a very heavy-handed way: 'we can't move or speak or think without legislation at *every* turn.' Equally heavy-handed is Xenophon's attempt in *Mem.* i. 1. 16 to impress us with the scope of Socrates' moral enquiry:

He himself conversed always about human concerns, examining what[14] is pious? what is impious? what is fair? what is foul? what is right? what is wrong? what is good sense? what is insanity? what is courage? what is cowardice? what is a city? what is an active citizen (πολιτικός[15])? what is rule over people? what is a leader of people (ἀρχικὸς ἀνθρώπων[16])? and about those other matters of which he thought that those who knew were good men (καλοὺς κἀγαθούς[17]) and those who did not could justly be called slavish.

We may well be reminded here of a current political style in which each of a succession of sentences begins with an identical sequence ('We have been able . . . We have been able . . . We have been able . . .'), a style which owes something to the Southern preacher. Plato seeks a comparable effect—needless to say, with a lighter touch—in *Rep.* 360 BC:

to take without fear whatever he wished (βούλοιτο) . . . to have intercourse with anyone he wished (βούλοιτο) . . . to kill . . . whoever he wished (βούλοιτο) . . .

and 362 B:

to marry from wherever (i.e. from whatever family) he wishes (βούληται), to give (sc. his daughters) in marriage to whomsoever he wishes (βούληται), to make contracts and partnerships with whomsoever he desires (ἐθέλῃ).

In the second passage, there is a twist in the tail, variation by substituting ἐθέλειν for βούλεσθαι, not an uncommon variation; cf. Hdt. vii. 10. θ. 1. In the former passage, there are alternative modes of

[13] Cf. the change from οὐ δεῖ to μή at the end of the Antiphon passage above.
[14] The direct interrogative τί is used throughout the passage.
[15] 'Politician' would be a little too specialized.
[16] ἀρχικός or ἱκανὸς ἄρχειν denotes an attribute to which Xenophon always attaches importance.
[17] On καλὸς κἀγαθός cf. Dover (1974) 41–5.

utterance: plainly the first βούλοιτο must be spoken with emphasis, but after that we have a choice between reiterated emphasis
and minimal emphasis, depending on the intonation we choose to
give to 'have intercourse' and 'kill'.[18] By contrast, the repetition of
δῆλον 'clear' in Xen. *Mem.* i. 1. 8 loses more force than it gains by
recurrence:

He said that the most important aspects of all those activities are reserved
by the gods for themselves, for to the man who plants land well it is not
clear (δῆλον) who will gather its crop, nor to the man who has built a house
well is it clear who will live in it, nor to the man of military talent is it clear
whether it is advantageous to him to be a general, nor to the man active
in politics is it clear whether it is advantageous to him to be a leader in
his city, nor to the man who has married a beautiful woman, looking for
happiness, is it clear whether he will be grieved because of her, nor to the
man who has acquired by marriage kinsmen influential in the city is it clear
whether because of them he will be deprived of his city.

Insensitivity, indifference, or bad judgement[19] may reasonably be
invoked to explain examples such as the following: Anon. *Ath.* i.
6 '. . . ought to allow only the best (ἀρίστους) and most intelligent
men to speak; but in this matter they (sc. the demos) take a very
good (ἄριστα) decision'; Hdt. i. 8. 4 καί σεο δέομαι μὴ δέεσθαι ἀνόμων
'I ask you not to ask unlawful acts (sc. of me)', where speaker and
addressee are so unequal in power that the first 'ask' means 'beg'
and the second 'require';[20] Xen. *HG* vii. 1. 26 'recognized that they
were treating their own arguments (λόγους) as being of no account
(ἐν οὐδενὶ λόγῳ)'; and Isoc. vii. 30 'not to suppress any ancestral
rites, nor to add any which departed from established custom (τῶν
νομιζομένων), for they did not consider (οὐκ . . . ἐνόμιζον) that piety
rested upon great expenditure'. I do not doubt that every such
example will find its defenders,[21] and they always deserve a hearing.

In poetry variation by synonymy went hand-in-hand with apparent indifference to recurrence,[22] and it is not surprising that fifth-

---

[18] It should be noted by English-speakers that the distribution of stress in utterances of this type is not the same in English as it is in (e.g.) French and Italian.

[19] But hardly lack of skill, despite Lilja's attribution (50) of recurrence to the
writer's 'negligence' or 'inability to construct the sentence properly'.

[20] Cf. *Wf* 151.

[21] e.g. Long 25–35, on the story of Kandaules and Gyges (but the semantic distinction he draws between ὁρᾶν and θεᾶσθαι is doubtful, since ὀφθῆναι functions as
the aorist passive of both).

[22] Jackson 220–2 assembles many instances from drama.

century prose also shows a mixture. This is true even of Anon. *Ath*., e.g. 1. 11 'they allow their slaves (δούλους) to live well' ~ 'to be the slaves of their servants (τοῖς ἀνδραπόδοις δουλεύειν[23])' ~ 'where there are well-to-do slaves (δοῦλοι)' ~ 1. 19 'they themselves and their servants (ἀκόλουθοι)' ~ 'both he himself and his slave (οἰκέτην)'; 1. 14 'they look after the good men (χρηστούς) in the allied cities' ~ 'to look after the best men (βελτίστους) in the cities'. Cf. Hdt. i. 9. 1 'apprehensive (ἀρρωδέων) that some ill (κακόν) might come to him from it' ~ 'do not be afraid (φοβεῦ) that some harm (βλάβος) may come to you from her'; 9. 3 'as soon as she has gone towards the bed (στίχῃ ἐπὶ τὴν εὐνήν) and you are behind her back' ~ 10. 2 'when he was behind the woman's back as she went to the bed (ἰούσης . . . ἐπὶ τὴν κοίτην)'.[24] Variation is in evidence even in scientific exposition, e.g. Hp. *VM* 8. 2. 'not a great quantity, but much less (ἔλασσον) than a healthy man would have been able to' ~ ibid. 'not a great quantity, but much less (μεῖον) than he could'.

Ros's exhaustive collection of putative instances of variation in Thucydides, invaluable for syntactical phenomena (cf. p. 152), is much less serviceable in its discussion of vocabulary, because it ignores not just nuances but distinctions for which 'nuance' would be too weak a word, e.g. in Thuc. i. 9. 3–10. 1, where it is wide of the mark to treat μοι δοκεῖ 'in my opinion', and φαίνεται 'it is apparent (sc. from the *Iliad*)' as variation.[25] I would not myself regard vii. 79. 5 ἐπίοιεν . . . ὑπεχώρουν . . . ἀναχωροῖεν . . . ἐπέκειντο, where the subject of the first and third verbs is the retreating Athenians and the subject of the second and fourth the cautiously but relentlessly pursuing Syracusans, as exhibiting variation.[26] None the less, it is easy, on any page of Thucydides, to observe the ingenuity—as a rule, effortless-seeming—with which he rings the changes on dif-

---

[23] The writer could have retained δούλοις and used a different verb (e.g. ὑπουργεῖν, ὑπηρετεῖν, θεραπεύειν), but presumably, having once given priority to δοῦλος, he shunned the paradoxical δούλοις δουλεύειν, which would have appealed strongly to some other writers.

[24] It is possible, in view of the epic φιλότητι καὶ εὐνῇ, that εὐνή seemed to Herodotus to have stronger erotic associations and therefore to be more appropriate in the mouth of Kandaules.

[25] Ctr. Ros 120.

[26] And in view of *IG* i³ 78. 33 μὲ ἐπιτάττοντας, κελεύοντας δέ it is particularly unfortunate that Ros 119 treats Thuc. i. 139. 1 ταῦτα ἐπέταξάν τε . . . ὕστερον δέ . . . ἐκέλευον δέ as variation.

ferent lexemes in the same semantic field, e.g. i. 3. 2–4, on the history of the name Ἕλληνες:[27]

I think that Greece as a whole did not yet have this name (τοὔνομα τοῦτο), but in the time before Hellen son of Deukalion this appellation (ἡ ἐπίκλησις αὕτη) did not even exist—individual tribes . . . provided the nomenclature (τὴν ἐπωνυμίαν)—but when Hellen and his sons had become powerful in Phthiotis and were called in as allies by other states, in one place and another . . . they were increasingly called (καλεῖσθαι) Hellenes. Homer is evidence for this, for . . . he nowhere gave the name (ὠνόμασεν sc. Ἕλληνας) to the combined forces (sc. of the Greeks), but calls them (ἀνακαλεῖ) Danaoi . . . (etc.) Nor indeed has he spoken (εἴρηκε) of 'barbarians', because the Greeks too had not yet been set apart under a single contrasting name (ὄνομα).

There are different ways of avoiding lexical recurrence, and synonymy is only one of them.[28] A lexeme may be replaced, at the point where its recurrence might be expected, by a demonstrative or anaphoric pronoun,[29] sometimes combined with a highly general lexeme (e.g. ποιεῖν, πάσχειν), such as Thuc. i. 10. 2 τὸ αὐτὸ τοῦτο παθόντων for 'being deserted' (~ 10. 1 εἰ ἡ πόλις ἐρημωθείη 'if the city were deserted') and Pl. *Rep.* 358 c τρίτον δὲ ὅτι εἰκότως αὐτὸ δρῶσι 'and thirdly, that it's understandable that they do so', sc. 'do right as something they can't avoid, not as a good thing in itself'. Cf. Thuc. i. 5. 1 'they turned to piracy (λῃστείαν) . . ., for this activity (τούτου τοῦ ἔργου, i.e. 'piracy') was not yet regarded as shameful . . . 2 those who are proud of doing this (τοῦτο δρᾶν, i.e. λῃστεία) well . . .'.

When positive and negative are juxtaposed in opposition,[30] recurrence can be (though it is not always) avoided by omission, e.g. Hdt. i. 139 Πέρσας μὲν αὐτοὺς λέληθε, ἡμέας μέντοι οὔ (sc. λέληθε). As a rule, omission poses no problem of understanding, but Thucydides pushes it rather further than other writers, e.g. vi. 79. 1 ὅταν ὑπ' ἄλλων (sc. ἀδικῶνται) καὶ μὴ αὐτοὶ ὥσπερ νῦν τοὺς πέλας ἀδικῶσιν.[31]

Yet despite the resources available in Greek for the avoidance of

[27] Ros 118.
[28] One way is 'hyponymy' (Lyons (1963) 69–71, (1977) 291–301), using a generic word rather than repeating a specific one. The normal Greek tendency to use a simple verb in preference to repeating a compound verb (KG i. 552, *GG* ii. 422) is one type of hyponymy.
[29] Cf. KG i. 35, *SPG* 125 = *GPS* 78, *Wf* 49 f., 140, 152.
[30] *Wf* 128 f.
[31] Spormann 32–5. This kind of brachylogy causes many problems for the grammarian (e.g. vi. 82. 4 δουλείαν δὲ αὐτοί τε (sc. φέρειν) ἐβούλοντο καὶ ἡμῖν τὸ αὐτὸ ἐπενεγκεῖν) and indeed for the reader/listener (e.g. ii. 62. 1 δηλώσω δὲ καὶ τόδε, ὅ μοι δοκεῖτε οὔτ' αὐτοὶ πώποτε ἐνθυμηθῆναι . . . οὔτ' ἐγὼ (sc. ἐδήλωσα) ἐν τοῖς πρὶν λόγοις.

recurrence, recurrence none the less obtrudes from time to time even in an author as plainly hostile to it as Thucydides, e.g. vii. 80. 5 f.:

. . . so that when *they came to the River* Kakyparis, they might go along *the river* into the interior . . . And when *they came to the river*, they found a Syracusan blocking-force . . . Having overcome it, they crossed *the river* and went further on to another *river*, the Erineos . . .

Hypersensitivity to recurrence is explicable, once we are past Thucydides, as the continuation of a fashion; continuation seldom needs explanation, and speculation on why it started in the first place is rarely profitable. One does not 'explain' tastes, i.e. choices of models. Plato's choice of the middle road, neither following a trend subserviently nor reverting to more primitive models, is to my mind (p. 138) easily explained as the product of his experience and observation of the effect of different styles on the relation between the originator and the recipient of a text. What is harder to explain is the sporadic loss of sensitivity in the normally hypersensitive, as in the Thucydidean passage quoted above.

B. STRUCTURE

In the Hippocratic *De Vetere Medicina* 3. 5 we read:

From wheat, having moistened, winnowed, ground, sifted, kneaded, and baked it, they manufactured bread, and from barley, *maza*; and having subjected that food to many other procedures, they boiled and baked and mixed and blended the substances which were strong and undiluted with the weaker, fashioning everything in conformity with man's nature and capacity, in the belief that whatever is too strong, one's nature will not be able to manage it if it is ingested, and from those materials sufferings and illnesses and deaths will result; but from whatever it can control, nourishment and growth and health. To this discovery and enquiry what more just and fitting name could one give than 'medicine', for it has been discovered for man's health and well-being and nourishment, a substitute for that diet from which those sufferings and illnesses and deaths came about?

In this short passage we have five sequences which can be symbolized as $A + B$, five $A + B + C$, and one $A + B + C + D + E + F$, where '+' signifies 'and', 'or', or 'nor', and the letters signify mobile tokens which in each sequence all stand in exactly the same syntactical relation to what lies outside the sequence. Moreover, the pairing or grouping is emphasized by assonance, thus:

βρέξαντές σφας καὶ πτίσαντες καὶ καταλέσαντές τε καὶ διασήσαντες καὶ
φορύξαντες καὶ ὀπτήσαντες
ἤψησάν τε καὶ ὤπτησαν καὶ ἔμιξαν
τὰ ἰσχυρά τε καὶ ἄκρητα
φύσιν τε καὶ δύναμιν
πόνους τε καὶ νούσους καὶ θανάτους
τροφήν τε καὶ αὔξησιν καὶ ὑγίειαν
τῷ δὲ εὑρήματι τούτῳ καὶ ζητήματι
δικαιότερον ἢ προσῆκον μᾶλλον
ὑγιείῃ τε καὶ σωτηρίῃ καὶ τροφῇ
οἱ πόνοι καὶ νοῦσοι καὶ θάνατοι

I propose to call sequences of the type A + B etc. 'multiples', and Table 7.3 shows, from some samples of c.1,000 mobile tokens, how their incidence varies. Taking the view that the stylistic effect of multiples is diminished by asymmetry, I have disallowed instances in which a single mobile is co-ordinated with an expression composed of two or more, e.g. *VM* 1. 3 οὔτ᾽ αὐτῷ τῷ λέγοντι οὔτε τοῖσιν ἀκούουσιν (where αὐτῷ 'himself' is fully mobile). I have, however, readmitted those in which just one out of three or more co-ordinated items has two mobiles, e.g. *VM* 3. 1 ἅπερ . . . ἐσθίουσί τε καὶ πίνουσι καὶ τἄλλα διαιτέονται 'what they eat and drink and the regime they follow in other respects', 3. 3 καὶ τρέφονται καὶ αὔξονται καὶ ἄπονοι διάγουσιν 'are nourished and grow and live free of ills', 6. 2 ξηρὸν σιτίον ἢ μάζαν ἢ ἄρτον 'dry victuals or barley-bread or wheaten bread'. Thus in the opening passage of *VM*

ὁκόσοι μὲν ἐπεχείρησαν περὶ ἰητρικῆς λέγειν ἢ γράφειν ὑπόθεσιν αὐτοὶ ἑωυτοῖσιν ὑποθέμενοι τῷ λόγῳ θερμὸν ἢ ψυχρὸν ἢ ὑγρὸν ἢ ξηρὸν ἢ ἄλλο τι ὃ ἂν θέλωσιν κτλ.

All those who have embarked upon speaking or writing about medicine, treating as a premiss of their argument hot or cold or wet or dry or whatever else they wish . . .

λέγειν ἢ γράφειν is clearly a simple multiple, but in the sequence θερμὸν κτλ. the fifth item, ἢ ἄλλο τι ὃ ἂν θέλωσιν, might be thought not to meet the criterion 'the same syntactical relation to what lies outside the sequence'; yet it is naturally taken as a unit (ἄλλο is in fact superfluous). On the other hand, in 3. 5 'and blended . . . with the weaker' is just too big to be counted as one item in a multiple; accordingly, I treat that not as 'A + B + C + D' but as a '3 +' multiple.

I also exclude from my statistics:

(*a*) Examples in which a mobile intervenes between the co-ordinated items, e.g. Pl. *Rep*. 360 E τά τε ἀδύνατα ἐν τῇ τέχνῃ καὶ τὰ δυνατά.

(*b*) Those in which different forms of the same lexeme are co-ordinated, e.g. *VM* 2. 2 ἐξηπάτηται καὶ ἐξαπατᾶται, Dem. xxi. 191 παθὼν καὶ πάσχων, Dem. xviii. 1, 8 πᾶσι καὶ πάσαις, Pl. *Smp*. 218 A ὑπὸ ἀλγεινοτέρου καὶ τὸ ἀλγεινότατον, *Rep*. 358 E, 359 A. Cf. p. 134.

(*c*) Different compounds of the same verb, e.g. Anon. *Ath*. 2. 3 εἰσάγεσθαί τι ἢ ἐξάγεσθαι, Pl. *Smp*. 217 E.

(*d*) Oaths, e.g. Pl. *Smp*. 219 C.

(*e*) Numerals, e.g. 'one or two', 'a hundred and fifty'.

(*f*) Where either of the items is a pronoun, ἄλλος, or πολύς, e.g. Anon. *Ath*. 1. 19 'himself and his slave'.

(*g*) Where the second member is 'and/but/or not'.

(*h*) Very common oppositions such as: 'do'/'say' (e.g. Dem. xxi. 190, Pl. *Smp*. 218 A), 'do'/'undergo' (e.g. Hdt. vii. 11. 3), 'give'/ 'receive' (satisfaction) (e.g. Anon. *Ath*. 1. 18), 'gods'/'mortals' (e.g. Pl. *Rep*. 362 C), 'Greeks'/'barbarians' (e.g. Anon. *Ath*. 2. 11), 'here or there' (*VM* 9. 3), 'person'/'property' (e.g. Dem. xviii. 20), 'private'/'public' (e.g. Pl. *Rep*. 362 B), 'speak'/'hear' (e.g. Pl. *Smp*. 219 B).

VM stands out from all the rest in respect of simple A + B multiples, and Anon. *Ath*. joins it for multiples of three or more items. In both texts one can sometimes see a rhetorical reason for the accumulation of items, e.g. Anon. *Ath*. 2.7 '. . . in Italy, or Cyprus, . . . (etc.)', where the point is 'absolutely *everywhere*' (cf. 3. 4 'the Dionysia and Thargelia and Panathenaea and Promethia and Hephaestia', sc. 'all those festivals *every* year'), or *VM* 1. 1, where the implication is that the variety of theories about 'hot or cold . . . (etc.)' is itself a bad advertisement for any of them. In fourth-century authors the rhetorical purpose of multiples exceeding two items is usually discernible without difficulty. In Pl. *Smp*. 216 E and 219 D Socrates is being praised magniloquently (in the former, passionately), and 218 A is probably a reminder that Alcibiades is drunk. Dem. xxi. 182 carries the implication '*no one*', 181 '*no* excuse', 195 '*everything* about him'. The accumulations in xviii. 12, 15 and xxi. 191 are designed to implant hostility towards the speaker's oppo-

TABLE 7.3. *Multiples in eleven texts*

No. of items in multiples	2	2+	3	3+	4	4+	5 or more
Anon. *Ath.* i. 1–2. 12	11		11	1[a]	2[b]		2[c]
Gorgias, *Helen*	26		2				1[d]
scaled up	33	3			1		
Hdt. vii. 8–11	9	1	1[e]			1[f]	
Hp. *VM* 1–10. 3	52	2	8	1[g]		1[h]	1[i]
Thuc. vi. 76–87. 2	13		1[j]				
Pl. *Smp.* 215 A 4–218 B 7, 219 B 3–221 D 1	14	1[k]		1[l]		1[m]	
Pl. *Rep.* 357 A 1–363 B 4	13	1	1[n]				
Isoc. iv. 1–37	8	1	2[o]				
Isoc. vii. 1–38	25		1[p]				
Dem. xxi. 175–200	22	1	2[q]	1[r]	1[s]		1[t]
Dem. xviii. 1–26	30	1	3[u]	1[v]			

[a] 1. 13   [b] 1. 13, 2. 9   [c] 1. 2; 2. 7 (proper names)   [d] *Hel.* 1   [e] 9. a. 1 (proper names)   [f] 9. 2 (proper names)   [g] 3. 5   [h] 1. 1   [i] 3. 5   [j] 82. 2   [k] 219 D 3   [l] 216 E 7   [m] 218 A 6 (proper names)   [n] 357 C 2   [o] 27, 29   [p] 14   [q] 185, 196   [r] 181   [s] 182   [t] 195   [u] 13, 15, 23   [v] 12

nent, and in xviii. 15 'heaping together (συμφορήσας) charges and gibes and abuse' the multiplicity of the object reinforces the verb.

The occasional occurrence of a simple A + B multiple gives the hearer the impression of unrehearsed utterance, as if the author felt some dissatisfaction with the lexeme he had just used and were seeking something better, e.g. *VM* 2. 2 ἀποβαλὼν καὶ ἀποδοκιμάσας 'discarding and rejecting'. This pleonasm often becomes an obtrusive mannerism, as e.g. in Isoc. vii. 19 καὶ τὴν αἵρεσιν καὶ τὴν κρίσιν αὐτῶν 'your choice and judgement between them', 20 ὀνόματι . . . τῷ κοινοτάτῳ καὶ πραοτάτῳ 'the most comprehensive and conciliatory . . . name' . . . μισοῦσα καὶ κολάζουσα 'detesting and punishing' . . . βελτίους καὶ σωφρονεστέρους 'better and more sensible', 22 τοὺς βελτίστους καὶ τοὺς ἱκανωτάτους 'the best and most competent'. In the same portion of text there are two simple multiples which are semantically of quite a different kind, because within each pair each item is the antonym of the other, but acoustically they can be classed with the rest: 21 τοὺς χρηστοὺς καὶ τοὺς πονηρούς 'the good and the bad', 22 τιμῶσαν καὶ κολάζουσαν 'honouring and punishing'.

In his portrayal of the First Congress at Sparta Thucydides (i. 70) makes his Corinthian speaker contrast Athens and Sparta as indicated schematically below (my literal translation takes little account of English usage). In a text designed to list the differences between opposing ways of life some antitheses are to be expected, and section V is, one might say, Lesson One in the art of antithesis: two sequences, each of three items, each item in the second sequence corresponding in position to its antonym in the first. Subsection Ia, on the other hand, is a multiple complement, and its second member is itself a subordinate multiple. In Subsections IIa and IIb the contrast of γνώμη with δύναμις has a strongly antithetical character (cf. i. 77. 3, ii. 89. 6, and passages contrasting γνώμη with παρασκευή or ἔργον), while τολμηταί and κινδυνευταί come close to synonymy but are dressed up as antithetical by incorporation in the sequence $(A_1 \, B_1) + (A_2 \, B_2) + (A_3 \, B_3)$.

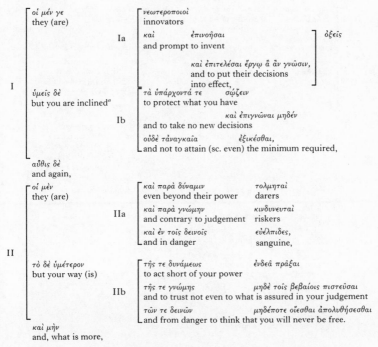

---

a It is often necessary, in translating Thucydides, to supply a verb similar to, but not identical with, a preceding verb; e.g. vi. 87. 4 ἀμφότεροι ἀναγκάζονται ὁ μὲν ἄκων σωφρονεῖν ὁ δ' ἀπραγμόνως σῴζεσθαι 'the one is compelled, against his wish, to restrain himself, and the other (sc. is enabled) to survive without having to act'.

III   (sc. they are)

καὶ ἄοκνοι   πρὸς ὑμᾶς μελλητὰς
unhesitating   against you (sc. who are) delayers

καὶ ἀποδημηταὶ   πρὸς ἐνδημοτάτους,
and venturers abroad against (sc. you, who are) more
stay-at-home than anyone,

IV   for they think

οἴονται γὰρ οἱ μὲν   τῇ ἀπουσίᾳ ἄν τι   κτᾶσθαι
that by going abroad they may acquire something

ὑμεῖς δὲ   τῷ ἐπελθεῖν   καὶ τὰ ἑτοῖμα ἂν βλάψαι.
but you (sc. think) that by an attack you may damage what you already have.

V

κρατοῦντές τε τῶν ἐχθρῶν   ἐπὶ πλεῖστον   ἐξέρχονται,
when they defeat their enemies, further than anyone they extend themselves,

καὶ νικώμενοι   ἐπ᾽ ἐλάχιστον   ἀναπίπτουσιν,
and when they are worsted,   less far than anyone they fall back,

ἔτι δὲ
and furthermore

VI

τοῖς μὲν σώμασιν ἀλλοτριωτάτοις   ὑπὲρ τῆς πόλεως   χρῶνται
their bodies   as wholly owed to others on their city's behalf   they
                                                                                             treat,

τῇ δὲ γνώμῃ   οἰκειοτάτῃ   ἐς τὸ πράσσειν τι ὑπὲρ αὐτῆς,
but their spirit   as absolutely their own   for an achievement on her behalf,

VII

καὶ ἃ μὲν ἂν   ἐπινοήσαντες   μὴ ἐπεξέλθωσιν   οἰκείων στέρεσθαι   ἡγοῦνται
and whatever, having conceived it,   they have not   they consider that
                                       followed up   they are robbed
                                                        of their own

ἃ δ᾽ ἂν   ἐπελθόντες   κτήσωνται   ὀλίγα πρὸς τὰ μέλ-
                                                  λοντα
                                                  τυχεῖν πράξαντες.
and whatever, having followed it up, they have gained, (sc. they consider)
                                                       that they have accom-
                                                       plished little this time
                                                       compared with what
                                                       is to come.

here follow five MCFs, comprising 27 mobile tokens and ending:

VIII

μήτε ἑορτὴν   ἄλλο τι ἡγεῖσθαι   ἢ τὸ τὰ δέοντα πρᾶξαι
. . . and not regarding as a holiday anything other than doing their duty

ξυμφοράν τε   οὐχ ἧσσον   ἡσυχίαν ἀπράγμονα
and as misfortune   just as much restful inaction

ἢ ἀσχολίαν ἐπίπονον
as laborious activity.

then an MCF of 11 mobile tokens, including:

IX

μήτε αὐτοὺς   ἔχειν ἡσυχίαν
. . . neither themselves   to stay inactive

μήτε τοὺς ἄλλους ἀνθρώπους ἐᾶν.
nor to allow other people (sc. to do so) . . .

It is clear from the examples given by Arist. *Rhet.* 1409^{b}36–10^{a}23
(cf. Demetr. 22 f.) that antithesis does not always and necessarily
entail antonymy,[32] as we can see for ourselves by constructing a
series of hypothetical examples graded on a scale (and using Greek
δέ throughout rather than choosing between 'but' and 'and') from

---

[32] Cf. Rehdantz 8, *Wf* 42–5, 295–307, *SPG* 112–15 = *GPS* 70–4, Hollingsworth
1–14. On the different types of opposition and contrast see Lyons (1977) 270–90.

'the rind is hard + the flesh is tender' at one extreme to 'the smell is fragrant + the flesh is delectable' at the other, via 'granular fruit + glossy leaves'. Most antitheses (in the Aristotelian sense) consist of sequences of identical syntactical status, which can be symbolized as $(A_1 B_1) + (A_2 B_2)$, but that is not true of them all, as we see from the example given in *Rhet*. 1410^{a}12 (lit.) 'being by birth citizens, to be deprived of their city by law' (cf. 34 f., 10^{b}29–31, Anaximenes 26). It would be wrong to deny the term 'antithesis' e.g. to Gorgias *Helen* 6 θεοῦ γὰρ προθυμίαν ἀνθρωπίνῃ προμηθίᾳ ἀδύνατον κωλύειν 'it is impossible to impede the determination of a god by human forethought', where the opposition of the two phrases is strongly reinforced by assonance. Except in its very simplest form, e.g. 'I saw it, you didn't', antithesis has intellectual and aesthetic appeal (cf. Arist. *Rhet*. 1410^{a}20–3) but lacks the forcefulness (cf. Demetr. 27) which multiples sometimes impart. No one would be inclined to characterize as 'spontaneous' or 'unrehearsed' (e.g.) Hdt. i. 4. 2:

τὸ μέν νυν ἁρπάζειν γυναῖκας ἀνδρῶν ἀδίκων νομίζειν ἔργον εἶναι, τὸ δὲ ἁρπασθεισέων σπουδὴν ποιήσασθαι τιμωρέειν ἀνοήτων, τὸ δὲ μηδεμίαν ὤρην ἔχειν
ἁρπασθεισέων σωφρόνων.

(sc. they say that) they consider that to carry off women is an action of unprincipled men; but when they have been carried off, to be zealous in avenging, of foolish men; and to make nothing of their being carried off, of sensible men.

To avoid fruitless vacillation over the placing of examples on the scale of antithesis (and, quite deliberately, to give aesthetics precedence over semantics), I propose to use the term 'symmetry' to cover all instances of $(A_1 B_1) (A_2 B_2)$, $(A_1 B_1) + (A_2 B_2)$, 'not A but B', and 'A and/but not B' (together, of course, with $(A_1 B_1 C_1)$ . . . etc.).[33] I treat a symmetrical sequence as beginning from the token to which the introductory particle (καί . . ., ἤ . . ., . . . μέν . . .) or the negative is attached. Thus e.g. in Pl. *Mnx*. 240 B τούτους ἐχειρώσατο μὲν ἐν τρισὶν ἡμέραις, διηρευνήσατο δὲ αὐτῶν πᾶσαν τὴν χώραν, where τούτους is related in sense to ἐχειρώσατο as πᾶσαν τὴν χώραν αὐτῶν is to διηρευνήσατο, I would ignore τούτους, treating the sequence $(A_1 BB_1) + (A_2 BB_2)$, strongly marked by assonance (-σατο), as symmetrical in respect of the number of mobile tokens it contains. In such instances I have relaxed the rule that all the

[33] Arist. *Rhet*. 1410^{a}24 uses the term παρίσωσις to denote the conjunction of kola of equal size (πάρισα 1410^{b}2).

components of a symmetry should stand in the same syntactical relation to what lies outside it.

Texts differ, and some of them differ very strikingly from the norm, in the frequency and scale of their use of symmetry, and may push it to a point at which it becomes monotonous (there are twelve instances in the passage from [Lys.] ii quoted on pp. 5–7). The comparison between texts which is quantified in Table 7.4 is founded on symmetries which are either perfect or only slightly imperfect; 'slight' imperfection in this case means that (i) one of the four items contained in a 2×2 symmetry, and not more than two of those in a larger one, comprise one more or one fewer mobile tokens than the rest, and/or (ii) one or two mobiles which stand in the same syntactical relation to both or all the members of a symmetrical sequence appear within one of them. So, for example, Pl. *Mnx.* 236 D κοινῇ μὲν ὑπὸ τῆς πόλεως, ἰδίᾳ δὲ ὑπὸ τῶν οἰκείων is a perfect symmetry; so is 238 E ἔνιοι μὲν δούλους, οἱ δὲ δεσπότας, because the tokens which complete the MCF, ἀλλήλους νομίζοντες, stand in the same relation to both members, and 241 D οἵ τε ἐπ᾽ Εὐρυμέδοντι ναυμαχήσαντες καὶ οἱ εἰς Κύπρον στρατεύσαντες καὶ οἱ εἰς Αἴγυπτον πλεύσαντες can be treated as 3×2, putting the cut-off point after πλεύσαντες and ignoring what follows, καὶ ἄλλοσε πολλαχόσε. 239 A ἡ ἰσογονία ἡμᾶς ἡ κατὰ φύσιν ἰσονομίαν ἀναγκάζει ζητεῖν κατὰ νόμον is imperfect, symbolizable as $(A_1\ B_1)\ (A_2\ \dots\ B_2)$; so too is 239 E πεζῇ μὲν μέχρι Σκυθῶν τὴν ἀρχὴν ὡρίσατο, ναυσὶ δὲ τῆς τε θαλάττης ἐκράτει καὶ τῶν νήσων $(A_1\ B_1\ CC_1) + (A_2\ B_2\ C_2 + B_2)$. On the other hand, 240 E τὰ μὲν οὖν ἀριστεῖα τῷ λόγῳ ἐκείνοις ἀναθετέον, τὰ δὲ δευτερεῖα τοῖς περὶ Σαλαμῖνα καὶ ἐπ᾽ Ἀρτεμισίῳ ναυμαχήσασι καὶ νικήσασι $(A_1\ \dots B_1\ \dots) + (A_2\ B + BB + B_2)$ exceeds the limits of permissible imperfection. Variation in the order of the responding elements does not justify exclusion; I therefore admit e.g. *Mnx.* 241 E τῇ ἑαυτοῦ σωτηρίᾳ τὸν νοῦν προσέχειν, ἀλλὰ μὴ τῇ τῶν Ἑλλήνων ἐπιβουλεύειν φθορᾷ $(A_1\ B_1\ CC_1) + (A_2\ C_2\ B_2)$.

The texts compared all contain many sequences which we readily recognize as being in some degree antithetical but cannot reasonably classify as symmetrical. However regretfully, we must exclude them from Table 7.4 by defining symmetry strictly; their turn will come, in a different form, in Table 7.6. The alternative would be to count every . . . μέν . . ./. . . δέ . . ., every οὐ(κ) . . ./ἀλλά . . ., and a good many . . . τε . . ./καί . . . or καί . . ./καί . . ., and that procedure would entail distinguishing between many different degrees of symmetry.

TABLE 7.4. *Symmetrical antitheses in ten texts*

	2×2	3×2	4×2	5×2	2×3	3×3	6×3	2×4	4×4	2×5
Gorgias	29	8	2	1	6			1[a]	1[b]	
	+4		+2		+5					
(scaled up)	39	11	3	1	8			1	1	
	+5		+3		+7					
Antiphon	4	1						1[c]		
	+7				+2			+1[d]		+1[e]
Hdt. vii	6				5					
	+5				+3		+1[f]			
Thuc. i	4									
	+8				+1					
Thuc. vi	6				2					
	+7				+4			+1[g]		
Lys. xii	8							2[h]		
	+5	+1	+2		+1		+1[i]			
Pl. *Mnx.*	13	1			2					
	+7				+4					
Pl. *Rep.*	11				1					
	+6	+1								
Isoc. vii	12				5	1[j]		1[k]		2[l]
	+5			+1[m]	+2					+1[n]
Dem. xviii	6							1[o]		
	1				+4					

[a] 14   [b] 4   [c] 1   [d] 5   [e] 16   [f] 10. η. 2   [g] 85. 2   [h] 7, 33   [i] 20   [j] 20   [k] 32   [l] 29   [m] 4, 34   [n] 5   [o] 15

Indeed, some sequences introduced by μέν run into the sand before ever reaching a δέ or ἔπειτα.

In Table 7.4 the headings, of the type $m \times n$, mean 'm members, each of n items'. Figures preceded by a plus sign refer to imperfect symmetries. The samples are selected from those in Table 7.3 with one fresh sample, Pl. *Mnx.* 236 D 4–242 C 2, in which Plato uses the style which he judges appropriate to a funeral oration.[34] Gorgias' use of symmetry is prodigious; it appears (from these samples) to have had some influence on the earlier forensic orators and a very marked influence on Isocrates; Dion. i. 90. 21–92. 1 comments on the extent to which its intrusion into the forensic speeches of Isocrates gives them an epideictic flavour. In respect of minimum symmetry, 2×2, Pl. *Rep.* and Isoc. turn out much alike; the difference is manifested in the more extensive symmetries.

Just as the recurrence of lexemes is avoided by the use of syn-

[34] Cf. the passage from [Lys.] ii quoted on p. 5.

152 *Variety*

onyms (p. 142), so the frequency and scale of multiples and symmetries can be reduced by syntactical variation.[35] We have encountered (p. 19) two examples in Pl. *Lys.* 207 E, δουλεύων τε καὶ ᾧ μηδὲν ἐξείη ποιεῖν ὧν ἐπιθυμοῖ 'if he were a slave and not allowed to do anything he desired' and εὐδαίμονά σε ἐπιθυμοῦσι γενέσθαι~προθυμοῦνται ὅπως ἂν εὐδαιμονοίης. No prose author, however, exploits variation as fully as Thucydides. There are three instances in the Thucydidean sample texts already used in this chapter: i. 2. 2 τῆς γὰρ ἐμπορίας οὐκ οὔσης οὐδ' ἐπιμειγνύντες ἀδεῶς ἀλλήλοις 'as there was no commerce and they had no secure intercourse with one another', i. 5. 1 οἵ τε ἐν τῇ ἠπείρῳ παραθαλάσσιοι καὶ ὅσοι νήσους εἶχον 'the dwellers on the mainland coasts and those who inhabited islands', and vi. 84. 1 σῳζομένων ἡμῶν καὶ διὰ τὸ . . . ὑμᾶς . . . ἀντέχειν Συρακοσίοις ἧσσον ἂν . . . βλαπτοίμεθα 'if you are preserved . . . and through your resistance to Syracuse, we would suffer less harm'. Cf. also vi. 8. 2 βοηθοὺς μὲν Ἐγεσταίοις . . . ξυγκατοικίσαι δὲ καὶ Λεοντίνους 'as supporters of Segesta and to join in the re-establishment of Leontinoi'.[36]

We have seen from the analysis of Thuc. i. 70 that some multiples and symmetries stand out because they are marked by assonance, i.e. the phonemic identity of the beginnings or ends of co-ordinated or contrasted items.[37] This phenomenon is treated as stylistic by Arist. *Rhet.* 1410ᵃ25–37 and labelled παρομοίωσις (cf. Demetr. 25–7). Plato's Apollodorus makes a joking reference to it in *Smp.* 185 C Παυσανίου δὲ παυσαμένου—διδάσκουσι γάρ με ἴσα λέγειν οὑτωσὶ οἱ σοφοί 'When Pausanias had finished—the professionals tell me I should speak equal (sc. lengths) like that'. Recurrence of initial syllables is prominent in Gorgias (there are a dozen examples in the *Helen*) and sporadic thereafter, but not widely enough distributed for statistical treatment: examples are Isoc. vii. 4 συντέτακται καὶ συνακολουθεῖ, 12 διεσκαριφησάμεθα καὶ διελύσαμεν, 13 καὶ παραγιγνομένας καὶ παραμενούσας, 16 κινδύνων ἀποτροπὴν καί . . . κακῶν ἀπαλλαγήν, Dem. xviii. 4 καὶ πεποίηκα καὶ πεπολίτευμαι, 11 πεπραγμένων καὶ πεπολιτευμένων, 14 διέβαλλε καὶ διεξῄει. Final assonance, on the other hand, is easily quantified for the purpose of comparing texts: observe how often a mobile token in a multiple or symmetry ends like the mobile of the preceding item (in a multiple) or the responding item (in a symmetry). For this purpose both

[35] *SPG* 115 f. = *GPS* 73 f.
[36] Ros 255 (i. 2. 2), 392 (i. 5. 1), 195 (vi. 84. 1), 153, 388 (vi. 8. 2).
[37] *SPG* 189–91, 204–9 = *GPS* 124 f., 135–8, Rehdantz 3–5, 23.

'multiple' and 'symmetry' should be defined more loosely than they were for Tables 7.3 and 7.4, so that such pairings as $(A_1 + BB_1$ or $AA_1 B_1) (A_2 BB_2$ or $AA_2 B_2)$ are admitted, because an awareness of multiplicity or symmetry is actually created by the presence of assonance. Because of the phonotactic constraints on final consonants in Greek, to take account of the recurrence of single final phonemes (e.g. -ν, -ε) would blur the difference between samples; a minimum of two (e.g. -ον, -τε) should therefore be required.[38]

Comparison would be distorted by including instances in which compounds of the same stem are co-ordinated or opposed, e.g. Thuc. vi. 76. 4 οὐκ ἀξυνετωτέρου, κακοξυνετωτέρου δέ, Pl. *Smp.* 217 E γνωσομένοις τε καὶ συγγνωσομένοις; it is not common enough for us to reckon with encountering at least one example in every 1,000-mobile sample. The recurrence of a lexeme, a phenomenon discussed on pp. 131–43, is not assonance. Regarding a short vowel as a different phoneme from the same vowel lengthened, I treat a diphthong as if it were a single phoneme (the poets, after all, normally scan it like a long vowel), and I ignore the presence or absence of ephelcystic *nu*, as if there were no such thing.

TABLE 7.5. *Recurrent phonemes at mobile-end in twelve texts*

	I	II		I	II
Gorgias	240	26	Thuc. i	56	1
(scaled up)	320	35	Thuc. vi	68	2
Hp. *VM*	170	14	Pl. *Mnx.*	143	10
Hp. *Flat.*	131	9	Pl. *Smp.*	54	6
Hdt. i	32	1	Isoc. vii	216	12
Hdt. vii	41	1	Dem. xviii	80	5
Antiphon	70	6			

In Table 7.5 most of the samples are selected from those used in Tables 7.3 and/or 7.4, with the addition of Hp. *Flat.* 1–10 and Hdt. i. pr.–14. 2. Column I gives the total number of recurrent phonemes at mobile-end, and column II the number of instances in which at least two complete end-syllables recur (e.g. ἁμαρτήματα . . . ἀπατήματα).

Again, Gorgias leads the field; and again, Isocrates is notably

[38] If a postpositive is treated as part of the mobile which precedes it, there is no assonance; πράττειν τε καὶ λέγειν would be a case in point, and it may be that postpositives should always be so treated.

'Gorgianic'. It is curious that assonance should play so prominent a part in the two samples from the Hippocratic corpus, but evidently, when we look at the Herodotean samples, it is not a distinctive fea-. ture of Ionic prose as such. The great difference between the two Plato samples reflects the difference between epideictic oratory and narrative, and there is a hint of the relevance of genre to assonance in the difference between Thuc. vi (speeches) and Thuc. i (generalizing narrative), as well as between Hdt. vii (speeches) and Hdt. i (narrative, with a little dialogue).

The concentration of symmetry and assonance in Thuc. i. 70 makes it a 'show-piece' of a kind unusual in Thucydides, and we may wonder why he chose to put it into the mouth of an unnamed Corinthian. The content, however, helps to explain the form. Given that the purpose of the passage is to emphasize and maximize the differences between Athens and Sparta, and the relevance of those differences to the situation in 432, Thucydides had a choice between (i) 'they are a, b, c, . . . n, but you are not-a, not-b, not-c, . . . not-n', (ii) 'they are a, you are not-a; they are b, you are not-b, . . . they are n, you are not-n', and (iii) 'they are a, b, and c, but you are not-a, not-b, and not-c; they are d, e, and f, but you are not-d, not-e, not-f . . .'. The disadvantage of (i) is that the hearer has to work too hard to pair each item of the 'Sparta' series with one of the 'Athens' series; and of (ii), that it quickly deteriorates into a monotonous list; (iii) was therefore the wise aesthetic choice.

A more obvious influence of content on form is apparent in Xen. *Mem.* i. 2. 24 f., on Socrates' innocence of the charge that he had corrupted Critias and Alcibiades. Alcibiades

διὰ μὲν κάλλος	ὑπὸ πολλῶν καὶ σεμνῶν γυναικῶν	θηρώμενος,
because of his beauty	by many women of high class	being pursued
διὰ δύναμιν δὲ τὴν ἐν τῇ πόλει καὶ τοῖς συμμάχοις	ὑπὸ πολλῶν καὶ δυνατῶν ἀνθρώπων	διαθρυπτόμενος,
and because of his influence in the city and the allies	by many powerful people	being indulged,
	ὑπὸ δὲ τοῦ δήμου	τιμώμενος, κτλ.
	and by the electorate	being honoured, etc.

and then the two of them

(1)	ὠγκωμένω μὲν	ἐπὶ γένει,
	made vain	by family,
(2)	ἐπηρμένω δ'	ἐπὶ πλούτῳ,

		overconfident	through wealth,
(3)		πεφυσημένω δ'	ἐπὶ δυνάμει,
		puffed up	by power,
(4)		διατεθρυμμένω δὲ	ὑπὸ πολλῶν ἀνθρώπων,
		indulged	by many,
(5)	ἐπὶ δὲ πᾶσι τούτοις	διεφθαρμένω	
	and on all these counts	corrupted	
(6)		καὶ πολὺν χρόνον ἀπὸ Σωκράτους γεγονότε κτλ.	
		and away from Socrates for a long time, etc.	

(Note: there is no English preposition which suits all those instances of ἐπί.) This looks like a show-piece without parallel in the *Memorabilia*, and it makes an interesting contrast with Xenophon's characterization of Clearchus, Proxenus, and Meno in *Anab*. ii. 6. Xenophon's point is that so many forces acted upon Critias and Alcibiades that no evil in them can be attributed to what he treats as their earlier acquaintance with Socrates. There is no Gorgianic 'playfulness' here; the assonance and symmetry (and note the variations in (4) and (6); cf. p. 139) are meant to have the effect of table-thumping in an argument which is very serious indeed for Xenophon.

The effect of frequent short symmetries on the hearer is somewhat like the rocking of a boat, whereas long sequences divided by μέν and δέ or by a negative and ἀλλά are more like the slow rise and fall of a swell; that is particularly so in Isocrates, where even the reader comes to recognize a negative as more often than not a signal that an ἀλλά is in the offing; for the hearer, sentence intonation could make the prediction even easier. Table 7.6 shows how texts can differ in the proportions of shorter and longer μέν/δέ and 'not'/'but' sequences. μέν/ἀλλά, μέν/μέντοι, and μέν/οὐ μὴν ἀλλά are included, but I have excluded πρῶτον μέν/ἔπειτα 'first . . . secondly . . .', πρῶτον μέν/δεύτερον δέ (etc.), and, of course, the 'solitary' μέν to which no adversative particle responds.[39] In counting the number of mobiles in a sequence, I have started from the mobile to which μέν is attached, and in the case of 'not/but' from the first negative (οὐ . . ./ οὐδέ . . ./ἀλλά . . . is not uncommon), treating the simple negative (and οὐδέ and οὔτε) as prepositive but any compound negative as mobile.[40] To decide when a sequence ends is not always easy, since its main clause(s) may be followed by subordinate or participial

---

[39] Denniston 380–4.

[40] This applies even when the compound negative is the first token of the negative member; hence οὐκ ἠθύμει would count as one mobile, οὐκέτι ἠθύμει as two.

clauses which take our attention away from the basic opposition, and other hearers may sometimes disagree with my choice of the pause which seems to me to serve as a boundary.[41]

TABLE 7.6. *Lengths of symmetries in five texts*

	No. of instances	Number of mobile tokens per instance				
		2–5	6–10	11–15	16–20	21 or more
Gorgias						
μέν/. . .	27	14	9	1	2	1
scaled up:	36	19	12	1	3	1
not/but	4	3	1			
Thuc, vi						
μέν/. . .	26	2	13	4	3	4
not/but[a]	25	8	9	2	5	1
Pl. *Smp.*						
μέν/. . .	19	1	7	4	2	5
not/but	10	3	5	1	1	
Isoc. vii						
μέν/. . .	38	4	15	11	6	2
not/but	23	3	7	5	6	2
Dem. xviii						
μέν/. . .	29	3	8	8	5	5
not/but	10		3	1	3	3

[a] In 18 of the 25 instances the second member is connected by δέ, not by ἀλλά; this is distinctively Thucydidean.

The striking feature of this table—in accord with our unquantified subjective impressions of the authors in question—are: first, that Gorgias differs from the rest in having his highest number of μέν sequences at the lower end (2–5) of the scale; secondly, that Isocrates differs in having as many μέν sequences in the higher ranges (11+) as in the lower, while Demosthenes actually has more; and thirdly, that whereas Thucydides and Isocrates are very close in their total of not/but sequences, Thucydides has many more in the lower ranges (2–10) than in the higher, but Isocrates fewer.

In any symmetry it is possible to change the order of items within a member, creating the forms $(A_1 B_1) (B_2 A_2)$, $(A_1 B_1 C_1) (B_2 C_2 A_2)$, etc. This 'chiasmus' appears early in gnomic utterances, e.g. *Il.* ii. 204:

οὐκ ἀγαθὸν πολυκοιρανίη· εἷς κοίρανος ἔστω.

[41] A short symmetry may be contained within a longer one; in such a case, both are entered in the table, so that the mobiles of the shorter sequence are counted twice.

(lit.) Not good (sc. is) multiplicity-of-kings; one king let-there-be.

Cf. Hes. *Op.* 334, 345, 346, 365, 375. Unsurprisingly, the feature persists in Heraclitus and Democritus,[42] e.g. Democr. DK 68 B 177:

οὔτε λόγος ἐσθλὸς φαύλην πρῆξιν ἀμαυρίσκει οὔτε πρῆξις ἀγαθὴ λόγου βλασφη-μίῃ λυμαίνεται.

Fine words do not hide mean action, nor is good action harmed by hurtful words.

And evidently it was available to the administrative officials who composed public documents. The boundary-stones of Attic trit-tyes in the late fifth century begin 'At this point the [*name*₁] trittys ends', but continue with either 'and the [*name*₂] trittys begins' (*IG* i³ 1129) or 'and begins the [*name*₂] trittys' (*IG* i³1127).[43] So too *IG* xii (v) 593. 14 ff. (Iulis, s. v), lit. 'purify the house a free man with sea-water first, then with hyssop a slave going in'. This being so, the rarity of chiasmus in our sample texts is noteworthy. Clear examples are: Anon. *Ath.* 1. 13 (A₁) γυμνασιαρχοῦσιν (B₁) οἱ πλούσιοι (C₁) καὶ τριηραρχοῦσιν, (B₂) ὁ δὲ δῆμος (C₂) τριηραρχεῖται (A₂) καὶ γυμνασιαρχεῖται; Hdt. vii. 11. 2 (A₁) Σάρδεις τε (B₁) ἐνέπρησαν (B₂) καὶ ἤλασαν (A₂) ἐς τὴν Ἀσίην; Thuc. i. 5. 1 (A₁) κέρδους (B₁) τοῦ σφετέρου αὐτῶν ἕνεκα (B₂) καὶ τοῖς ἀσθενέσι (A₂) τροφῆς; Ant. 5. 12 (A₁) τὸν αὐτὸν ὅρκον σοὶ (B₁) διομοσαμένους (B₂) καὶ ἁπτομένους (A₂) τῶν σφαγίων; Lys. xii. 33 (A₁) πάντα τὰ κακὰ (B₁) εἰργασμένοις (C₁) τὴν πόλιν (A₂) πάντα τἀγαθὰ (C₂) περὶ αὐτῶν (B₂) λέγειν. There are a few more to be found among the *c.*240 symmetries entered in Table 7.4, especially in Pl. *Mnx.* 237 A 6, 239 D 2, 240 D 3, 241 E 3, which accords with Plato's (comparative) readiness to use chiasmus elsewhere,[44] but it seems that authors who make a significant use of symmetry fight shy, most of the time, of reducing the monotonous effect of repeating responding items in the same order. This cannot be attributed to primitive lack of skill, nor, as we have seen, to the absence of precedent. Herodotus knew very well how to use chias-mus with subtlety when he judged it appropriate to a show-piece, and in the first of the three speeches in the 'Persian debate' (iii. 80–2) we find (80. 3–5):

καὶ γὰρ ἂν τὸν ἄριστον ἀνδρῶν πάντων
(A₁) στάντα (B₁) ἐς (C₁) ταύτην τὴν ἀρχὴν
(B₂) ἐκτὸς (C₂) τῶν ἐωθότων νοημάτων (A₂) στήσειε.

---

[42] *SPG* 117 f. =*GPS* 74 f.   [43] Dover (1968a) 53.
[44] *SPG* 118–20=*GPS* 75–7.

For even the best of all men, if he were put into that position of power, it (sc. monarchy) would put outside his usual mind.

(A₁) ἐγγίνεται μὲν γὰρ οἱ (B₁) ὕβρις (C₁) ὑπὸ τῶν παρεόντων ἀγαθῶν,
(B₂) φθόνος δὲ (C₂) ἀρχῆθεν (A₂) ἐμφύεται ἀνθρώπῳ . . .

For arrogance is engendered in him by the blessings available to him, and jealousy is inborn in a human from the start . . .

(A₁) φθονέει γὰρ (B₁) τοῖσι ἀρίστοισι περιεοῦσί τε καὶ ζώουσι,
(A₂) χαίρει δὲ (B₂) τοῖσι κακίστοισι τῶν ἀστῶν
(A₃, B₃) διαβολὰς δὲ ἄριστος ἐνδέκεσθαι.

For he is jealous of the best (sc. men) so long as they live and survive, and he rejoices in the worst of the citizens, and (sc. he is) (lit.) best at being receptive to allegations of wrongdoing.

Herodotus could have said *διαβολὰς δὲ ἐνδέκεται μάλιστ' ἀνθρώπων 'and he is more receptive than anyone to allegations of wrongdoing', but after the straightforward symmetry of (A₁ B₁) (A₂ B₂), with its assonance of -ίστοισι reinforcing the antonymy 'best'/'worst', he preferred a twist in the tail (cf. p. 139), at the same time echoing the superlatives ironically, as one might say of a lout 'What he's *best* at is hurting people'.

ἀναρμοστότατον δὲ πάντων·
(A₁) ἤν τε γὰρ αὐτὸν μετρίως (B₁) θωμάζῃς,
      (C₁) ἄχθεται (D₁) ὅτι οὐ κάρτα θεραπεύεται·
(B₂) ἤν τε θεραπεύῃ τις (A₂) κάρτα,
      (C₂=C₁) ἄχθεται (D₂) ἅτε θωπί.

And what is most unacceptable of all: if you show him a reasonable degree of respect, he resents not being given complete attention, and if anyone attends to him completely, he resents him as being a toady.

The contrastive framework 'Reasonable respect—not enough! Abject respect—too much!' is complicated here by cross-currents, where θεραπεύειν from D₁ surfaces in B₂ and κάρτα also from D₁ in A₂. Variation is an added complication: the change from second-person θωμάζῃς to θεραπεύῃ τις, and the reversal of order in κάρτα θεραπεύεται~θεραπεύῃ τις κάρτα.

τὰ δὲ δὴ μέγιστα ἔρχομαι ἐρέων·
(A₁ₐ) νόμαιά τε (B₁) κινέει (A₁ᵦ) πάτρια
(B₂) καὶ βιᾶται (A₂) γυναῖκας
(B₃) κτείνει τε (A₃) ἀκρίτους.

And I will tell you the most important things:

He upsets long-established usages
and violates women
and executes without trial.

The three A-items are varied not only by the division of A₁ but
by the fact that although ἀκρίτους responds formally to γυναῖκας,
semantically it is very different; 'people who have not been tried'
do not constitute, as women and usages do, an ingredient of society
which is necessarily there already when the monarch takes power,
and ἀκρίτους is not an object of κτείνει, but a complement, the object
being understood as 'some people'.[45]

Herodotus crafted this passage—knowing when to stop—in a
way which makes the style of his younger contemporary Gorgias
sound adolescent.[46]

---

[45] There is a 'lurking' symmetry in many passages of Thucydides, e.g. (with
chiasmus) vi. 80. 2 (A₁?) τήν τε κοινὴν ὠφελίαν (B₁) τῇ Σικελίᾳ (C₁) φυλάξαι (B₂) καὶ
τοὺς Ἀθηναίους (A₂?) φίλους δὴ ὄντας (C₂) μὴ ἐᾶσαι ἁμαρτεῖν.

[46] Dion. i. 437. 4 calls Thuc. i. 70. 3 μειρακιώδης. Cf. Lucilius fr. 187, where
symmiraciodes (coupled with *Eisocration* and *Ierodes*) seems, as C. M. Francken saw,
to be the Latin prefix *sub-* (not, as in LSJ, συμ-) combined with μειρακιῶδες.

8

RHYTHM

ONE of the earliest passages of Greek literary prose which we possess—perhaps *the* earliest—is the opening of the theogonic work of Pherecydes Syr. (DK 7 B 1). Its rhythm is strongly dactylic, a formal reinforcement of the affinity of its content to Hesiodic poetry.

$$Ζὰς \ μὲν \ καὶ \ Χρόνος \ ἦσαν \ ἀεὶ^{1} \qquad -- \ -\cup\cup \ -\cup\cup \ -$$
$$καὶ \ Χθονίη· \ Χθονίη \ δέ \ . . . \qquad -\cup\cup \ -\cup\cup \ -\cup \ . . .$$

In B 2, a papyrus fragment of the same work, we find a sustained run of anapaestic rhythm:

$$καὶ \ χρήματα \ καὶ \ θεράποντας \qquad --\cup\cup- \ \cup\cup-- \ \text{(paroemiac)}$$
$$καὶ \ θεραπαίνας \ καὶ \ τἀλλ(α) \ ὅσα \ δεῖ \ . . . \qquad -\cup\cup-- \ --\cup\cup- \ \text{(anapaestic}$$
$$\text{dimeter)}$$

There is an abundance of comparable passages in Heraclitus,[2] notably B 61 on sea-water ('drinkable' by fishes but deadly to humans):

$$ἰχθύσι \ μὲν \ πότιμον \ . . . \qquad -\cup\cup-\cup\cup-$$
$$ἀνθρώποις \ δ(ὲ) \ ἄποτον \ καὶ \ ὀλέθριον \qquad -- \ -\cup\cup-\cup\cup-\cup\cup$$

Here, in the second member, word-end after the fourth dactyl is especially reminiscent of the hexameter—provided (and we don't know) that δέ was elided, καί shortened by correption, -λέθρι- treated as -λέθ'ρι-, and -ριον followed by a word beginning with a vowel and not by pause.[3] Many potentially dactylic and anapaestic sequences in Heraclitus require us to choose between alternative assumptions.[4] Is hiatus acceptable in B 31 τὸ μὲν ἥμισυ γῆ, τὸ δὲ ἥμισυ

---

[1] Assuming ἀεί; but that assumption may be wrong.

[2] Cf. Haberle 8, de Groot 28–33, and particularly Deichgräber (1962)—who, however, does not hesitate to emend (e.g. 524 on B 121) in order to give the rhythm he wants.

[3] Cf. McCabe 4 f., 129 on the prosody of final syllables at pause in Demosthenes; given the universal practice of the poets, the a priori assumption of *brevis in longo* at pause should be adopted.

[4] Blass (1901) 59 reminds us that we are in fact guessing, in every instance, how the author himself chose to treat that instance.

πρηστήρ, B 54 ἁρμονίη ἀφανὴς φανερῆς κρείσσων, B 62 ἀθάνατοι θνητοί, θνητοὶ ἀθάνατοι, B 99 εἰ μὴ ἥλιος ἦν, B 117 ἄγεται ὑπὸ παιδὸς ἀνήβου? And correption in B 26 ἅπτεται εὕδοντος? What is the prosody of -νέου- and τοι- in B 17 οὐ γὰρ φρονέουσι τοιαῦτα? Is it possible (I greatly doubt it) that μαρτυρέει was intended in B 34 μαρτυρεῖ παρεόντας ἀπεῖναι? That is just a sample of the occasions on which we have to make a prosodic choice, but enough to show that accurate assessment of the extent to which an early prose writer adopts poetic rhythms is not straightforward. One thing which does emerge from the putative examples, however, is that the writer tends to draw back from sustaining such a rhythm for more than seven or eight syllables. Heraclitus B 61, after the dactylic ἰχθύσι μὲν πότιμον, breaks away rhythmically by continuing καὶ σωτήριον. So too in Pherecydes Syr. B 2 the long anapaestic run καὶ χρήματα . . . ὅσα δεῖ is both preceded and followed by πάντα. A little later in the same passage we are told that Zeus made 'a great and splendid robe', φᾶρος . . . μέγα τε καὶ καλόν. Those acquainted with Homer are likely to recall the formulae κᾱλός τε μέγας τε, κᾱλὴν καὶ μεγάλην, etc.,[5] but Pherecydes has done what he could to discourage reminiscence.

Dactylic and anapaestic rhythms have a double association: with moralizing dicta and proverbs, and with heroic narrative. Dicta may be single hexameters separable in content from their narrative context, e.g. *Il.* ii. 204 οὐκ ἀγαθὸν πολυκοιρανίη· εἷς κοίρανος ἔστω, 'a multitude of kings is not good; let there be one king', or half-hexameters (a traditional form in self-standing proverbs), e.g. Hes. *Op.* 218 παθὼν δέ τε νήπιος ἔγνω ⟨even⟩ a fool understands after the event' ≃ *Il.* xvii. 32 ῥεχθὲν δέ τε νήπιος ἔγνω. In Heraclitus we sometimes find, as in poetic dicta, dactylo-anapaestic rhythm combined with a compression which verges on the enigmatic, as in B 52 αἰὼν παῖς ἐστι παίζων, πεσσεύων· παιδὸς ἡ βασιληΐη, 'life is a child enjoying itself, playing with counters; rule ⟨over us⟩ is a child's' and B 34 ἀξύνετοι ἀκούσαντες κωφοῖσιν ἐοίκασι[6] φάτις αὐτοῖσι μαρτυρεῖ παρεόντας ἀπεῖναι, 'those who have heard without understanding are like deaf people' (or 'people without understanding resemble deaf people even when they have ⟨apparently⟩ heard'); 'their speech testifies that they are there but not there'. This imparting of a

---

[5] *ELDH* 437 f.

[6] I adopt the translation of Nussbaum 12. I have also assumed that Heraclitus said -ᾱσι, not the Attic -ᾶσι (but cf. Chantraine i. 471), in the third person plural of the active perfect. κωφοῖσιν ἐοίκασι then reminds one of the fourth-dactyl diaeresis in hexameters.

poetic charge to moralizing dicta[7] was less favoured later in the fifth
century; the sense of the epic dictum about the fool whose understanding comes too late is spelled out more plainly in Democritus
B 54 οἱ ἀξύνετοι δυστυχέοντες σωφρονέουσι, 'those who lack understanding acquire sense when they meet with misfortune', and B 76
νηπίοισιν οὐ λόγος ἀλλὰ ξυμφορὴ γίνεται διδάσκαλος, 'it is not reason
but mishap that is teacher to fools'—where, however, (non-gnomic)
rhythms are strong: $-\cup\cup-$ $-\cup\cup--$ $-\cup\cup-\frown$ and $-\cup-\cup$ $-\cup\cup---\cup-$
$-\cup-\cup-\cup\frown$. But we still catch the gnomic note in the long passage of
Antiphon the Sophist (DK 87 B 49) on marriage, notably in μέγας
γὰρ ἀγὼν γάμος ἀνθρώπῳ, 'marriage is a great moment of decision
for a man', expressed in the form of an anapaestic dimeter (with
initial $\cup$). This is immediately preceded by αὕτη ἡ ἡμέρα, αὕτη ἡ νύξ,
καινοῦ δαίμονος ἄρχει, καινοῦ πότμου, 'that day, that night, is the start
of a new destiny, a new fortune', where the word πότμος is poetic,
and repetition with asyndeton comes close to incantation—as a few
words later, ἴσα φρονοῦντας, ἴσα πνέοντας, 'united in mind, united in
spirit'. Yet the passage is by no means wholly poetic in character: its
symmetries are familiar enough in epideictic prose (cf. the passage
of [Lys.] ii cited on pp. 5–7),[8] and a substantial part of it, from ἐν τῷ
αὐτῷ δέ γε τούτῳ (p. 358, l. 8) to καὶ τῆς εὐκλείας (p. 359, l.13), could
fairly be called 'prosy' in the usual sense of the word. The author
has simply used poetic rhythm and vocabulary as an ingredient to
lend the authority of the poet to admonitory dicta.

Snatches of dactylic rhythm appear occasionally in the citations
from the early historians,[9] e.g. Pherec. Ath. 35 F 35 θητεύσων ἐνι-
αυτόν, F 64 καὶ ἔρχεται εἰς Δελφοὺς περὶ παίδων χρησόμενος, and
Hecataeus F 6 καὶ Ψωφιδίους κακὰ πολλὰ ἔοργε. In *Il.* v. 175 we find
κακὰ πολλὰ ἔοργε; but the text of F 6 as transmitted by Stephanus
Byz. has πόλλ' ἔοργε, and that may well have been intended by
Hecataeus in order to avoid excessive versification. Cf. Hellanicus
FGrHist 4 F 26 ἀνδράσιν εἰδόμενοι ἐπὶ μισθῷ. It is, however, no-
ticeable that some geographical data in Hecataeus begin with the
hemiepes ἐν δ' αὐτοῖσι πόλις (e.g. F 163) or the like, and it is rea-

---

[7] Cf. *ELDH* 441. Norden (1915) 22 notes echoes of Heraclitus in Democritus, but
the clearest examples do not exemplify poetic rhythms. Havelock 55 hears a 'solemn
lilt' in Heraclitus.

[8] *Wf* 204, 210.

[9] Lilja 22–4.

sonable to suppose that metrical form in such cases is accidental.[10]
How often, then, ought we to attribute to mere accident sequences
in prose which are familiar to us in poetry? Statistical considerations suggest that the right answer is: quite often. Out of a possible
256 sequences of eight long and short syllables, no less than 32, one
in eight, are familiar in poetry, viz.:

– ∪ – x – ∪ – x	trochaic dimeter	(four possibilities)
x – ∪ – x – ∪ –	iambic dimeter	(four)
x – ∪ – – ∪ ∪ – – ∪ ∪ – x – ∪ – }	iambo-choriambic dimeter	(four)
o o – ∪ ∪ – ∪ –	glyconic	(three)
o o – x – ∪ ∪ –	wilamowitzian	(six)
∪∪∪ – x – ∪ – – ∪ ∪∪ x – ∪ – – ∪ – x ∪∪∪ – }	lekythion with one longum resolved	(six)
∪ ∪ – – ∪ ∪ – –	ionic dimeter	(one)
∪ ∪ – x – ∪ – x	anacreontic	(four)

If we add to these the commonest dactylic and anapaestic sequences
of six to ten syllables,[11] some single-short sequences of six syllables
(e.g. the cretic dimeter – ∪ – – ∪ – and the ithyphallic – ∪ – ∪ – –),[12]
and all the possibilities created by resolution of longa in trochaics
and iambics, we can see that it is impracticable to avoid familiar
poetic rhythms in composing Greek prose.[13]

This is illustrated by the fact that the seven double-short sequences listed in Table 8.1 actually occur more often in a set of
three Attic decrees (*IG* i³ 40, 52, and 78),[14] totalling 797 mobile
tokens, than in Heraclitus, whose citations contain approximately
890.

An even more striking illustration is afforded by a simple experi-

[10] Lilja 21 f., Dion. ii. 127. 7 f. observes that 'Nature often produces metres spon-
taneously'. Cf. de Groot 6–8 and the articles of Broadhead and Shewring.
[11] Itsumi 72 f. lists 24 forms (not all textually certain) which the wilamowitzian
may take in Euripides.
[12] Conomis 23–8 lists 32 forms of dochmiac.
[13] There is no sequence of (say, a dozen) longs and shorts of which anyone could
say, 'This sequence *cannot* occur in Greek lyric.' We can say that of putative *respon-
sions*, but that is another matter.
[14] I chose these documents for their good state of preservation, before knowing
what their rhythmical yield would be.

TABLE 8.1. *Double-short sequences in four texts*

| | Heraclitus | *IG* i³ | | |
		40	52	78
–⏑⏑–⏑⏑–	54, 61	21		
–⏑⏑–––	26, 32, 57, 61	6, 23, 48, 52	16, 21, 27	
–––⏑⏑–	45, 57, 58, 61 *bis*, 99	33,[a] 56, 75	19	52
×–⏑⏑–⏑⏑–	51, 76			
–⏞–⏞–×	30, 74, 107	32	4, 13	21, 37
anapaestic				
dimeter	15		B13	8, 38, 44[b]
paroemiac	5, 30, 117		23	23, 60

[a] Admitting one hiatus, μὲ ὀμόσει.
[b] Admitting one hiatus, καὶ ℎελλένōν.

ment. Take a prose text and invert the first two mobile tokens after pause and the last two before pause, converting (e.g.):

Thuc. i. 1. 1 Θουκυδίδης Ἀθηναῖος ξυνέγραψε τὸν πόλεμον τῶν Πελοποννησίων καὶ Ἀθηναίων, ὡς ἐπολέμησαν πρὸς ἀλλήλους, ἀρξάμενος εὐθὺς καθισταμένου καὶ ἐλπίσας μέγαν τε ἔσεσθαι καὶ ἀξιολογώτατον τῶν προγεγενημένων, κτλ.

into:

*Ἀθηναῖος Θουκυδίδης . . . τῶν Ἀθηναίων καὶ Πελοποννησίων, ὡς πρὸς ἀλλήλους ἐπολέμησαν, εὐθὺς ἀρξάμενος . . . τῶν προγεγενημένων ἀξιολογώτατον, κτλ.

Then compare the rhythmic sequences of the original with those of the artificially manipulated text; if the score in the original is significantly[15] higher, it promotes the suspicion that the author deliberately sought poetic rhythms, but if significantly lower, that he deliberately avoided them. Herodotus is not a suitable subject for this experiment, because there is far too much doubt about the relation between his pronunciation and the spelling of the transmitted text, but the experiment can be performed on Attic prose texts, and Table 8.2 (p. 168) shows its results for Thuc. i, Plato *Rep.* ii, Isoc. vii, and Dem. xviii. The quantity of text in each case is the first hundred pauses, 'pause' being defined as the point at which the modern editor punctuates (Stuart Jones for Thucydides, Burnet for Plato, Mathieu for Isocrates, Butcher for Demosthenes).[16]

The very first sentence of Thucydides poses a problem. Did he

[15] Statisticians rightly warn us against the idle use of this word (cf. p. 45), but that is not an excuse for ignoring great disparities as if they necessarily lacked significance.

[16] I have adhered to this principle even when I disagree with the editor. The disagreements do not make much difference to the results.

pronounce καὶ Ἀ- in καὶ Ἀθηναίων with hiatus (-‿), correption (‿‿), or synecphonesis (-)? Since hiatus and its avoidance are an aspect of prose style to which importance was attached from the late fifth century onwards, we have to reckon with ancient as well as modern editorial decisions founded on theory or aesthetic preference. We can well envisage circumstances in which a pause after ὅμως δέ or ἔπειτα would be appropriate and the printing of an elision mislead-ing, to say nothing of hiatus at the boundary of a phrase, e.g. Dem. xviii. 7 καὶ τὰ τοῦ λέγοντος ὑστέρου δίκαια ⋮ εὐνοϊκῶς προσδέξεται. To avoid begging any questions, I confine myself in the experiment to sequences of syllables in which there is no prosodic ambiguity at all—no opportunity for elision, hiatus, correption, or synecphone-sis, no creation of a long syllable by ephelcystic *nu*,[17] and no syllables (e.g. πόεῖν, πατρός) whose scansion affects the rhythmical classifica-tion of the sequences in which they occur. These exclusions apply equally to the manipulated text. It follows that some of the original sequences allow of no admissible transposition, and the originals of some of the transpositions are equally inadmissible. I do not admit any transposition which violates normal Greek practice in respect of the placing of appositives. I leave out of account sequences which contain only one mobile each or cannot undergo transposition with-out being grossly un-Greek, e.g. Thuc. i. 1. 1 τὸ μὲν εὐθύς, τὸ δὲ καὶ διανοούμενον.

In the following list the (A)-rows present those instances of cer-tain selected rhythmical sequences which are bounded on one side by pause and on the other by token-end (or on occasion by pause on both sides). The (B)-rows show what would result from trans-position on the principles described. '|' marks pause.

anapaestic dimeter (≈ – ≈ – ≈ – ≈ –)
Isoc. (B) 6 *συμβάντων καὶ Λακεδαιμονίοις |
    (B) 9 *ἀπολωλεκότες τὰς ἐπὶ Θρᾴκης |

paroemiac (≈ – ≈ – ‿‿ – –)
Thuc. (A) 5. 3 λῃστείας ἐμμεμένηκε(ν) |

ionic dimeter (‿‿ – – ‿‿ – – , ‿‿ – ‿‿ – – , ‿‿ – – ‿‿ –)
Thuc. (A) 8. 1 | ὑπὲρ ἥμισυ Κᾶρες (κ-)
    (B) 2. 4 *| διὰ γὰρ γῆς ἀρετήν

---

[17] On the problems created by ephelcystic *nu* cf. McCabe 67–72. It makes no difference, of course, when it occurs in a syllable occupying *anceps* position, and such instances are included in my list.

Pl. (A) 358 B 4 | ἐπιθυμῶ γὰρ ἀκοῦσαι
   (B) 359 C 5 *| ὃ φύσις πᾶσα διώκειν

ionic trimeter (∪∪– ∪∪–– ∪∪–)

Isoc. (B) 12 *| χρόνον οὐδένα τὰς εὐτυχίας

anacreontic (∪∪–×–∪––)

Thuc. (B) 2. 4 *ἐπεβουλεύοντο μᾶλλον |
Pl. (A) 359 A 4 νόμιμόν τε καὶ δίκαιον |
Dem. (B) 9 *περὶ τούτων πρῶτον εἰπεῖν |

dactylic trimeter (–⏖–∪∪––)

Isoc. (A) 12 καὶ διελύσαμεν αὐτάς |
   (B) 10 *πραττόντων τὰ δέοντα |
Dem. (A) 7 τῷ φεύγοντι παρελθεῖν |
   (A) 12 | τοῦ δὲ παρόντος ἀγῶνος

hemiepes (–∪∪–∪∪–, –––∪∪–, –∪∪–––)

Thuc. (B) 2. 6 *τὴν πόλιν ἀνθρώπων
   (B) 4 *| ἐξελάσας Κᾶρας (κ-)
   (B) 6. 6 *τῷ νῦν βαρβαρικῷ |
Isoc. (A) 1 | ὥσπερ τῆς πόλεως
Pl. (A) 358 C 1 | καὶ πρῶτον μὲν ἐγώ
   (B) 357 B 5 *τῶν ἀποβαινόντων |
Dem. (A) 1 | τοῦτο παραστῆσαι
   (A) 3 | τῶν μὲν λοιδοριῶν
   (A) 6 ᾤετο δεῖν εἶναι |
   (B) 4 *καὶ πεπολίτευμαι |

hagesichorean (×–∪∪–∪––)

Dem. (A) 5 | πάντων γὰρ ἀποστερεῖσθαι

glyconic (∘∘–∪∪–∪–)

Thuc. (A) 6. 3 τῶν ἐν τῇ κεφαλῇ τριχῶν |
   (B) 2 *ἐξέπεμψαν ἀποικίας |
Isoc. (B) 9 *ἀνθρώποις διακειμένοις |
Pl. (A) 357 D 3 τὴν δικαιοσύνην τιθείς |
Dem. (A) 7 | αἷς ἐκ τοῦ πρότερος λέγειν

pherecratean (∘∘–∪∪––)

Isoc. (A) 13 | οὐδὲ τοῖς μετὰ πλείστων
   (B) 6 *| ἤλθομεν παρὰ μικρόν
   (B) 10 *δὶς τεθύκαμεν ἤδη |
   (B) 10 *πραττόντων τὰ δέοντα |
Pl. (A) 357 A 3 τυγχάνει πρὸς ἅπαντα |
Dem. (A) 12 ἡ προαίρεσις αὕτη |
   (A) 12 | εἴπερ ἦσαν ἀληθεῖς |

aristophanean (–◡◡–◡––)
Pl. (B) 359 C 5 *ὡς ἀγαθὸν πέφυκε(ν) |
   (B) 359 D 2 *| ποιμένα μὲν γὰρ εἶναι

ibycean (–◡◡–◡◡–◡–)
Dem. (A) 11 τῆς ἀνέδην γεγενημένης |

iambo-choriambic (×–◡– –◡◡–, –◡◡– ×–◡–)
Thuc. (A) 2. 3 τὰ πολλὰ πλὴν Ἀρκαδίας |
Isoc. (B) 6 *ἐκ πραγμάτων τῶν ἰδίων |
Pl. (B) 357 C 8 *οὐκ ἂν ἔχειν δεξαίμεθα |
Dem. (A) 7 εὐνοϊκῶς προσδέξεται |
   (A) 11 | τοὺς περὶ τῶν πεπραγμένων
   (A) 12 | οὐκ ἔνι τῇ πόλει δίκην
   (B) 1 *εἰς τὸν ἀγῶνα τουτονί |
   (B) 8 = 1

choriambic dimeter (–◡◡– –◡◡–)
Pl. (A) 358 A 6 φευκτέον ὡς ὂν χαλεπόν |

wilamowitzian (∘∘–× –◡◡–)
Thuc. (A) 3. 3 τοὺς ξύμπαντας ὠνόμασε(ν) |
   (A) 5. 1 | οἱ γὰρ Ἕλληνες τὸ πάλαι
   (A) 8. 1 | Δήλου γὰρ καθαιρομένης
   (B) 5. 1 *καὶ τροφῆς τοῖς ἀσθενέσι(ν) |
Isoc. (A) 3 κινδύνους καθισταμένας |
   (A) 3 ταῦτα τυγχάνω δεδιώς |
   (A) 14 | ἔστι γὰρ ψυχὴ πόλεως
Pl. (A) 358 A 8 ὡς τοιοῦτον ὂν ψέγεται |
Dem. (A) 7 | καὶ παρασχὼν αὐτὸν ἴσον
   (A) 12 | τῶν μέντοι κατηγοριῶν

Alcaic enneasyllable (×–◡–×–◡–×)
Isoc. (A) 14 οἷανπερ ἂν ταύτην ἔχωσι(ν) |

trochaic dimeter (–◡–× –◡–×)
Thuc. (A) 6. 1 | καὶ ξυνήθη τὴν δίαιταν
   (B) 3. 2 *μᾶλλον Ἕλληνας καλεῖσθαι |
Isoc. (A) 8 | ὅστις οὖν εἰδὼς τοσαύτας
   (B) 12 *ἠδυνήθημεν κατασχεῖν |
Dem. (A) 10 οἷον οὗτος ἠτιᾶτο |
   (B) 9 *Αἰσχίνης κατηγόρησε(ν) |

iambic dimeter (×–◡– ×–◡–)
Pl. (B) 357 A 1 *ᾤμην ἀπηλλάχθαι λόγου

lekythion (–◡–×–◡–)
Isoc. (B) 9 *| οἵτινες τὰς μὲν πόλεις
Dem. (A) 5 ἄξιον σπουδῆς ἐμοί |

cretic dimeter ($-\cup-\ -\cup-$)

Thuc. (A) 6. 1 ὥσπερ οἱ βάρβαροι |
  (A) 6. 5 | καὶ διεζωμένοι

Isoc. (A) 5 | ἐκ δὲ τῆς κρείττονος
  (B) 11 *τῆς διοικήσεως |
  (B) 13 *εἰς τὸν αὐτὸν τόπον |
  (B) 15 *| ἧς διεφθαρμένης

Pl. (A) 359 B 4 | ἡ μὲν οὖν δὴ φύσις
  (A) 359 C 1 | δόντες ἐξουσίαν

Dem. (A) 1 | τοῖς θεοῖς εὔχομαι
  (A) 5 καὶ φιλανθρωπίας |

iambic + bacchiac ($\times-\cup-\ \cup--$)

Thuc. (B) 2. 1 *οἰκουμένη βεβαίως |

Pl. (B) 357 D 1 *| χάριν δὲ τῶν τε μισθῶν

Dem. (A) 5 τούτων μέγιστόν ἐστι(ν) |

ithyphallic ($-\cup-\cup--$)

Thuc. (A) 2. 1 | φαίνεται γὰρ ἡ νῦν

Isoc. (A) 4 | ἀλλὰ συντέτακται

Dem. (B) 3 *ἡδέως ἀκούειν |
  (B) 10 *καὶ λέγω δίκαια |

bacchiac dimeter ($\cup--\ \cup--$)

Thuc. (A) 6. 5 ἐπειδὴ πέπαυται |
  (B) 3. 3 *Ὅμηρος μάλιστα |

Isoc. (A) 7 κατέστησαν ἡμῖν |
  (A) 19 διελθεῖν πρὸς ὑμᾶς |
  (B) 19 *πρὸς ὑμᾶς διελθεῖν |

Dem. (A) 9 | ἀναγκαῖον εἶναι

TABLE 8.2. *Poetic
rhythms in four texts*

	A	B
Thucydides	12	10
Isocrates	12	15
Plato	9	7
Demosthenes	21	7

The sample is too small to justify firm conclusions about the
rhythmical preferences of the four authors, but in the case of three
of them it is enough to suggest that the occurrence of poetic rhythms
is a matter of chance; and this is a strong warning against imagining

aesthetic reasons in particular instances. We would expect to find a predominance of poetic rhythms in the actual text over those created by mechanical transposition of mobiles at pause only when there is some positive indication that the author wishes to invest his prose with poetic colour. This is the case in Pl. *Phdr.* 245 C–256 E, the Myth of the Soul, where Plato tells us that the vocabulary is poetic (cf. p. 103). There, the rhythms are sustained;[18] but any author may on occasion yield to the temptation, and Thucydides was surely right to do so in vii. 87. 5, where the annihilation of the Athenians at Syracuse is described as being (for the Syracusans) the most decisive victory in Greek history, καὶ τοῖς διαφθαρεῖσι δυστυχέστατον,[19] 'and for those destroyed, the most grievous'—a perfect, sombre iambic trimeter which implicitly likens tragic events to tragic myth in drama.[20]

The most striking concentration of poetic rhythms is to be found in the peroration of Agathon's encomium on Eros, Pl. *Smp.* 197 DE, which is susceptible of the following metrical analysis:

(1) οὗτος δ' ἡμᾶς

– – – –

anapaestic

(2) ἀλλοτριότητος μὲν κενοῖ,   (3) οἰκειότητος δὲ πληροῖ,

– ⌣⌣ – – ⌣ –   – – ⌣ – – ⌣ – –

iambic dimeter   iambic + trochaic

(4) τὰς τοιάσδε συνόδους μετ' ἀλλήλων   (5) πάσας τιθεὶς συνιέναι,

– ⌣ – ⌣⌣ – ⌣ – – –   – – ⌣ – ⌣⌣ –

cretic dimeter + ⌣ – – –   iambic + cretic

(6) ἐν ἑορταῖς, ἐν χοροῖς, ἐν θυσίαισι(ν)

⌣ ⌣ – – – ⌣ – – ⌣ ⌣ – ⌴

ionic trimeter (anacreontic + ionic)

(7) γιγνόμενος ἡγεμών· (8) πραότητα μὲν πορίζων, (9) ἀγριότητα δ' ἐξορίζων,

– ⌣⌣ – ⌣ –   – ⌣ – ⌣ – ⌣ – –   ⌣⌣ – ⌣ – ⌣ – –

cretic dimeter   trochaic dimeter   trochaic dimeter

(10) φιλόδωρος εὐμενείας,   (11) ἄδωρος δυσμενείας·

⌣ ⌣ – ⌣ – ⌣ – –   ⌣ – – – ⌣ – –

anacreontic   acephalous anacreontic

[18] For the details see Dover in Ayres 13–22.
[19] δυστυχεῖν, -ής, -ία are abundant in Euripides but not so common in prose; of 29 examples in Lysias, 12 are in the *Epitaphios*, and there are none in Antiphon i, v, vi or Andocides i and iii.
[20] Lamb 266; Hornblower 115.

(12) ἴλεως ἀγανός· (13) θεατὸς σοφοῖς, (14) ἀγαστὸς θεοῖς·

‒∪‒∪∪‒   ∪‒‒∪‒   ∪‒‒∪‒

dodrans   dochmiac   dochmiac

(15) ζηλωτὸς ἀμοίροις, (16) κτητὸς εὐμοίροις·

‒‒∪∪‒‒   ‒∪‒‒‒

reizianum   syncopated cretic dimeter

(17) τρυφῆς, ἁβρότητος, (18) χλιδῆς, χαρίτων, (19) ἱμέρου, πόθου πατήρ·

∪‒∪∪‒‒   ∪‒∪∪‒   ‒∪‒∪‒∪‒

reizianum   lekythion

(20) ἐπιμελὴς ἀγαθῶν, ἀμελὴς κακῶν· (21) ἐν πόνῳ, ἐν φόβῳ, ἐν πόθῳ, ἐν

∞∞∪‒∪∪‒∪∪‒∪‒   ‒∪◡‒∪◡‒∪◡‒∪‒ [λόγῳ

expanded glyconic   expanded ibycean[21]

(22) κυβερνήτης, ἐπιβάτης, (23) παραστάτης τε καὶ σωτὴρ ἄριστος,

∪‒∪‒   ‒∞∞‒   ∪‒∪‒   ∪‒‒   ‒∪‒‒

bacchiac + iambic   iambic + bacchiac + trochaic (=no. 30)

(24) συμπάντων τε θεῶν καὶ‿ἀνθρώπων κόσμος,

‒‒‒∪∪‒   ‒‒‒‒‒

two hemiepe

(25) ἡγεμὼν κάλλιστος καὶ ἄριστος, (26) ᾧ χρὴ ἕπεσθαι

‒∪‒   ‒‒‒◡∪‒⌒   ‒◡∪‒‒

cretic + pherecratean   adonean

(27) πάντ' ἄνδρ' ἐφυμνοῦντα καλῶς, (28) ᾠδῆς μετέχονται

‒‒∪‒∪∪‒   ‒‒∪∪‒

iambo-choriambic   reizianum

(29) ἦν ᾄδει θέλγων (30) πάντων θεῶν τε καὶ‿ἀνθρώπων νόημα·

‒‒‒‒‒   ‒‒∪‒   ∪‒‒   ‒∪‒⌒

hemiepes   iambic + bacchiac + trochaic (=no. 23)

The lyric character of the passage is reinforced by the trio (7)–(9) and the pairs (10)–(11) and (13)–(14). Twenty-two of the thirty 'verses' are marked off from the next by punctuation in modern editions, and there is no punctuation required within a verse except to distinguish the components of a pair or list: (6), (17), (18), (19), (20), (21), (22). There is no hiatus which cannot be avoided by positing verse-end (2/3), normal elision, correption (21 and—more doubtfully—26), or commonplace synecphonesis with καί (24, 25, 30). Socrates says (198 C) 'the speech put me in mind of Gorgias', and indeed it puts us in mind of Gorgias long before the peroration, because of its reference to its own organization: 194 E 'I wish first

---

[21] Cf. Ar. *Lys.* 1283/4; Dale 167.

to speak of how I should speak, and then to speak', 195 A 'So it is right that we too should first praise Eros himself for the kind of god he is, and then praise his gifts to us', 196 B 'I have said enough about the beauty of the god, though there is still much more that could be said; I come now to the admirable character of Eros'. Compare Gorgias *AS* B VII 42 = DK 82 B 6, 'May I be able to say what I wish to say, and may I wish to say what I should', *AS* B VII 39. 15 = DK 82 B 11. 15, 'I have explained how, if she was persuaded by words, she did not commit a wrong but suffered a misfortune; I will now, in my fourth argument, expound the fourth cause.' But were lyric passages like Agathon's peroration characteristic of Gorgias? In Gorgias' *Defence of Helen* (*AS* B VII 39 = DK 82 B 11) and the famous citation from his *Funeral Speech* (*AS* B VII 42 = DK 82 B 6) there are sequences of words which permit, even encourage, metrical analysis, e.g. 39. 1 κόσμος πόλει μὲν εὐανδρία ($--\cup- \quad \cup--\cup-$ = iambic + dochmiac), 39. 8 εἰ δὲ λόγος ὁ πείσας καὶ τὴν ψυχὴν ἀπατήσας ($-\cup\sim\sim-- \quad ----\cup\cup--$ = ithyphallic + paroemiac), 42 Διὸς μὲν ἀγάλματα, τούτων δ(ὲ) ἀναθήματα (two telesilleans = $\cup-\cup\cup-\cup\cap \mid --\cup\cup-\cup\cap$). However, the frequent occurrence of somewhat intractable hiatus is an obstacle to scansion, to a degree quite different from anything that we encounter in Agathon's peroration, e.g. 39. 6 βίᾳ ἁρπασθεῖσα . . . ἄξιος αἰτιᾶσθαι ὁ αἰτιώμενος . . . ὑπὸ τοῦ ἥσσονος . . . τὸ ἧσσον, 42 νόμου ἀκριβείας and οὖτ(ε) ἐμφύτου Ἄρεως . . . οὖτ(ε) ἐνοπλίου ἔριδος οὖτε φιλοκάλου εἰρήνης. Since Agathon was a tragic poet, and has burst into impromptu hexameters immediately before (197 C) his peroration, it is understandable that in addition to parodying his Gorgianic style in the greater part of his encomium Plato should also have given his hymn in praise of Eros, a long chain of phrases of a kind very unusual in prose, a heavy charge of poetic language and rhythm.[22]

If all occurrences of poetic rhythm in prose were to be explained either as a deliberate attempt to exploit the associations of poetry or as mere accident, we would be hard put to it to explain the very high count of poetic sequences in the opening portion of Demosthenes xviii. In the experiment made above, in which all ambiguities of

---

[22] Agathon describes his speech as part παιδιά, 'fun', part σπουδὴ μετρία, 'a fair degree of seriousness', but I do not think there is a sharp division between the two at 197 C (as there might have been but for μετρία). The παιδιά is the strand of provocative ingenuity which runs through his arguments; Gorgias, after all, described his own defence of Helen as an encomium of her and 'a conceit (παίγνιον) of my own' (*AS* B VII 39. 21 = DK 82 B 11. 21).

scansion were eliminated at the start, we found in that portion fifteen instances of 'double-short' rhythms (dactylic, anapaestic, ionic, choriambic) as against only four that could be created by manipulation.[23] If we now admit all the obvious elisions and synecphoneses, the single section (§13) which follows the sample contains the following:

| οὐ γὰρ ἀφαιρεῖσθαι (hemiepes)
| οὐδ' ἐν ἐπηρείας (hemiepes)
οὔτε δίκαιόν ἐστιν | (aristophanean)
| ἀλλ' ἐφ' οἷς ἀδικοῦντά μ' (pherecratean)
| οὐσί γε τηλικούτοις (aristophanean)
　(followed by a dactylic trimeter, ἡλίκα νῦν ἐτραγῴδει)
τἀδικήματα χρῆσθαι | (pherecratean)
καθιστάντα παρ' ὑμῖν | (pherecratean)
αὐτὸν οὐκ ἂν ἐγράψατο | (glyconic)

The most probable explanation is that Demosthenes, as an individual (not 'the orators' in general), developed his rhythmic preferences for prose in its own right,[24] as if poetry did not exist. One consequence of this was that he was indifferent to the accidental creation of whole verses in cases where poetry would have been totally out of place, e.g. xviii. 71 | καὶ καθιστὰς ἐν μὲν Ὠρεῷ[25] Φιλιστίδην τύραννον | (acatalectic trochaic tetrameter), xxi. 4 | ἃ δ' ἐν ὑμῖν μετὰ ταῦτ' ἔσθ' ὑπόλοιπα | (ionic trimeter), xxi. 179 | ταῦτ' ἔλεγεν μὲν ἐκεῖνος, ἐχειροτονήσατε δ' ὑμεῖς | (dactylic hexameter),[26] ibid. 180 ὅ τε δῆμος ἅπας κατεχειροτόνησ' ἀδικεῖν περὶ τὴν ἑορτήν | (iambo-anapaestic),[27] ibid. | καὶ τούτῳ μεθύων ἐπάταξέ τιν' ἐχθρὸν ὑπάρχονθ' ἑαυτῷ | (dactylo-epitrite).[28]

The first we hear from the Greeks about prose rhythm[29] is Isocrates' reference (v. 27, written in 346) to ταῖς περὶ τὴν λέξιν εὐρυθμίαις

---

[23] Cf. Blass (1901) 160–7.

[24] Cf. ibid. 1 (*Wetteifer*), Martin 324 (*Konkurrenz*), on the ambition of prose-writers to *rival* poetry. Demosthenes' range of options is, of course, limited by his avoidance of tribrachs.

[25] For the absence of word-end at the mid-point of a trochaic tetrameter cf. (e.g.) Ar. *Eq.* 266, 275, 278, 279.

[26] ἐχειροτονήσατε and κατεχειροτονήσατε are variants here, and I follow Goodwin (against MacDowell) in preferring the former.

[27] The immediately preceding words are ἑτέρου τοίνυν, and τοίνυν is not impossible, as in (e.g.) Ar. *Pl.* 567, 1161.

[28] It has affinities with Soph. *Aj.* 172–4, Eur. *Alc.* 591 f., *Med.* 433 f.

[29] The ῥυθμοί studied by Hippias of Elis (Pl. *Hp. Ma.* 285 D, *Hp. Mi.* 368 D) were pretty certainly (McCabe 12) those of poetry, not prose.

καὶ ποικιλίαις ('the attractive rhythms and elaborations of language') 'which I used and taught when I was younger', and Alcidamas' assumption (*AS* B XXII 15, 16, cf. 17) that the pupils of a rhetorician learn μετ᾽ ἀκριβείας καὶ ῥυθμοῦ τὰ ῥήματα συντιθέναι ('put their words together with precision and ⟨attention to⟩ rhythm'). Aristotle *Rhet.* 1409ᵃ1–3 regards Thrasymachus—already well known at Athens by 427 (Ar. fr. 205. 8)—as having established a preference for paeonic rhythm (–∪∪∪ and ∪∪∪–). As it happens, we have a fairly substantial citation from Thrasymachus in Dion. i. 132. 19–134. 14, and its distribution of initial and final four-syllable sequences is shown in Table 8.3, where all (and only) the points at which Radermacher punctuates (*AS* B IX 10 = DK 85 B 1) are treated as pause. Where I give a total in the form '*x* + *y*', *x* refers to the instances in which there is no room for argument, *y* to those whose classification I have made dependent on adoption of the elision and synecphonesis normal in Attic comic dialogue. There being 16 possible ways of arranging four longs and shorts after pause (but only 8 preceding pause, the fourth syllable in such a case being always notionally long), I have added in square brackets the figures which would be statistically expected.[30] This gives no support at all to the statement that Thrasymachus favoured paeonic rhythm.[31] Maybe Aristotle made a mistake and said 'Thrasymachus' when he had someone else in mind; more probably, our sole citation happens to be untypical. Paeonic rhythm may have been recommended by Thrasymachus in his technical treatise (*AS* B IX 1–5 = DK 85 B 3–7a) and oral teaching.

TABLE 8.3. *Rhythms in Thrasymachus*

| ×–∪–	8	[4]	×–∪⌒ |	4 + 1	[8]
| –∪–×	4	[4]	–∪–⌒ |	5	[4]
| –∪∪∪	2 + 1	[2]			
| ∪∪∪–	1 + 1	[2]	∪∪∪⌒ |	2	[4]
others	15	[20]	others	20	[16]

Aristotle's reason for commending paeonic rhythm is to be sought

[30] Calculation of rhythmic probability is necessarily rough, because the ratio of long syllables to short in Greek is 4:3 (Broadhead 36) and syntactical rules do much to determine which lexemes are particularly likely to occur after (and even before) pause.

[31] Ephorus too was regarded as favouring the paeon (*AS* B XXXIII 2, 3, 5), but the surviving citations from his work do not bear this out.

in his insistence that listening to poetry and listening to prose
are different experiences and belong to different kinds of occasion. While a little seasoning of poetry in prose is attractively pi-
quant, whether rhythmical or lexical, too much (i.e. what Aristotle
would judge too much) creates a conflict in the hearer. Hence (*Rhet.*
1408^{b}21–6, 30 f., 9^{a}22 f.) a speech should be εὔρυθμος ('attractive in
rhythm') but not ἔμμετρος ('in ⟨recognizable⟩ metres'),[32] because
repetition of a unit of familiar rhythm creates the expectation that
completion of a metrical unit is coming, and this ἐξίστησι ('throws',
I suggest)[33] the hearer. The three stichic metres best known to
any audience in Aristotle's time were the dactylic hexameter (as
in epic), the iambic trimeter (as in most dramatic dialogue), and
the trochaic tetrameter (as in some dramatic dialogue); the anapaestic tetrameter and iambic tetrameter were peculiar to comedy.
Aristotle regards trochaic rhythm as κορδακικώτερος 'appropriate to
vulgar dancing', τροχερός, 'running' or 'bustling' (*Rhet.* 1408^{b}36 f.),
dactylic rhythm as 'impressive' (σεμνός) but not 'appropriate in
speech' (λεκτικός), and iambic rhythm as lacking that degree of
σεμνότης which a speech needs, for it is 'the language of the majority' (1408^{b}32–6; cf. Demetr. 42 f.). 'There remains', says Aristotle,
'the paeon'—which was never a stichic metre, and concentrations
of it in lyric are confined to comedy—and Demetr. 39–41 follows
suit, adding that the opening long syllable in initial ‒◡◡◡ 'strikes
(πλήσσει) the hearer at once' and the final long in ◡◡◡‒ 'leaves an
impression of grandeur'.

Those of us who recall the exodos of *Oedipus Tyrannus* or the
Persian Queen's dialogue with the ghost of Darius may well be
puzzled by Aristotle's dismissal of trochaic rhythm as vulgar. We
must, I think, believe that it was indeed the rhythm characteristic of
popular dancing-songs at Athens; yet the prejudice engendered in
rhetorical theory by that association does not seem to be reflected in
rhetorical practice. Antisthenes, for example, exhibits a very strong

---

[32] Demetrius 180 f. advocates that the pleasure generated in the hearer by metrical
units should be effected λανθανόντως, 'without his perceiving them', and Dion. ii.
125. 2 echoes this (ἀδήλως, 'surreptitiously'). The modern English use of 'metre' to
cover everything to do with the art of arranging long and short syllables obscures
the clear difference between ῥυθμός and μέτρον which is apparent (e.g.) in Ar. *Nu.*
638–52. An iambic tetrameter has the same μέτρον as a trochaic tetrameter but the
same ῥυθμός as an iambic trimeter.

[33] But in *Rhet.* 1408^{b}36 ἐκστῆσαι is 'impress', 'strike (favourably)'.

TABLE 8.4. *Rhythms in Antisthenes*

	Ajax (*AS* B xix 11)		Odysseus (ibid. 12)	
| x‒∪‒	12+8	[8‒9]	26+19	[15‒16]
| ‒∪‒x	4+3	[8‒9]	9+5	[15‒16]
| ‒∪∪∪	4	[4‒5]	6+4	[7‒8]
| ∪∪∪‒	2	[4‒5]	4+1	[7‒8]
others	33	[41‒2]	51	[78]
x‒∪⌒ |	4+3	[16‒17]	18+3	[31‒2]
‒∪‒⌒ |	27+3	[8‒9]	40+5	[15‒16]
∪∪∪⌒ |	7	[8‒9]	9	[15‒16]
others	22	[33]	50	[62]

preference for initial iambic and final trochaic, as shown in Table 8.4.

Tables of this kind can be compiled for any prose work of any Greek author. The individual work rather than the author is the appropriate unit, not only because many speeches are of disputed authorship, but also because an author may not compose all his works with the same ἀκρίβεια (see below on hiatus), and his practice may in any case change with time. Those works of Plato which are nowadays generally treated as comparatively late (Brandwood's Group III) have been arranged chronologically in accordance with the decreasing affinity of their clausulae with those of *Republic* and increasing affinity with *Laws*.[34] Enquiries of this kind, and hypotheses founded upon their outcome, are modern. The rarity of initial \| ‒∪∪∪ and final ∪∪∪‒\| in Demosthenes alerted Blass to the fact that sequences of three or more short syllables in any position within a sentence are far rarer in Demosthenes than in any other Classical prose author.[35] No one in antiquity draws attention to this, but

[34] See Cox and Brandwood. Wishart and Leach show that within any given work of Plato there is a certain degree of consistency of preference (taking five syllables at a time) not just in clausulae but overall, and that in this respect also a chronological order of works, in accordance with their affinity with *Laws*, may be constructed. These stylometric studies have pushed *Phaedrus* up to a rather earlier date than some Platonists would have wished, but they leave it subsequent to *Republic*.

[35] Blass (1887–98) iii/1. 105 ff. Treatment of Blass's generalization as a 'law' has had undesirable consequences (as the concept of 'laws' often does), particularly in tempting editors to emend for the sake of conformity; cf. Vogel 87–96, 107. It also leads to question-begging in the treatment of elision and ephelcystic *nu* (cf. McCabe 42–73), in which the manuscript tradition is inconsistent.

since avoidance is characteristic also of Aelius Aristides, who held a
very high opinion of Demosthenes, it seems likely that Aristides did
notice it.[36] Table 8.5 shows how many syllables, in the first 1,000
syllables of two Demosthenic texts (xviii and xxi) and four others
(Antiphon v, Lys. xii, Isocr. vii, and Pl. *Lg.* v), are short syllables
keeping company with at least two other shorts.[37] The printed texts
of the editions used have been modified in one respect: whenever
ᾰ, ε, or o (except in the definite article) would be elided in dramatic
dialogue, I have elided them, and regular synecphonesis of τό and τά
with ἁ- and ὁ- has also been assumed. In all other cases where there
is room for doubt about elision, synecphonesis, or hiatus (over hiatus after τί, ὅτι, and περί there is no doubt) the syllables concerned
have simply been left out of the count; thus e.g. Pl. *Lg.* 727 B 6
τότε οὐ τιμᾷ ὑπείκων is treated as τότ' οὐ τῑ[   ]πείκων, and ibid. D 7
ἕτερον ἢ ἡ τῆς ψυχῆς as ἕτερον [   ] τῆς ψυχῆς, but in the latter case
-ον is counted as short because it would be so however ἢ ἡ was managed. The figures in brackets show how many short syllables would
have to be subtracted from the totals in the main row when a syllable scanned short by virtue of the initial vowel which follows it is
treated as long because it immediately precedes pause. Thus in Pl.
Lg. 728 A 8 κατὰ δύναμιν, οὐκ οἶδεν I treat κατὰ δύνα as four shorts but
μιν as a contribution to the bracketed figure, whereas at ibid. 726. 3
θειότατον, οἰκειότατον ὄν· τὰ κτλ. I treat both instances of οτατον as
three shorts, but the first of them puts three into the brackets.

TABLE 8.5. *Short syllables*
adjoining two or more other shorts

Ant.	Lys.	Isoc.	Pl.	Dem. xviii	Dem. xxi
125	106	129	206	38	51
(4)	(3)		(24)	(6)	(4)

Within the Demosthenic corpus there is a 'general coincidence'[38]
between a low proportion of sequences of more than two short
syllables and the absence of grounds adduced (in antiquity or our

[36] McCabe 2, 7, 37; Vogel 109.
[37] There are other ways of counting. Vogel, for instance (90), looks at the number
of occurrences of three or more shorts in succession per hundred lines of Teubner
text. What matters is that, whatever comparisons are made, the same method should
be used for all the items compared.
[38] McCabe 128.

own day) for doubting the authenticity of the speech; but there is enough variation to rule out the practicability of using a high proportion as a firm criterion of false attribution. Three of Demosthenes' speeches on his own inheritance (xxvii, xxviii, xxx) show the same proportion as (on average) Isaeus, a little higher than speech vii, which was reasonably attributed to Hegesippus.[39] It seems that the elimination of tribrachs was something that Demosthenes had to work at, and he did not always put the same effort into it.

Another striking feature of Demosthenes' style is the avoidance of hiatus. Table 8.6 shows the incidence of hiatus (after its removal, in many cases, as indicated in connection with Table 8.5) in the six texts of Table 8.5 plus Lys. xxiv. 1 ff., Plato's Myth of Er (*Rep.* 614 B 4 ff.), and *Tim.* 29 D 7 ff. (all texts of 1,000 syllables). It is clear that with Isocrates the avoidance of hiatus, even at pause, amounted to an obsession,[40] and that Demosthenes, while admitting hiatus at pause, or after καί or the article, tended to eschew it elsewhere. Plato's attitude to hiatus is plainly variable, a fact which can be used for the chronological grouping of his works.[41] The striking difference between Lys. xii and Lys. xxiv in respect of the ratio of pausal hiatus to other instances might be an indication of different authorship or of a change in his practice, but neither can be assumed;[42] the speeches of Isaeus, for example, all on very similar disputes over inheritance, show very great variation in respect of hiatus, which cannot be accounted for chronologically,[43] and it seems more reasonable to believe that an orator who had any inclination to avoid hiatus did not always devote equal time and trouble to its avoidance.

Whether or not Isocrates ever 'published' (i.e. allowed to go into circulation) a handbook on rhetorical technique,[44] it is inconceivable that he failed to preach avoidance of hiatus to his pupils, and

---

[39] McCabe 122, 126–8, 149.

[40] Dion. i. 57. 9–12 observes the importance which Isocrates attaches to the avoidance of hiatus. Norden (1913) i. 67 n. 1 remarks that in iv. 80 Isocrates writes τῷ ποιεῖν εὖ, whereas ibid. 63 he adheres to the normal order in τῶν εὖ ποιησάντων. Cf. Blass (1887–98) ii. 158–60.

[41] Ritter i. 238. There is great variation within the Platonic corpus in respect of sequences of three or more shorts (Vogel 101 f.), and a tendency for the number to be high in works regarded on other grounds as late, but no very clear correlation with the frequency of hiatus outside the late group.

[42] Vogel 97 sets out the remarkable differences existing within the Lysian corpus.

[43] Vogel 99, Wyse 178 f.

[44] On this problem see Kennedy 71 f., McCabe 14 f., 21.

TABLE 8.6. *Hiatus in nine texts*

	Ant.	Lys. xii	Lys. xxiv	Isoc.	Pl. *Rep.*	Pl. *Tim.*	Pl. *Lg.*	Dem. xviii	Dem. xxi
ὦ ἄνδρες[a]	3	2						3	4
after καί	8	4	4		16	5	8	3	6
after the article	9	1	2		15	2	9	1	5
at pause	11	20	7		10		7	11	9
others	27	10	17		28		8	1	3

[a] Dion. ii. 78. 1–7, 126. 16–127. 5, assumes hiatus between ὦ and ἄνδρες.

in the course of the fourth century his teaching and example were taken to heart. He is treated as the originator by Demetrius 68 and Cic. *Or.* 151 (cf. Dion. i. 57. 9–12). There are reasons, however, for thinking that avoidance of hiatus was important to Thrasymachus;[45] the one continuous piece of Thrasymachus which we have (*AS* B IX 10) contains just under 600 syllables, and we find therein only six instances of hiatus: one ὦ Ἀθηναῖοι, one with καί, one at pause, and three non-pausal (λυπεῖσθαι ἐπί, λόγῳ ἐνόντα, αὐτοὶ ἐπεῖδον); converted to percentage, this would mean a grand total of 10 in Table 8.6, by far the smallest total (not counting Isocrates) after the *Timaeus*. If avoidance started with Thrasymachus, it was a technique available to Lysias, and he may on occasion have adopted it deliberately, though not necessarily for a whole speech.

But why? It has been argued by Lionel Pearson that the incidence of hiatus in forensic and political oratory is explicable in terms of the speed and style of delivery, determined by the vehemence, solemnity, or casualness with which a speaker wished to develop a particular stage of his argument.[46] There are, however, some objections to this interpretative principle, and not the least is the unsoundness of the idea that a concentration of hiatus 'cannot

[45] Blass (1901) 37–9.
[46] Especially Pearson (1975) 148 f., (1978) 140–3. His assumptions about the alternative dispositions of words available to the speaker do not always take account of the constraints on word-order (e.g. (1978) 134 on πολλοῦ ἄν in Lys. i. 1) or (ibid. 137. f.) the normal treatment of nuclear ingredients such as ἐξέβην in Ant. v. 26.

be due to accident'.[47] A National Lottery draw of six numbers out of
1–50 'surprisingly' often produces three numbers which fall within
the same decad. Secondly, there is considerable room for disagreement over assessment of the speaker's tone, speed, and emotion
from moment to moment. One further important consideration is
that such an approach to hiatus does not seem to have occurred to
the ancient critics. Anaximenes (*Rhet.* 25), in a context devoted to
the avoidance of obscurity and ambiguity, recommends that vowels
should not be put next to each other 'unless it is impossible to make
one's meaning clear otherwise, or there is some ἀνάπτυξις or other
διαίρεσις' (terms which seem to refer to *internal* combinations of
vowels);[48] and that is all. Demetrius takes the line 'Some like it,
some don't' (68), and judges particular instances by criteria which
are 'aesthetic' in the narrowest sense, smoothness of flow and mu-
sicality, while decrying 'excessive' smoothness. Dionysius declares
(ii. 76. 21–77. 1) that 'a speech made up entirely of good (καλός)
rhythms must necessarily be a good (καλός) speech', a doctrine to
which it is easy to give the lie. Demetrius sees in *Od.* xi. 598 λᾶαν
ἄνω ὤθεσκε, 'he pushed the stone uphill', an imitation of Sisyphus'
straining to move the stone (72; cf. Dion. ii. 90. 1–91. 9); but when
he goes on to say that 'in the same way too (καὶ ὡσαύτως) Thucydides says τὸ μὴ ἤπειρος εἶναι, 'from being mainland' (Thuc. vi.
1. 1), it is hard to see 'sameness' except in the sound itself. It is
just that Demetrius regards the 'clash' of vowels as characteristic
of the 'grand' (μεγαλοπρεπής) style, of which both Homer (cf. 52,
56 f.) and Thucydides (cf. 40, 44 f., 49) are notable examples. When
it comes to the (comparative) virtue of different rhythms, Dionysius does not hesitate to characterize them in terms which have a
moral colouring (e.g. ii. 70. 5 'lowly, frivolous, ignoble' of a long
sequence of short syllables), or ii. 69. 12, where trochaic is called
'less firm' (μαλακώτερος) than iambic. Such obsession with rhythm
is occasionally redeemed by a spark of awareness that words have
meanings. The treatment of καλά ἐστιν as three syllables in πάντα
μὲν τὰ νέα καὶ καλά ἐστιν, 'all that is young is beautiful too', seems to

---

[47] (1978) 144 on Lys. xiii. 40–2, where he treats the concentration of hiatus as
representing the speaker 'choking with emotion'.

[48] ἀναπτύσσειν certainly refers to the internal structure of a word in the scholia
on *Il.* xiii. 340*a* and xxi. 1 (*P.Oxy.* 221, p. 80 in Erbse), and LSJ must be wrong
in translating Anaximenes' ἀνάπτυξις as 'explanation'. διαιρεῖν and διαίρεσις are used
both of internal vocalization (e.g. Σ *Il.* i. 272) and of abstention from elision (e.g.
Dion. ii. 76. 11).

Demetrius (70) 'not to sound so good' (δυσφωνότερον ἔσται); it may
well be thought that it diminishes the weight of the utterance that
should lie on καλά. And it is possible to forgive Dionysius something, even if not much,[49] for his observation (ii. 31. 9–17) that
χάρις and πάθος would be lost if the order of words were changed in
Thuc. iii. 57. 4 ὑμεῖς τε ὦ Λακεδαιμόνιοι, ἡ μόνη ἐλπίς, δέδιμεν μὴ οὐ
βέβαιοι ἦτε, 'And you, Spartans, our only hope, we fear are not to
be relied on..

Most of us cannot easily put ourselves in the position of people
who noticed, let alone cared, whether two short syllables are followed by a third, or whether a final vowel is followed by an initial
vowel, unless there is so extraordinary an accumulation of such
phenomena as to make us realize that we are listening to something abnormal.[50] The ancient critics give us the impression that
an orator attended to words as a professional musician does to
the quality, volume, and tempo of sounds,[51] and that his audience
was (whatever else it may have been in addition) a concert audience. Unfortunately, these critics give us little or no help in understanding detailed rhythmical effects, because their treatment of
examples is arbitrary and sometimes, we must venture to say, wrong.
It is unhelpful on the part of Demetrius (41, explicitly following
Theophrastus) to classify as 'having, I feel, a paeonic character'
(παιωνικόν τι ἐστί) a phrase which actually scans − − ∪ ∪ ∪ − ∪ ∪ − ∪ ∪
∪ ∪ ∪ − −.[52] Dionysius is a blind guide because he makes so many
puerile errors in scansion, e.g. εὖνοῖᾱν (ii. 78. 7–14 and 130. 20–
131. 4), Χέρρόνησος (ii. 129. 8–15) and τουτονῑ́ τὸν ἀγῶνα (ii. 78.
15–17, blandly calling τουτονί 'bacchiac[53] or cretic'). His decisions
on phrasal pause and hiatus are subjective, and unashamedly so,
as when he decides (ii. 76. 2–16)[54] to scan Pl. *Mnx.* 236 D 4 ἔργῳ

[49] Norden (1915) i. 79–91, 96 f., 104, is vehemently contemptuous.
[50] Personally, I care a lot about some configurations of sound, and find myself
fully in sympathy with Denniston in his adverse reaction (*SPG* 190 f. =*GPS* 124 f.)
to Aesch. *Cho.* 848 ἠκούσαμεν μέν. I would never say 'in innumerable cases', through
dislike of unstressed *in in-*, but would not object to 'in instances such as those',
where the second *in-* is stressed.
[51] In respect of tempo a conductor or performer may sometimes defy the composer's instructions with excellent effect.
[52] Users of Grube's translation of Demetrius should note that there are three
gross errors of prosody (ἡλικίᾱν, θῡμοειδές, λῡρα) in his footnotes on pp. 182, 184,
185.
[53] Dionysius uses βάκχειος of − − ∪, ὑποβάκχειος of ∪ − − (e.g. ii. 75. 3, 76. 20, 78. 9,
16).
[54] He thinks − − ∪ − − more appropriate than the iambic rhythm − − ∪ − − to the

μὲν ἡμῖν οἵδε ἔχουσιν τὰ προσήκοντα σφίσιν αὐτοῖς as − − ◡ − − − ◡ ◡ − −
− ◡ − (or ◡ ◡ −) − − ◡ − − (or ◡ ◡ −) − .

Prosodic errors aside, it is plain that one and the same sequence of words was open to more than one rhythmical interpretation, and that a given interpretation might or might not—how could one know?—recognize the author's intention. That is one important difference between poetic and prosaic rhythm. The former, in the Classical period, was rule-bound, but prose rhythm was free to experiment as a creative art in its own right.[55]

Although Aristotle (*Rhet.* 1408ᵇ21–6) expresses disapproval of sequences in which identical repetition reminds the hearer of stichic verse, there are many passages of Isocrates and Demosthenes, and some of Plato, in which, as Blass observed, such repetition is in evidence, and on occasion the rhythm recurs in a manner analogous to responsion in lyrics.[56] For example:[57]

Dem. xviii. 306	Αἰσχίνη, τὸν καλὸν κἀγαθὸν	− ◡ − − ◡ − − ◡ −
	πολίτην ἔδει,	◡ − − ◡ −
	ὧν κατορθουμένων μὲν μεγίστοις ἀναμ-	− ◡ − − ◡ − − ◡ − − ◡ −
	-φισβητήτως κτλ.	− − − − . . .
ibid. 308	πηνίκ' ἔσεσθε μεστοὶ	− ◡ ◡ − ◡ − −
	τοῦ συνεχῶς λέγοντος	− ◡ ◡ − ◡ − ◡
	ἢ παρὰ τῆς τύχης τι	− ◡ ◡ − ◡ − ◡
	κτλ.	
id. xv. 25	τὰ δίκαια λέγειν	◡ ◡ − ◡ ◡ −
	ὑπὲρ τῶν ἄλλων πρὸς ὑμᾶς	◡ − − − − ◡ − −
	. . . (*46 syllables*) . . .	
	ἄτοπον περὶ τῶν	◡ ◡ − ◡ ◡ −
	δικαίων ὑμᾶς διδάσκειν	◡ − − − − ◡ − −
Pl. *Tim.* 26 E	οὐκ ἔστιν, ἀλλ' ἀγαθῇ τύχῃ	− − ◡ − ◡ ◡ − ◡ −
	χρὴ λέγειν μὲν	− ◡ − ◡

solemnity of a funeral speech. But did he really make even a minimal pause between μέν and ἡμῖν?

[55] Isoc. ix. 8–11 takes no account at all of this in his melancholy recognition of the problems faced by prose in competing with poetry for the attention and goodwill of an audience.

[56] Cf. Ch. 2 n. 35.

[57] I found the first two examples in a moment by opening Demosthenes at random. The second two are from Blass (1887–98) iii. 131 (Demosthenes) and (1901) 105 (Plato). I have not cited any of Blass's Isocratean examples, because his decisions on both metre and prosody are too often arbitrary, but the sporadic appearance of recurrent rhythmical sequences in Isocrates, even if their identity is only approximate, cannot be denied.

ὑμᾶς, ἐμὲ δ᾿ ἀντὶ τῶν   – – ∪∪ – ∪ –

χθὲς λόγων νῦν   – ∪ – –

ἡσυχίαν ἄγοντ᾿   – ∪∪ – ∪ –

ἀντακούειν.   – ∪ – –

The distribution of this phenomenon is not explicable in terms of any obvious requirements of genre, function, or affect.

APPENDIX: POETRY AND PROSE: ANCIENT TERMINOLOGY

In modern languages which use alphabetic scripts the definition of poetry presents no problem. If in a printed or written text the majority of lines end before they reach the right-hand margin, the author is signalling, 'I am a poet, and this is poetry.' It may be very bad poetry, and commonly is, but that is a different matter; badly cooked meat is still meat. Advertisements can be turned into 'found poetry' by staggering the lines,[58] and sometimes sound quite attractive in that format, just as accidentally spilled paint can make a more enchanting shape than many abstract pictures; so too an editor can be hoaxed into publishing as poetry a sequence of prose sentences selected at random and suitably arranged,[59] and the result may be charged with resonances for one reader or another; but a hoaxer who pretends to be a poet is no more a poet than a child wearing a Hallowe'en mask is a hobgoblin.

At least from the third century BC (and no doubt from the Classical period, in the case of stichic metres)[60] Greek poetry and prose were distinguishable in writing by a similar formal difference. They were also distinguishable by ear. A sung text was poetry. A spoken text was recognized as poetry if it was organized rhythmically in one or other of a limited number of familiar rhythmical units, i.e. metres.[61] Except (some of the time) in comic dialogue, such a text also differed significantly from everyday conversation, oratory, nar-

---

[58] Examples given by Gross.

[59] See Heyward on the famous affair of 'Ern Malley'.

[60] The clear implication of Dion. ii. 140. 18–20 is that colometry of lyrics began with Aristophanes of Byzantion, and that is supported by early Hellenistic papyri (*P.Lille* 76 of Stesichorus is the earliest instance of lyric colometry). The Timotheus papyrus (s. iv) shows considerable variation in length of line, but the inequalities do not accord with any metrical principles, ancient or modern, and I suspect that the copyist was trying to imitate the appearance of texts of poetry κατὰ στίχον.

[61] On the distinction between ῥυθμός and μέτρον see above, n. 32.

rative, or instruction in its vocabulary, morphology, and syntax (cf. pp. 98 f.). These linguistic features, however, were not the primary differentia of poetry.

Poetry is ἔμμετρος 'in a metre', prose ἄνευ μέτρου 'without metre'. Gorgias *AS* B VII 39. 9=DK B 11. 9 calls poetry λόγον ἔχοντα μέτρον (echoed in Pl. *Grg.* 502 C, where Socrates secures the agreement of Callicles that if poetry is stripped of its melody, rhythm, and metre what is left is λόγος). So too Isoc. ix. 10, 'poets do everything in metres and rhythms, while prose-writers have no part in those means'.[62] Aeschines i. 141 refers to 'what has been said ἐν τῷ μέτρῳ' (i.e. 'in metrical form' = 'in poetic form'),[63] and ibid. 147, after paraphrasing a passage of Homer, he tells the clerk to read the original aloud, so that 'you may hear the thought' (γνῶμαι, i.e. the content of the passage) 'in its metrical form (διὰ τοῦ μέτρου)'; cf. iii. 136 'if you take away the metre and examine his thought'.

Since in speaking we do not sustain long metrical sequences which are familiar in poetry, though we may utter brief sequences accidentally (cf. p. 163), composition in metre is a deliberate act comparable to the carving of a statue or the painting of a picture. Classical Greek therefore denoted the composition of poetry by ποιεῖν, 'make',[64] and though the verb continued to flourish in its very wide general use, the derived nouns ποιητής, 'poet', ποίησις, 'poetry', ποίημα, 'poem', and ποιητικός, 'poetic', usually, though not invariably,[65] had those special denotations (as remarked in Pl. *Smp.* 205 BC). By contrast, written composition in prose was treated implicitly as compilation rather than creation, being denoted by συγγράφειν,[66] συγγραφεύς, συγγραφή, and σύγγραμμα. The referents of these words include reports, plans and recommendations (*IG* i³

[62] The statement of Isoc. ix. 10 that 'metres and rhythms' are not available to prose-writers, and his clear implication that εὐρυθμίαι are confined to poetry, are hard to reconcile with his claim in v. 27 that in his youth he had sought to achieve εὐρυθμίαι. Presumably by 'metres and rhythms' he means 'sequences which constitute recognizable units of familiar poetic rhythms'.

[63] τῷ is puzzling, and τῷ =τινι would not help, since 'in metre' is ἐν μέτρῳ in Xen. *Mem.* i. 2. 21. Presumably Aeschines has the dactylic hexameter in mind, as he goes on (144) to quote from Homer.

[64] Cf. Scots *makar*. 'Portray ⟨in poetry⟩' is ποιεῖν (the selection of examples in LSJ s.v. ποιέω A.4.b–c is good), but 'portray ⟨in prose⟩' seems to be γράφειν, to judge from Pl. *Phdr.* 227 C 'Lysias γέγραφε an attempt to seduce a good-looking boy'.

[65] These words can refer to the creation or manufacture of anything, if the context precludes misunderstanding, e.g. Hdt. iii. 22. 3, iv. 5. 3, Pl. *Euthd.* 305 E, *Rep.* 597 D.

[66] On the distinction between active and middle in this verb see Dover (1987) 31–3. I take συγγραφικῶς ἐρεῖν in Pl. *Phd.* 102 D to mean 'talk like a treatise'.

45. 6 f., 78. 3 f., 47 f., 79. 16), contracts (Isoc. xvii. 20), historiography (Thuc. i. 1. 1, 97. 2, cf. ibid. ξυνετίθεσαν), philosophy and
science (Diog. Apoll. DK 64 B 4), and simply 'describing', 'relating'
(Hdt. i. 93. 1, iii. 103; vi. 14. 1 οὐκ ἔχω ἀτρεκέως συγγράψαι οἵτινες
κτλ.) or 'putting in writing' (Thuc. v. 35. 3 χρόνους τε προύθεντο
ἄνευ ξυγγραφῆς ἐν οἷς χρῆν κτλ.). The opposition between ποι- and
συγγραφ- is illustrated by Pl. *Lys.* 205 A μὴ ποιεῖν εἰς τὰ παιδικὰ
μηδὲ συγγράφειν, *Prm.* 128 A, comparing what Zeno had written
τῷ συγγράμματι with what Parmenides wrote ἐν τοῖς ποιήμασιν, and
Dem. lx. 9 τούς . . . ποιητὰς καὶ πολλοὺς τῶν συγγραφέων. The
only passages in which the opposition is overridden are : (1) Pl.
Lg. 810 B, where compositions μετὰ μέτρων and those which are
συγγράμματα κατὰ λόγον εἰρημένα μόνον are both brought under
ποιητῶν γράμματα, a usage partially justified by the speaker's later
(811 C) observation that the arguments in which he has been en-
gaged 'since early morning' ἔδοξαν . . . μοι παντάπασι ποιήσει τινὶ
προσομοίως εἰρῆσθαι 'seemed to me to have been expressed throughout in a sort of poetic form'; (2) 858 D, where συγγράμματα are
simply 'writings', including both poetry and prose; (3) Demetr.
215 on Ctesias: 'This poet—for one could fairly call him poet—
. . .'.

In the fourth century the συγγραφ- words are sometimes joined
with καταλογάδην; Isoc. ii. 7 τῶν μετὰ μέτρου ποιημάτων καὶ τῶν
καταλογάδην συγγραμμάτων establishes the denotation 'not in verse'
for καταλογάδην, and in Pl. *Smp.* 177 AB the composition of ὕμνοι
and παιῶνες by ποιηταί is contrasted with ἐπαίνους ('encomia') καταλογάδην συγγράφειν, predicated of 'the good σοφισταί'. Written prose
and unwritten speech possess in common the feature 'not in verse',
and this is recognized in Pl. *Lg.* 957 D ὅσοι τε ἐν ποιήμασιν ἔπαινοι
λέγονται καὶ ὅσοι καταλογάδην εἴτ' ἐν γράμμασιν εἴτε καθ' ἡμέραν ἐν
ταῖς ἄλλαις πάσαις συνουσίαις, 'the encomia which are uttered in
poems and those uttered καταλογάδην, whether in written works
or in all kinds of everyday intercourse', while in *Lys.* 204 D καταλογάδην must refer to speech alone, excluding συγγράμματα: 'what
he relates καταλογάδην . . ., but when he tries to deluge us with his
poems and συγγράμματα'.

What I have described is the usage of the fourth century and the
late fifth; earlier terminology was different. In the Archaic period
poetry is ἀοιδή, 'song', and the poet is an ἀοιδός who ἀείδει. When
Theognis in his prooemium (1–4) tells Apollo that he will always

'sing' (ἀείσω) of him, he plainly refers to composition, not merely to performance, and this is even plainer in Solon fr. 1, where the poet proclaims that he brings news from Salamis κόσμον ἐπέων ᾠδὴν ἀντ' ἀγορῆς θέμενος, literally, 'having made the ordered form of my utterance song instead of public speech'.[67] However, ποιεῖν makes its first appearance side by side with ἀείδειν in Solon fr. 3, apostrophizing Mimnermus: καὶ μεταποίησον . . . ὧδε δ' ἄειδε, 'change what you have composed . . . and sing thus . . .'. ἀοιδός (Attic ᾠδός) is used in Hdt. i. 24. 5 of Arion, who was both composer (cf. 23) and performer, but the four occurrences of the word in Plato refer to performance (*Phdr.* 262 D (cicadas!), *Lg.* 670 B, 800 E, 812 B), and so probably does Heraclitus B 104.[68]

Herodotus calls portions of his own work λόγοι (e.g. i. 5. 3, 184), and he speaks of the λόγοι of Hecataeus (vi. 137. 1). Accordingly, Hecataeus (ii. 141. 1 *al.*) and Aesop (ii. 134. 3) are λογοποιοί. This usage survived: in Pl. *Rep.* 390 A ἐν ποιήσει is contrasted with ἐν λόγῳ, in Isoc. ix. 9 f. τοῖς ποιηταῖς with τοῖς περὶ τοὺς λόγους, and in *Rep.* 392 A and Isoc. v. 109 ποιηταί and λογοποιοί seem to constitute an exhaustive division of writers. But the denotation 'prose' did not have much hope of establishing itself firmly as yet one more of the things to which λόγος could refer,[69] and λογοποιός, -εῖν developed specialized denotations: the composition of forensic speeches (Pl. *Euthd.* 289 D) and the spreading of rumours and gossip (Thuc. vi. 38. 1, Lys. xvi. 11, Dem. xxiv. 15 *al.*).

In the Hellenistic period λογοειδής makes its appearance as a term for prose: Posidonius fr. 44 Kidd, defining poetry as λέξις ἔμμετρος . . . τὸ λογοειδὲς ἐκβεβηκυῖα, and Strabo i. 2. 6 τὸ λογοειδὲς νῦν καλούμενον. In that period πεζός, 'on foot', and lexemes derived from it, are regular for 'prose', e.g. Demetr. 167 (contrasted with ποιητικός), Dion. ii. 9. 20 (contrasted with ἔμμετρος), but the first appearance of this denotation is much earlier, Pl. *Sph.* 237 A πεζῇ τε . . . λέγων καὶ μετὰ μέτρων, and it is so unobvious that it cannot have been created by Plato for that occasion without warning. It implies a mildly negative evaluation, made more explicit in Strabo

[67] Cf. West (1974) 12–14 on the singing of elegiacs. (In *IEG* ii. 140, however, West obelizes ᾠδήν as a gloss.)

[68] Eur. fr. 955g (Snell) ἀνθηρὸς ᾠδός is cited by Allen and Italie s.v. ποιητής, but it is obvious from Photius' wording (s.v. ἀνθηρός) that ποιητής is his gloss on ᾠδός.

[69] It can be the 'theme', 'subject', or 'plot' of a play (Ar. *Pax* 148), though in *Vesp.* 54, *Pax* 50 it would more probably be taken by the hearer to mean 'explanation (sc. of what you have seen so far)'.

i. 2. 6 (on the historical priority of poetry) ἀπὸ ὕψους τινὸς καταβάντα
καὶ ὀχήματος εἰς τοὔδαφος 'coming down on to the ground from an
elevated position, from a carriage',[70] and Plu. *Pyth. Orac.* 406 E
κατέβη μὲν ἀπὸ τῶν μέτρων ὥσπερ ὀχημάτων ἡ ἱστορία,[71] and it was
presumably determined by a confluence of the superior speed and
directness of sea-travel (e.g. *Od.* xi. 57 f.) with the superior status
of mounted men over infantry and with the poet's 'chariot of song'
(e.g. Pi. *Ol.* 1. 110).

Before Aristotle's *Poetics* the only explicit allusions to poetic *language* are Isoc. ix. 9 f. and Pl. *Phdr.* 257 A, the former offering a brief
characterization of it (cf. p. 96) and the latter not (cf. p. 103). The
reference in Pl. *Rep.* 332 B to Simonides' verses on moral integrity
as 'allusive' or 'indirect' (ἠνίξατο . . . ποιητικῶς, cf. *Tht.* 180 CD and
p. 101) accords with the judgement in *Alc. II* 147 B that poetry is
by nature αἰνιγματώδης[72] but tells us nothing, except perhaps by
implication (on 'semantic stretch' and metaphor cf. p. 122), about
poetic vocabulary and syntax.[73]

---

[70] Strabo is referring here to the direction in which comedy diverged from tragedy.

[71] A good thing, according to Plutarch, for the health of rational communication;
but the implication of 'came down' remains. In Xen. *An.* v. 6. 1 πεζῇ is 'by land' (as
opposed to 'by sea'), and in Xen. *Oec.* 5. 5 'on one's own feet' (as opposed to 'on
horseback')—and so elsewhere.

[72] Aristotle's insistence on 'clarity' in poetry (*Po.* 1458ᵃ18, 34, ᵇ1–5) as in λέξις
generally (*Rhet.* 1404ᵇ1 f.) was evidently not shared by Tolstoy, in whose diary for
9–10 Nov. 1909 we find: 'And yet, like Andreyev, [Gorky] has nothing to say. They
ought to write poetry or . . . dramas. With poetry the permissible obscurity would
save them . . .'.

[73] Russell (1981) rightly says (149 f.) that the ancient critics' view of the differentia
of poetry was 'rather naïve'.

ADDENDA

p. 11 n. 10 'more for the ear than for the eye' and p. 40 'in reading
. . . as a producer necessarily does'. When my book went to the
publisher I had my own contribution to Ayres (ed.), *The Passionate
Intellect*, and was therefore able to refer (p. 169 n. 18) to its page-
numbers, but I had not then received a copy of the volume and
therefore did not know of Professor Yaginuma's important article
'Did Thucydides Write for Readers or Hearers?' (Ayres 131–42).
It is certainly clear from Thuc. i. 22. 4 that Thucydides envisaged
a 'market' from which he himself would be absent, and Yaginuma
argues that the complexity of some of his sentences requires analysis and dismemberment by a careful reader if they are to be understood. I am not sure about that; could Thucydides really have
believed that a complex sentence would be better understood from
scrutiny of an unpunctuated and unaccented text than from the
flexible articulation of the human voice? I suspect that, accustomed
as he was to the voice, he simply underrated the problems of understanding sentences which he had 'heard' in his mind. Cf. *HCT*
iv. 231, 260.

p. 46 n. 20. These stylometric tests have been criticized on aprioris-
tic grounds, and even as 'contrary to common sense', a criterion on
which (e.g.) psychology and quantum physics would fare ill. Critics
would be well advised to consider cases in which conclusions drawn
from stylometric tests have been vindicated later by the disclosure
of data (e.g. the results of electrostatic tests, which have nothing
to do with language or style) not known at the time of the original
tests.

p. 49, on nouns in -σις in Thucydides; see Yaginuma 137–9.

p. 50, on average sentence-length; see Yaginuma 133.

pp. 80, 87, on forms of the dative plural; see Threatte ii (1996)
25–32, 96–101.

p. 139, 'twist in the tail'. Cf. Gorgias DK 82 B 6, quoted on p. 136, and Sections IIa and IIb of the Thucydidean passage displayed on p. 147. The aesthetic effect καταστρέφει the period (cf. pp. 38–40) in a way which somewhat resembles the closure of a lyric passage by catalexis.

p. 163 n. 12. Some theoretically possible forms of dochmiac, however, are not exemplified in extant literature, and others are very rare; see L. P. E. Parker, *The Songs of Aristophanes* (Oxford, 1997), 65–6.

p. 173 'Maybe Aristotle made a mistake'; as Denniston did in *GPS* 15 in saying 'Thucydides' for 'Thrasymachus' (corrected in *SPG*) and Bowra in saying 'Hieron' for 'Theron' twice in *Problems in Greek Lyric Poetry* (Oxford, 1953) 79.

pp. 183–4, on ποιεῖν and συγγράφειν; the distinction is not always observed in later Greek, e.g. Diog. Laert. ix. 110 ποιήματα συνέγραφε— a fact to be taken into account when using late authors as evidence for the work of early authors, as observed by E. L. Bowie, *JHS* 106 (1986) 32 n. 104.

INDEXES

1. GREEK

-ā, -ή 85
ἀ- (negative) 101
α+ο, α+ου, α+ω 87, 88
ἀγ-, ἀμ-, ἀν-=ἀνα- 92, 94
ἀγάλλεσθαι 122
ἄγγελμα 117
ἀγορά 185
ἀγορὰ ἐφορία 79
ἀγοράσθαι 88, 110
ἀγροῖκος 105
ἀγυρτής 104
ἀδηνής 93
ἀεικίνητος 105
ἀζήμος 79 n. 3
ἄθετος 117
ἀθῷος 79 n. 3
αἱματώδης 116
αἰνιγματώδης 101 n. 17, 186
-αισ(ι)(ν) 86
αἴσθησις 42
ἄκαιρος 102
ἀκατάξεστος 117
ἀλίζειν 93 n. 61
ἄλλως 65
ἄλογος 42
ἀμείβεσθαι 68, 92, 94
ἄν (frequentative) 65
ἀναγελᾶν 92
ἀναγιγνώσκειν 83
ἀνακηκίειν 104
ἀναλέγειν 93
ἄναξ 98, 99
ἀναπτύσσειν, ἀνάπτυξις 179
ἀνατροπεύς 118
ἀξιοθαύμαστος 105
ἀξιοκοινώνητος 105
ἀοιδ-ή, -ός 184–5
ἀπαθής 105
ἀπήμων 104
ἀπίλλειν 79
ἀποδέκται 117
ἀποθνήσκειν 99
ἀποκτείνειν 99
ἀπολλύναι 99

ἄποτος 117
ἄπους 113–14
ἀποφυσᾶν 92
ἀπρόσκλητος 117
ἆρα γε 64
ἀργυριοκόπιον 117
ἀρράβδωτος 117
ἀρτιτελής 105
ἄσημος 101 n. 17
ἀσθένεια 116
-ᾱσι, -ησι 80, 82
-ᾱσι, -ᾱσι 161 n. 6
ἀσσότερος 92, 94
ἀτέραμνος 122 n. 58
ἀτρεκής 93
αὐδᾶν 99
αὐτάρκης 105
ἀφαιρετεῖν 92
ἀφελής 37
ἄψορρος 82 n. 14

βάκχειος 180 n. 53
βήξ 116
βούλεσθαι 90
βραχυτράχηλος 105
βρίθειν 104

γάρ (parenthetic) 72
γίγνεσθαι 67
γλαυκόμματος 105
γλῶττα 96
γνήσιος 123

δαιμονᾶν 104, 108
δαίνυσθαι 93
δαίς 104
δάμαρ 79, 81
δημότης, δημοτικός 36
διαιρεῖν, διαίρεσις 38, 179
διάνοια 16–17, 37
διασπείρειν 124
διαφέρων 102
διαφθείρειν 99
διδάσκαλος 121

192 Indexes

2. AUTHORS AND PRINCIPAL TEXTS CITED

3. GENERAL